The Beauty of Today

Also by Gary Hardy

Look Back, Don't Stare

The Power of Love

The Time of Your Life

Learn more at www.gary-hardy.com

The Beauty of Today

365 Fresh Perspectives & Wisdom For Your Most Transformative Year

Gary Hardy

Copyright © 2024 by Gary Hardy

All rights reserved.

No part of this book may be reproduced in any form or by any electronic or mechanical means, including information storage and retrieval systems, without written permission from the author, except for the use of brief quotations in a book review.

For my wonderful family, old and new

Foreword

When I first began collecting quotes that moved me, I noticed something. While the well-known wisdom of historical figures and celebrated thinkers certainly held value, it was often the unexpected insights - the ones that hadn't been shared thousands of times on social media or printed on countless coffee mugs - that truly resonated with me and sparked real change in my life.

André Gide once wrote, "Everything that needs to be said has already been said. But, since no one was listening, everything must be said again." This paradox struck me deeply. Yes, many fundamental truths about life, love, healing, and growth have been expressed before. But sometimes we need to hear these truths in a new voice, from a different perspective, or at exactly the right moment in our lives for them truly to sink in.

That's why I created this book. I was tired of seeing the same quotes circulated endlessly, their power diminished through repetition. I wanted to share fresh voices and perspectives - words that might make you pause, think, and see your life from a new angle. More

Foreword

importantly, I wanted to share my own thoughts on these insights, drawn from years of observing how wisdom works in real lives, in real situations.

Each day's quote in this collection comes with my personal reflection - not as someone claiming to have all the answers, but as a fellow traveler on life's journey who has gathered some insights along the way. Some of these quotes come from unexpected sources; parents watching their children grow, friends supporting each other through difficult times, or individuals who found clarity in their darkest moments.

My hope is that as you read these pages, day by day, you'll find words that speak directly to your heart, that may arrive at exactly the moment you need them. Whether you're healing from past wounds, seeking daily inspiration, or working to transform any aspect of your life, may these fresh perspectives offer you the guidance and encouragement you need.

This book isn't meant to sit on your shelf as a collection of pretty words. It's designed to be a daily companion in your journey of growth and healing. Each quote and reflection is an invitation to pause, consider, and most importantly, take action in your own life. Some days, you might find exactly the wisdom you've been seeking. Other days, you might discover a perspective that challenges your thinking in necessary ways.

As you begin this year-long journey through these pages, I encourage you to approach each day's reading with an open heart and mind. Take what resonates with you, reflect on what challenges you, and most importantly, find ways to apply these insights in your daily life. True transformation doesn't come from merely reading wise words... it comes from living them.

Foreword

May these pages be a source of inspiration, comfort, and guidance as you navigate your own path towards healing and growth. Remember, every day offers a new opportunity to begin again, to see things differently, and to take one small step towards the life you envision.

Gary Hardy

Introduction

"I love quotations because it is a joy to find thoughts one might have, beautifully expressed with much authority by someone recognised wiser than oneself."

— Marlene Dietrich

This book is designed to be your daily companion for growth and reflection throughout the year. Each day features a carefully selected quote followed by a thoughtful exploration of its meaning and practical application to your life.

Introduction

How to get the most from this book:

- Read one entry a day, and start wherever you are in the year. If you bought this book on March 12th start it on that day.
- Take a few moments to reflect on the message you read that day.
- Try and implement the practical actions that I suggest.
- Use the reflective questions at the end of many of the days messages as journal prompts
- Revisit previous days that particularly resonated with you.

While you can read straight through, this book is most powerful when used as intended - one day at a time, allowing each entry's wisdom to sink in and shape your daily experience. Let each day's message be a starting point for deeper contemplation and personal growth.

The quotes and reflections are arranged to build upon each other while still standing independently, making this book both a structured journey and a collection of individual insights you can return to whenever needed.

Remember, transformation happens not in great leaps but in small, daily steps. Let this book be your guide in taking those steps, one day at a time.

Now, let's begin your journey.

Getting More From Your Journey

While this book serves as a powerful daily guide, many readers find they benefit from additional support and deeper exploration of these concepts. That's why I've created a space where we can grow together.

As a reader of "The Beauty of Today," you're invited to enhance your journey by joining me on YouTube at:

https://www.youtube.com/@officialgaryhardy

Here's what you'll find on the channel:

- Weekly Videos: Join me as I read quotes from this book, share personal stories about its meaning, and offer practical ways to implement these insights into your life.
- Exclusive Members Content: Get access to in-depth discussions, behind-the-scenes content, and special Q&A sessions where I address your questions and challenges directly.

How to Join:
1. Visit YouTube and search for @officialgaryhardy
2. Click the "Subscribe" button
3. Hit the notification bell to stay updated with new content

Remember, true transformation happens not just through reading, but through consistent application and support. Let's walk this path together.

Subscribe today and discover how these daily reflections can become powerful catalysts for change in your life.

January 1st

"January, the first month of the year, a perfect time to start all over again, changing energies and deserting old moods, new beginnings, new attitudes."

— Charmaine J Forde

January invites us to press the reset button on our lives. It's not just another month - it's like opening a fresh notebook where every page is crisp and clean, waiting for your story.

What I like about Forde's words is the emphasis on attitudes, not just actions. We can often get caught up in making ambitious resolutions, but the real magic happens when we shift our inner world first before attempting what we want to change in our outer world. It's like clearing out a cluttered room in your mind to make space for new ideas and possibilities.

Today, I suggest taking 5 minutes to sit and ask yourself, "What am I holding on to that no longer serves me?" Maybe it's lingering resentment from last year, doubt that's been weighing you down, or the old stories you keep telling yourself about what you can and can't do. Identify just one of these old attitudes you're ready to let go of, and consciously choose something new to replace it with. It could be as simple as replacing "I'm always behind" with "I'm exactly where I need to be."

Remember, transformation doesn't always require dramatic changes. Sometimes it's just about looking at thing just a little differently. What matters is taking that first step, however small it might be.

January 2nd

"It is not good enough for things to be planned, they still have to be done; for the intention to become a reality, energy has to be launched into operation."

— Walt Kelly

I've seen many people (myself included) get caught up in the planning phase - making to-do lists, crafting detailed game plans, dreaming up grand schemes. But Walt Kelly hits on something crucial here: plans are just the blueprint. They're not the house itself. You have to actually build the house.

When you are getting ready for a trip, you may spend hours looking for the perfect route, packing your bags and double sometimes triple checking them, and looking what the weather is doing and checking what the traffic is like on your route, but at some point, you have to actually step out the front door, get in your car, start the car, and drive away from home.

Today, I'd like to encourage you to look at one thing you've been planning or thinking about doing. Maybe it's starting a workout routine, learning a new skill, or even having an important conversation with someone. Now, instead of refining that plan even further than what you already have done, actually take one action towards that goal today - no matter how small.

When we transform our genuine intentions into actions that is when things begin to change. And remember - it doesn't have to be perfect. Taking imperfect action today is better than waiting for perfect conditions tomorrow, which usually never arrive. I have been caught in this loop many times, and not only was it a waste of my precious time, but it was also counterintuitive to any growth that could have accomplished, if I had only just taken the action needed.

What's one thing that you've been planning that you could take action on today?

January 3rd

"Gratitude makes sense of our past, brings peace for today, and creates a vision for tomorrow."

— Melody Beattie

This quote really resonated with me because Melody Beattie captures something about gratitude, that it's not just about saying "thank you", it is also how we can also use it as a tool to transform how we view our life journey.

When we look back and can be grateful, even for all the struggles and hardships we have experienced, they take on a while new meaning. Those challenging experiences shaped who we are, taught us lessons, and led us to exactly where we are today. I've seen this play out many times in my own life, there have been many things that I am extremely grateful for now that were devastating at the time. When we shift from feeling resentment to gratitude, our past becomes a source of wisdom rather than pain.

Today, I'd encourage you to identify one "difficult" thing from your past that you can now feel grateful for. Maybe it's a toxic relationship that ended but taught you about love and what you deserve, or something you think you failed at that actually redirected you to something much better. Then notice how this small shift in your perspective brings a sense of peace about where you've been and what you have experienced.

This also extends to the now - when we're grateful, we stop fighting what we're currently experiencing and find peace in the present moment. And perhaps most importantly, gratitude opens our eyes to possibilities ahead, because it's hard to envision a compelling future when we're stuck in negativity, but a grateful heart sees abundance, possibilities and opportunity.

Remember, you should never wait for perfect circumstances to be grateful, because you will be waiting forever. Start right now, where you are, with what you have. Let gratitude be your guide to making sense of what happened yesterday, finding peace with what's happening today, and dreaming about what you will make happen tomorrow.

January 4th

"A budget tells us what we can't afford, but it doesn't keep us from buying it."

— William Feather

I love this observation by William Feather! This quote points out the gap between knowing what the wise thing is to do with our money and actually following through and doing it. I've seen this many times - we plan our budgets, yet when temptation strikes, those carefully laid plans can crumble in an instant. It has happened to me, and I am sure it has happened to you.

Today, when you're about to buy something, stop for just a moment and ask yourself, "Is this in my budget? And if it's not, what's making me to buy it anyway?" This isn't about judging yourself, it's about understanding yourself better.

Maybe you're looking for comfort after a rough day, or perhaps you're trying to keep up with others, which is never a good thing to do. By recognising the motivations for spending beyond your budget, you can start finding better ways to address what you're really looking for. Sometimes, what we think we want to buy isn't what we truly need, its not the item its a feeling.

Remember, the power of a budget isn't in the numbers - it's in the better decisions it helps us make.

Your future self will thank you for each moment you stopped to think.

January 5th

"She picked up the broken pieces of her life and created something beautiful. From that day forth she shone like the sun and changed the definition of broken."

— Randall M. Gore

You may have at some stage heard someone talk about being "broken" as if it's the end of their story. But in reality, sometimes being "broken" is the beginning of something remarkable. I have first hand experience of this in my own life. I have felt "broken" many times but have used the breaks to my advantage.

There is an art form called Kintsugi in Japan, where they repair broken pottery with gold, making it more beautiful than before. The same can happen with us – those cracks and breaks we experience don't have to leave us feeling less than. Instead, these breaks can become the places where our light shines through the brightest.

Here's a suggestion for today: If you're dealing or have dealt with something that felt like it broke you – whether it's a relationship, trauma, loss or failure, try looking at those broken pieces differently. Instead of seeing them as proof of what's been lost, consider them the raw materials to create something new. Think about what feels broken to you and how you could transform it into something worthwhile and meaningful.

This isn't about toxic positivity or pretending the pain isn't real, I do not believe either of those things is the right way to deal with anything. It's about recognising that being broken isn't the opposite of being whole – sometimes it's the very beginning of creating something even more authentic and stronger than before. Your breaks don't define you; what you choose to bring into existence with them does.

Your worth isn't diminished by what you've been through. As is true in my case, sometimes it's through our deepest wounds, that we find our strength to shine.

January 6th

"It's beautiful to be alone. To be alone does not mean to be lonely. It means the mind is not influenced and contaminated by society."

— J Krishnamurti

This quote is talking about the transformative power of solitude - not the kind that leaves us feeling alone and empty, but the kind that enriches our lives and helps us to reconnect with our authentic selves. I have used this very practice many times in my life to rebalance and revitalise myself, so I can vouch for its value.

Nowadays we are always contactable and connected, so we are bombarded by social media feeds, and the opinions and the expectations of others. These external voices drown out our own inner voice that has all the wisdom you need. True solitude gives us the space we need to hear ourselves think, to understand what we truly want and believe, rather than what we've been conditioned to want and believe.

Today, try to spend at least 15 minutes alone, yes completely alone - not scrolling on your phone, chatting on WhatsApp, watching TV or reading a book, yes not even this one, but simply be with you. You go could choose to sit in nature, take a quiet walk, or find a peaceful corner in your home, whatever feels right for you. You will notice how your thoughts become clearer when they're not being stifled by the incessant noise of the world. When you give yourself this gift of uncontaminated mental space, insights will emerge that would have may have never seen the light of day.

You don't need to run from true solitude or feel that you need to fill every moment with a distraction. Some of life's most beautiful epiphanies come when we dare to be contented with being completely alone with ourselves.

January 7th

"There is a cost to staying on one path, especially if it doesn't feel like the one you should be on. But there is also a cost to walking away and venturing into the unknown. The real question that was embedded in each one of my concerns was, What price am I willing to pay?"

— Cait Flanders

One of the most difficult decisions we are faced with in life, is to either stay on the path we are on or venture onto an unknown one. Having faced many crossroads myself, and have had to make difficult decisions, I deeply resonate with what Cait Flanders' says about the costs of both of these choices.

Change is scary on many levels, and the uncertainty of it is enough to make you stay somewhere you no longer belong. However staying in a situation that doesn't align with your values or what you want in life will slowly drain your spirit, but taking a leap into complete uncertainty is full of risk and fear. I am sure you understand that there is no cost-free option. Every choice we make has its price, and it will inevitably be paid.

So today, I encourage you to sit quietly and ask yourself, "In my current situation, the one I have chosen to stay in, what price am I paying by staying where I am? What dreams or potential am I sacrificing?" Then consider the price of changing and leaving that situation - what would you need to give up or risk to walk a different path? Be honest with yourself and don't judge your answers. Sometimes clearly seeing the "prices" helps us realise which one we're more willing to pay. Courage isn't about choosing the easy, painless path - it's about choosing the path whose cost you can look in the eye and say, "Yes, this is worth it to me" and then take action to enable you to start walking that path.

January 8th

"Dear Life, I am slowly falling in love with you again."

— Conee Berdera

This quote talks about how we understandably can sometimes lose our love for life after a prolonged period of struggle, but we can rediscover it again.

We have all gone through phases where life has felt heavy or tedious. We get caught up in the daily routines, stress, or constant disappointments. But, usually in quiet moments, we may notice something - maybe our pet cuddling up to us and we feel that spark again. That's what this quote captures - the gentle awakening to life's magic.

Today, notice when you feel even a tiny flutter of joy or appreciation. It could be as simple as the taste of your favourite food or a moment of connection with someone. These are love notes from life itself. By acknowledging these moments, we strengthen our capacity to fall in love with life again and again.

Remember, love - even with life itself - isn't always a dramatic passion. Sometimes it's a slow, quiet recognition of beauty in the ordinary. How are you falling in love with life today?

January 9th

"It's time to distance yourself from the people who let you down, the inconsistent ones."

— Billy Chapata

This speaks to an important aspect of self-care and emotional well-being. It's not about anger or blame - it's about recognising patterns and making conscious choices about where we invest our emotional energy.

Sometimes it's not an outright betrayal that drains us, but the subtle exhaustion of never knowing where we stand with someone, of constantly adjusting our expectations, of making excuses for their inconsistency. It's like trying to build a house on shifting sand.

Today, think about your relationships and notice where you feel most steady and where you feel unsteady. Where do you find yourself constantly explaining away someone's behaviour or making excuses for them? This isn't about making dramatic declarations or suddenly cutting people off - it's about beginning to create healthy distance where needed. Remember, creating distance doesn't always mean completely ending relationships. Sometimes it means adjusting your expectations, reducing your emotional investment, or simply being more mindful about how much of yourself you share with certain people. It's about protecting your peace while still maintaining compassion - both for yourself and others.

The goal isn't to wait for perfect people (they don't exist), but to surround yourself with those who show up consistently in ways that matter to you.

January 10th

"Just because things hadn't gone the way I had planned didn't necessarily mean they had gone wrong."

— Ann Patchett

This quote is about life's unexpected twists and turns and how we deal with them. We often have such a firm grip on our plans and expectations that we mistake "different" for "wrong."

I've seen how this perspective can transform people's lives. Sometimes what feels like a detour or a disappointment is actually opening doors we never knew existed. Think about the job you didn't get that led to something better, or the relationship that ended but taught you exactly what you needed to learn.

Today, look back at a moment when life veered away from your plans. Maybe it's something happening right now. Instead of labelling it as "wrong," ask yourself, "What possibilities might this new direction hold? What have I learned or gained that I couldn't have if everything had gone according to plan?"

Remember, life often has a wisdom that extends beyond our carefully laid plans. Sometimes its greatest gifts come wrapped in unexpected packages. What unplanned turn in your life might actually be leading you somewhere meaningful?

January 11th

"I looked at everyone and wondered where they came from, and who they missed, and what they were sorry for."

— Jonathan Safran Foer

I found this to be a deeply empathetic and human observation. This quote is about the hidden depths within every person we pass, each of them carrying their own universe of loves, regrets, and longings.

In our busy lives, we often see others as just background characters in our own story. But this quote reminds us that every person we encounter - the barista making our coffee, the stranger in the car next to you on the motorway, our coworkers - has their own rich inner world. They all have someone they're missing, something they wish they'd done differently, dreams they're chasing.

Today, try this: When you're out today, look at the people around you with this lens of curiosity and compassion. Not in a judgemental way, but with the understanding that each person you see is living a life as complex and meaningful as your own. Maybe they're carrying grief, celebrating a private joy, or wrestling with a difficult decision.

This kind of perspective can transform how we interact with others. It reminds us to be kinder, more patient, more understanding. Because really, aren't we all carrying our own collection of missed people and quiet regrets?

What might change in your daily interactions if you remembered that everyone you meet has their own story of love and loss?

January 12th

"Make your life a mission, not an intermission."

— Arnold H. Glasgow

What a powerful reminder about living with purpose! This quote really strikes at something essential about how we approach our daily existence.

Think about it - an intermission is just a pause, a temporary break where we're essentially waiting for the next act to begin. But Glasgow is telling us that life itself is the main act. Too often, we catch ourselves living in a waiting pattern - waiting for the perfect job, the right relationship, or some future moment when things will finally "begin." We treat our present as just a gap between meaningful moments.

Today, ask yourself, "Where in my life am I treating the present as an intermission?" Are there dreams or actions your postponing, telling yourself someday or when the time is right?

Choose one small action today that moves you from waiting to doing. It doesn't have to be dramatic - maybe it's sending that email you've been putting off, starting that book you want to write, or having that conversation you've been avoiding. Make today part of your mission, not just a break between important moments.

Life is happening right now, in this moment. What will you do to make it count?

January 13th

"You can be a good person with a kind heart, and still say no."

— Danielle Koepke

This is a liberating truth that many kind-hearted people need to hear. There's this common misconception that being good means always saying yes, always being available, always putting others first. But that's not kindness - that's self-neglect.

The beauty of this quote lies in its permission to maintain your boundaries while still honouring your compassionate nature. Being kind doesn't mean being a doormat. In fact, sometimes the kindest thing you can do - both for yourself and others - is to say no.

Today, consider this: Where in your life are you saying yes when your heart is whispering no? Maybe it's extra projects at work, social obligations that drain you, or friendships that take more than they give. Remember that every time you say yes to something that doesn't align with your values or energy, you're saying no to something that might.

Try practicing a kind but firm "no" today. Notice how it feels. Notice that the world doesn't end, and that most people respect clear boundaries. Most importantly, notice how protecting your peace allows you to show up more genuinely for the things and people that truly matter to you.

What would become possible in your life if you believed - really believed - that you can be both kind and boundaried?

January 14th

"There are far too many silent sufferers. Not because they don't yearn to reach out, but because they've tried and found no one who cares."

— Richelle E. Goodrich

This quote hits at something deeply painful in our human experience - the loneliness of suffering in silence after finding our vulnerability met with indifference. It's a heartbreaking reality that many people close themselves off not because they want to, but because reaching out and finding no response hurts more than staying quiet.

In a world of social media and surface-level connections, we often miss the quiet cries for help. Someone might be posting happy photos while carrying immense pain. That colleague who seems "fine" might be struggling deeply. We've created a culture where everyone's expected to be okay all the time.

Today, consider two things: First, who around you might be suffering silently? Look beyond the smiles and "I'm fine" responses. Practice being that person who really listens, who asks twice, who creates safe spaces for truth.

Second, if you're one of those silent sufferers, please know this: Your previous experiences of not being heard don't define your worth or right to support. Sometimes it takes trying several times, with different people, to find those who can truly hear and hold your story.

Could you make space today to really listen to someone? Or if you're hurting, could you give reaching out another chance, maybe to someone new who might better understand?

Remember, sometimes the most powerful thing we can say to someone is simply "I'm here, and I care."

January 15th

"Create your own style... let it be unique for yourself and yet identifiable for others."

— Anna Wintour

This is a brilliant insight about authentic self-expression from someone who's shaped much of modern fashion culture. What I love about this quote is how it balances personal authenticity with connection to others - it's not just about being different for difference's sake.

Think about it - your style isn't just about clothes. It's about how you express yourself in everything: your work, your relationships, your creative pursuits, even how you solve problems. It's that unique fingerprint that makes you, uniquely you.

Today, consider: Where in your life are you perhaps following others' templates instead of developing your own approach? Maybe you're writing in someone else's voice, decorating your home like a magazine spread that doesn't feel like you, or handling situations the way others say you "should" rather than in ways that feel authentic.

Try this: Pick one area of your life and ask yourself, "If I were to do this completely my way, what would that look like?" Then take one small step towards that vision. Remember, developing your own style is a journey of experimentation and refinement.

What's one authentic expression of yourself that you could lean into more fully today?

January 16th

"Life becomes a lot more peaceful and less complicated when we decide what we will and won't accept in our lives, from ourselves and others."

— Gary Hardy

Here I talk about the importance of setting clear boundaries - both with ourselves and others. When we take the time to define our values and standards, we naturally filter out a lot of unnecessary drama and stress from our lives.

Think about it: How often do we find ourselves in situations that don't align with our values simply because we never drew that line in the sand? Whether it's tolerating disrespectful behaviour from others or continuing habits that we know aren't serving us well, lack of clear boundaries often leads to inner turmoil.

Today, I encourage you to take a quiet moment and ask yourself, "What am I currently accepting in my life that doesn't align with my values?" Maybe it's a friendship that constantly drains your energy, a habit that you know isn't good for you, or a situation at work that crosses your personal boundaries.

Choose one thing you'll no longer accept, and make a conscious decision to set that boundary today.

Remember, it's not about being rigid or harsh - it's about honouring yourself and creating space for what truly matters in your life.

January 17th

"Self-respect is the root of discipline: The sense of dignity grows with the ability to say no to oneself."

— Abraham Joshua Heschel

This is an insight about the relationship between self-discipline and self-worth. It turns the common view of discipline as punishment or restriction completely on its head. We often think of discipline as something harsh we impose on ourselves, but Heschel reveals it as something that actually grows from honouring ourselves. When you can say no to immediate gratification or easy choices that don't serve your higher good, you're essentially telling yourself, "I respect you enough to protect your long-term wellbeing."

For today's reflection, consider: Where in your life do you need to exercise this dignified "no" to yourself? Maybe it's setting boundaries with work hours, resisting the urge to check social media when you should be resting, or choosing not to engage in self-defeating behaviours or relationships that diminish you.

Try this: The next time you're faced with a choice between immediate gratification and long-term wellbeing, pause and ask yourself, "What would someone who deeply respects themselves do?" Then notice how choosing the more dignified path, even when it's harder, builds your sense of self-trust and worth. What small act of self-respect could you commit to today? Remember, each "no" to what lessens you is a "yes" to your own dignity.

January 18th

"Never, ever underestimate the importance of having fun."

— Randy Pausch

What a wonderful quote from Randy Pausch. As someone who has spent years observing how people navigate life's complexities, I find wisdom in these simple words.

Fun isn't just a luxury – it's essential nourishment for our spirit. When we're caught up in deadlines, responsibilities, and the serious business of life, we often dismiss fun as frivolous. But joy and playfulness keep us resilient, creative, and connected to what makes life worth living.

Today, ask yourself, "When was the last time I did something purely for the joy of it?" It doesn't need to be grand – maybe it's taking a different route home to enjoy new scenery, having a silly dance break while cooking, or calling an old friend just to share a laugh.

Try to incorporate one small moment of pure fun into your day, even for just five minutes. You'll likely find that these moments of lightness make you more productive and present in everything else you do.

Remember, the most successful and impactful people often maintain their childlike capacity for wonder and play.

It's not despite their success, but often because of it.

January 19th

"Maybe we are broken. But we put ourselves back together. We survived. That's what makes us so powerful."

— V.E. Schwab

This quote touches on the deep truth about human resilience. I've seen how our hardest moments, while painful, often forge us into stronger, more compassionate versions of ourselves. This is certainly true for me.

When V.E. Schwab speaks about being "broken," she acknowledges something we often try to hide – our wounds and struggles. But notice how she immediately pivots to the incredible power of human resilience...*how we put ourselves back together*. This isn't about pretending the breaks never happened. It's about honouring them as part of our story.

Take a moment today to acknowledge your own journey of healing and rebuilding. Think about a challenge you've overcome – it doesn't have to be huge. Maybe it was a difficult conversation you finally had, a habit you changed, or a fear you faced. That moment of putting yourself back together, however small, is evidence of your inner strength. Consider starting a "resilience journal" where you document not just your challenges, but more importantly, how you overcome them.

Over time, this becomes a powerful reminder of your ability to heal and grow stronger through adversity. When new challenges arise, you'll have tangible proof of your capacity to rebuild. Your breaks and repairs aren't flaws – they're testaments to your strength. Like the Japanese art of kintsugi, where broken pottery is repaired with gold, sometimes our mended places become our most beautiful features.

January 20th

"Never bend your head. Always hold it high. Look the world straight in the eye."

— Helen Keller

Coming from Helen Keller, these words carry extraordinary weight. As someone who has witnessed countless lives transformed by the simple act of standing tall in the face of adversity, I find this message particularly powerful.

When Keller talks about holding your head high, she's not just speaking about physical posture – she's addressing the very essence of self-worth and courage. Remember, this wisdom comes from a woman who faced unimaginable challenges yet refused to be defined by them.

Today, practice this principle in a literal and metaphorical sense. Start with your physical posture – shoulders back, chin up, eyes forward. Notice how this simple adjustment affects your mood and how others respond to you. Then, go deeper. When faced with a challenging situation – whether it's a difficult conversation, a presentation, or just walking into a crowded room – resist the urge to shrink yourself.

Choose one situation today where you'd normally want to look away or minimise yourself, and instead *look it straight in the eye*. It might be as simple as maintaining eye contact during a conversation or speaking up in a meeting when you'd usually stay quiet. Pay attention to how this small act of courage changes both your experience and the outcome.

True confidence isn't about being fearless – it's about maintaining your dignity and self-respect even when you're afraid. Remember, you have every right to take up space in this world.

January 21st

"Try to be like the turtle, at ease in your own shell."

— Bill Copeland

What a wonderfully simple metaphor from Bill Copeland. Having observed how many of us struggle with self-acceptance, I find the turtle's wisdom particularly touching.

Think about the turtle for a moment – it carries its home wherever it goes, never trying to be anything other than exactly what it is. It doesn't wish for feathers like a bird or speed like a cheetah. The turtle's strength lies in its complete acceptance of its nature.

Today, notice the moments when you feel the urge to be something different, to fit someone else's mould. Are you constantly adjusting your personality depending on who you're with? Do you apologise for parts of yourself that don't need apologies? Take a few quiet minutes to identify one aspect of yourself that you often try to change or hide.

Practice being *at ease in your own shell* by consciously accepting this part of yourself, just for today. Maybe it's your laugh, your enthusiasm for something others find boring, or your need for quiet time. Whatever it is, try carrying it with the turtle's quiet dignity.

Remember, your "shell" – your authentic self – has been shaped by your unique experiences and journey. It's not meant to look like anyone else's, and that's exactly what makes it perfect for you. Comfort with oneself isn't achieved overnight, but like the turtle, we can move towards it steadily, one small step at a time.

January 22nd

"Until you're ready to look foolish, you'll never have the possibility of being great."

— M.C. Escher

I love this quote's raw honesty about the price of achievement. As someone who has watched many people navigate their path to success, I can tell you that Escher captured something essential here – the intimate connection between vulnerability and greatness.

Think about any skill you've mastered or any meaningful achievement in your life. Chances are, you had to go through a period of looking less than graceful. Whether it was learning to ride a bike, speaking in public, or trying a new career path, the willingness to be imperfect in front of others was your entry ticket to eventual mastery.

Today, identify one thing you've been hesitating to try because you're afraid of looking foolish. Perhaps it's taking a dance class, sharing your writing, starting a business, or speaking up in meetings. Now, reframe that fear of looking foolish as a positive signal – it's pointing you towards something that matters to you.

Choose one small action that puts you in that uncomfortable space of potential foolishness. Maybe send that rough draft to a friend, sign up for that class, or raise your hand with that "silly" question. When the discomfort hits, remind yourself: this feeling isn't a warning sign – it's the sensation of growth.

Remember, those who appear effortlessly successful now all went through their own awkward phases. They just didn't let the fear of looking foolish stop them from becoming who they needed to be.

January 23rd

"Let our hearts and hands be stretched out in compassion towards others, for everyone is walking his or her own difficult path."

— Dieter F. Uchtdorf

This quote resonates deeply with my experience observing human nature. Uchtdorf captures something profound here – the universal truth that beneath our different exteriors, we're all navigating our own complex journeys.

The imagery of stretched-out hearts and hands is particularly powerful. It suggests that compassion isn't just an internal feeling – it requires action, reaching out, making ourselves available to others. Yet what makes this quote especially wise is how it links this outward compassion to the understanding that everyone, even those who seem to have it all together, is facing their own struggles.

Today, practice looking beyond the surface of people's behaviours. When someone is short-tempered in line at the store, or a colleague seems unusually withdrawn, pause and remember: they're walking their own difficult path. Instead of reacting with judgement, try one small act of reaching out – maybe a genuine smile, a patient moment, or a simple "How are you really doing?"

Make it practical by choosing one person in your life who's been challenging to deal with lately. Consider what unseen battles they might be fighting. Then find one way, however small, to extend compassion to them today. It might be as simple as sending a thoughtful message or offering to help with a task.

Remember, compassion doesn't mean taking on everyone's burdens. Sometimes it's just about acknowledging that we're all doing our best to navigate our paths, and showing a little more gentleness to ourselves and others along the way.

January 24th

"I hope you find yourself out there. I hope you figure out your heart. I hope you figure out your mind. I hope you learn how to be kind to yourself. How to embrace the journey you are on. I hope you learn to be proud of the person you are becoming. I hope you learn to be proud of where you are - even if it isn't exactly where you want to be."

— Bianca Sparacino

This quote is a gentle reminder of one of life's most important journeys – the one to find and accept ourselves. From my experience mentoring others, I've noticed how many of us are harder on ourselves than we'd ever be on a friend.

What's particularly beautiful about Sparacino's words is how she acknowledges that self-discovery is a gradual process. Notice how she says "the person you are becoming" – not "became." This suggests an ongoing journey rather than a destination, giving us permission to be works in progress.

Today, take a moment to pause and acknowledge where you are in your journey. Think about how far you've come rather than how far you still have to go. Try this exercise: Write down three things that would have seemed impossible to you five years ago but are now part of your daily life. They don't have to be big achievements – maybe it's being able to say "no" without guilt, or taking better care of your health, or speaking up more often.

Then, practice what I call "compassionate presence" – sit quietly for a few minutes and imagine treating yourself with the same kindness you'd show a dear friend who's trying their best. Can you look at your current challenges and say, "I'm proud of you for showing up, for trying, for not giving up"?

Remember, being proud of where you are doesn't mean you've stopped growing. It means you've learned to honour your journey, including the detours and the slow periods. You're exactly where you need to be right now, learning exactly what you need to learn.

January 25th

"There is nothing better than seeing your children become good, strong and confident people, who have achieved so much more than you ever did at their age."

— Gary Hardy

This quote beautifully captures one of the deepest joys of parenthood - watching your children not just grow, but thrive and surpass your own early achievements. There's such humility and pride woven into these words. It speaks to how true parental love is about wanting our children to soar beyond our own heights.

I particularly love how it emphasises character traits - "good, strong and confident" - before mentioning achievements. It suggests that while accomplishments are wonderful, the development of these core qualities is what truly matters in raising children. These are the foundations that enable all other successes.

For today, if you're a parent, I'd suggest taking a moment to write down one quality you've noticed developing in each of your children that makes you especially proud - not their grades or achievements, but who they're becoming as people. Then, find a way to acknowledge this quality to them, perhaps over dinner or during a quiet moment. Sometimes naming these strengths helps children recognise and build upon them.

There's something particularly touching about the joy expressed in seeing our children exceed our own early accomplishments. It's the ultimate expression of wanting better for the next generation - finding happiness not in our own success, but in seeing our children reach higher than we did. It shows how parenthood can transform us from being the protagonist of our own story to being the proud witness of our children's journeys.

January 26th

"Letting go doesn't mean that you don't care about someone anymore. It's just realising that the only person you really have control over is yourself."

— Deborah Reber

This quote touches on one of life's most challenging truths. Having watched many people struggle with letting go, I find Reber's insight particularly powerful because it reframes letting go not as an act of giving up, but as an act of wisdom and self-awareness.

The key insight here is the distinction between caring and controlling. So often, we confuse the two, thinking that if we truly care about someone or something, we must be able to influence or change it. But real love and caring can exist – and often exist more purely – when we release our need to control outcomes.

Today, identify one situation where you're trying to control something that's ultimately not yours to control. It might be someone else's decisions, their feelings, or their journey. Take a moment to acknowledge that your desire for control likely comes from a place of caring deeply.

Then, practice what I call "loving release" – consciously choosing to step back while maintaining your care and compassion. You might try this simple exercise: When you feel the urge to step in and fix or control, take a deep breath and say to yourself, "I care about this, AND I recognise that this isn't mine to control."

Remember, letting go isn't a one-time event but a daily practice. Each time you choose to focus on what you can control – your own responses, boundaries, and actions – you're not just freeing others; you're freeing yourself to live more authentically and peacefully.

January 27th

"My point is this: the more you have to lose, the braver you are for standing up."

— Craig Silvey

This is a powerful observation that challenges our usual understanding of bravery. From years of observing human courage, I've seen how having more at stake often makes acts of courage even more meaningful, not less.

Think about it – it's one thing to take a stand when you have nothing to lose. But to speak up, to act, to stand firm in your values when you have a comfortable life, a reputation, or relationships that could be affected? That requires a special kind of courage.

Today, take inventory of what you've built in your life – your relationships, career, reputation, stability. Now think about a situation where you've held back from speaking up or taking action because you were worried about risking these things. This awareness isn't meant to make you feel guilty, but to help you recognise that your hesitation comes from a place of having built something valuable.

Choose one small act of standing up for what you believe in today, being fully aware of what you're risking. Maybe it's respectfully disagreeing with a superior at work, setting a boundary with a long-term friend, or speaking an uncomfortable truth in a relationship you value. Notice how this consciousness of what's at stake doesn't make you less brave – it makes your action more meaningful.

Remember, true courage isn't about being fearless about what you might lose; it's about choosing to act despite those very real and valid fears. Your stake in life doesn't diminish your courage – it amplifies it.

January 28th

"Have nothing in your house that you do not know to be useful or believe to be beautiful."

— William Morris

This quote from William Morris offers wisdom that extends far beyond home decoration. Having observed how our physical spaces deeply affect our mental and emotional well-being, I find this principle both practical and transformative.

Morris gives us two powerful criteria for what deserves space in our lives: Utility and beauty. Notice how he doesn't force us to choose between them – something can earn its place through either purpose or pleasure, acknowledging that both have genuine value in our lives.

Today, choose one small space in your home – perhaps a drawer, a shelf, or even just your desk. Look at each item there and ask yourself Morris's two simple questions: "Is this useful to me?" and "Do I find this beautiful?" Be honest with yourself about both questions. Something might be theoretically useful but hasn't served a purpose in years. Another item might have been beautiful to you once but no longer brings you joy.

Try removing items that don't meet either criterion, even temporarily. Put them in a box for a week and notice how their absence affects you. Does the space feel lighter? Do you function more efficiently? Does your eye rest more peacefully on what remains?

Remember, this principle can extend beyond physical objects. Consider applying it to your digital space, your schedule, or even your relationships. Not to oversimplify complex human connections, but to remind yourself that everything you maintain in your life should serve a purpose or bring beauty in some way.

January 29th

"There's nothing like music to relieve the soul and uplift it."

— Mickey Hart

Ah, Mickey Hart's words resonate with me on multiple levels. As a former DJ, music store manager, and now a mentor, I've experienced the transformative power of music from every angle. I've seen it work its magic not just on packed dance floors, but in countless one-on-one conversations with people seeking guidance and light in their lives. Having recommended healing songs to individuals during their darkest moments, I know firsthand how the right music can shift someone's entire emotional state in minutes.

Drawing from my years of experience both behind the turntables and in mentoring sessions, I've learned that music is one of our most powerful tools for emotional transformation. When I work with people who are struggling, one of my first questions is often about what they're listening to, because I know how profoundly it affects our mental state.

Today, try approaching music as the healing force I've watched it be for so many others. Create your own emotional soundtrack – something I've helped countless mentees do. Think of it as prescribing music for different emotional needs, just as I used to curate sets for different moments in the night while DJing, and now recommend specific songs to help people through specific challenges.

Build a playlist for motivation, another for processing grief, one for celebration, and one for finding peace. Having guided many people through their personal transformations, I've seen how the right song at the right moment can be the catalyst for profound change.

Remember, you don't need to be a music professional or mentor like I am to harness this power. Sometimes, the simplest melody can be your guide back to centre. Music has been my own constant companion and a tool I use in helping others find their way, and it's always there, waiting to lift you up – you just need to let it in.

What piece of music speaks to your soul right now? As a mentor, I've found that this question often opens the door to our deepest truths.

January 30th

Of this be sure: You do not find the happy life...you make it.

— Thomas S. Monson

What a powerful truth Monson shares here. I particularly appreciate how this quote cuts through the common misconception that happiness is something we stumble upon or that simply happens to us.

Think about this: How often do we catch ourselves waiting for happiness to arrive? "I'll be happy when I get that promotion" or "I'll be happy once I'm in a relationship." But happiness isn't a destination - it's more like a garden we tend to daily through our choices and actions.

Today, I'd encourage you to ask yourself: "What's one small action I can take today to actively create happiness rather than wait for it?" It could be as simple as spending 10 minutes doing something you love, reaching out to a friend you've been meaning to call, or tackling that task you've been putting off.

Remember, happiness isn't about grand gestures - it's built through these small, intentional choices we make each day.

January 31st

"We do not learn from experience...we learn from reflecting on experience."

— John Dewey

What a great insight from John Dewey. Having spent years observing how people grow and develop, I've seen this truth play out countless times. Many people go through experiences without extracting their deeper lessons, while others turn even simple moments into powerful learning opportunities through thoughtful reflection.

Experience alone is like having an unread book on your shelf – it's only when we open it, examine its contents, and consider its meaning that it becomes valuable to us. Think of how many times we might repeat the same patterns until we actually pause to understand why.

Today, try this simple but powerful practice: Set aside 10 minutes of quiet time and choose one recent experience – it doesn't have to be dramatic or life-changing. It could be a conversation that left you feeling unsettled, a project that went particularly well, or even a small decision you made. Ask yourself: What actually happened? (Just the facts). How did I feel about it? What worked and what didn't? What does this tell me about myself or others? How might I use this insight going forward?

Remember, reflection doesn't mean dwelling on the past. It means mining your experiences for the gold of understanding. Each evening, try asking yourself, "What did today teach me?" You might be surprised at how much wisdom is hidden in your ordinary experiences, just waiting to be discovered through reflection.

February 1st

"In February, there is everything to hope for and nothing to regret."

— Patience Strong

What a beautifully hopeful perspective from Patience Strong. This quote captures something special about February - it sits at this unique intersection of winter and the promise of spring, much like how our lives often balance between where we've been and where we're heading.

There's profound wisdom in approaching life with this mindset of forward-looking optimism while letting go of past regrets. February, despite its cold and grey days in many places, carries within it the subtle hints of renewal - the first bulbs pushing through the soil, slightly longer days, the quiet preparation for spring.

This month, consider approaching your days with this "February spirit." What hopes can you plant, no matter how small? Maybe it's starting a new habit, rekindling an old friendship, or simply looking at a challenge through fresh eyes. And equally important - what regrets might you be ready to release?

Remember, just as February holds the promise of spring within its winter days, every moment holds the potential for a fresh start. We don't need to wait for January 1st to begin anew - sometimes the most powerful new beginnings happen on ordinary Tuesday afternoons in February.

February 2nd

"Never Stop Learning. Because Life Never Stops Teaching."

— Kirill Korshikov

There's something deeply encouraging about this quote from Korshikov. It reminds us that every experience, every challenge, every joy and setback - they're all opportunities for growth if we remain open to their lessons.

You know what's beautiful about this perspective? It takes the pressure off of having to "arrive" at some final destination of knowledge or wisdom. Instead, it invites us to view life as this amazing ongoing classroom, where every day brings new opportunities to learn and grow. Sometimes the lessons are gentle, sometimes they're tough, but they're always there if we're willing to see them.

Today, try approaching your experiences with the curiosity of a lifelong student. What might today be trying to teach you? It could be through a conversation that challenges your perspective, a mistake that shows you a better way, or even a moment of joy that deepens your understanding of what matters most to you.

Perhaps pause at some point today and ask yourself: "What lesson is life offering me right now?" Sometimes the most profound teachings come in the most ordinary moments - we just need to be awake to them.

The beauty is, as long as we're breathing, we're learning. And there's something incredibly hopeful about that, isn't it?

February 3rd

"We can complain because rose bushes have thorns, or rejoice because thorns have roses."

— Alphonse Karr

This is such a powerful reminder about the transformative power of perspective. Karr captures a fundamental truth about life - that often, our experience isn't shaped by what happens to us, but by how we choose to see it.

It's fascinating how the same exact reality - a rose bush with both thorns and flowers - can be seen as either a source of frustration or a gift of beauty. It's not about denying the thorns exist - they're very real, just like life's challenges. But it's about choosing where we place our focus and what story we tell ourselves about what we see.

Today, consider taking a moment to identify one "thorny" situation in your life right now. It could be a challenging project at work, a difficult relationship, or even just a daily frustration. Now, ask yourself: "What's the rose here? What's the beauty or opportunity I might be missing because I'm focused on the thorns?"

Sometimes the simple act of looking for the roses - the lessons, the growth opportunities, the hidden blessings - can completely transform our experience. Remember, we all face thorns in life, but we get to choose whether we let them overshadow the roses.

What "rose" might you be overlooking in your life right now?

February 4th

"You have to make mistakes to find out who you aren't. You take the action, and the insight follows: You don't think your way into becoming yourself."

— Anne Lamott

What a liberating perspective from Lamott! There's something deeply reassuring about framing mistakes not as failures, but as essential steps in discovering our authentic selves.

We often get caught in this trap of trying to think and plan our way to perfection, as if we could somehow figure everything out in our heads before taking action. But life doesn't work that way, does it? It's through trying, stumbling, getting up, and trying again that we truly learn who we are - and perhaps more importantly, who we aren't.

Today, consider embracing one thing you've been hesitating to try because of fear of making mistakes. Maybe it's learning a new skill, expressing a feeling, or taking on a challenge. Remember that each "wrong turn" on your path isn't really wrong at all - it's just helping you map out your authentic journey. Think of it like this: Every mistake is actually a clarifying moment, telling you "Okay, that's not quite me" or "That's not quite my way." These insights are invaluable, and you can only gain them through action, through living, through doing.

Perhaps today, instead of seeking perfection, you might choose to seek experience. What action could you take that would help you learn more about yourself, even if it means risking a mistake?

February 5th

"As you read my stories of long ago I hope you will remember that things truly worthwhile and that will give you happiness are the same now as they were then. It is not the things you have that make you happy. It is love and kindness and helping each other and just plain being good."

— Laura Ingalls Wilder

What profound wisdom Wilder shares here, drawn from a simpler time yet so deeply relevant to our modern lives. She cuts through all the noise and complexity of our world to remind us of what truly matters - those timeless human connections and values that have always been the real source of joy.

In our current age of constant upgrades, social media highlights, and pressure to acquire more, there's something deeply refreshing about this reminder. Happiness isn't wrapped up in the latest gadget or achievement - it's found in those moments of genuine connection, in small acts of kindness, in being there for each other.

Today, consider taking a moment to identify one simple way you could add more of these timeless sources of happiness into your day. Maybe it's sending a heartfelt message to someone you care about, helping a neighbour with a small task, or simply choosing to respond with kindness in a challenging situation.

Think about the happiest moments in your life - chances are they're not about things you bought or owned, but about times you felt deeply connected, times you made a difference in someone's life, or times when someone showed you unexpected kindness.

Remember, sometimes the most meaningful way forward is actually a step back to these fundamental truths: love, kindness, helping others, and, as Wilder so beautifully puts it, "just plain being good."

February 6th

"In the case of good books, the point is not to see how many of them you can get through, but rather how many can get through to you."

— Mortimer J. Adler

This is such an insightful observation from Adler about the true value of reading. It challenges our modern tendency to rush through books like items on a checklist, reminding us that real reading is about absorption and transformation.

It's interesting how we sometimes get caught up in counting the books we've read or racing to finish them, as if reading were a competition. But Adler reminds us that meaningful reading is more like having a deep conversation with the author - it's not about speed, but about allowing the ideas to truly sink in and change us.

Today, consider approaching whatever you're currently reading with this mindset of depth over breadth. Maybe pause after a meaningful paragraph and ask yourself: "How is this getting through to me? What's shifting in my understanding?" If you're not reading anything right now, perhaps choose a book that's been meaningful to you in the past and reflect on how it got "through to you" - how did it change your thinking or your life?

Remember, one book that deeply influences your life is worth more than a hundred that you simply skim through. It's not about the quantity of pages turned, but the quality of insights gained. What's the last book that truly "got through" to you?

February 7th

"Half of the troubles of this life can be traced to saying yes too quickly and not saying no soon enough."

— Josh Billings

This observation from Billings cuts right to the heart of so many of our daily struggles. This wisdom feels especially relevant in today's world, where we're constantly bombarded with requests for our time, energy, and attention. Many of us have been conditioned to see "yes" as the kind, helpful answer and "no" as somehow negative or selfish. But there's a profound truth here about how our quick "yeses" and delayed "nos" can gradually overwhelm us, dilute our ability to fully commit to what truly matters, and steal or focus and time.

Today, consider taking stock of your current commitments. Where might you be suffering from a "yes" that came too quickly? Perhaps it's time to practice what I like to call the "thoughtful pause" - that brief moment between being asked something and responding, where we can check in with ourselves about whether this aligns with our values and capacity.

Remember, every time you say yes to something, you're inherently saying no to something else - often to your own time, peace of mind, or ability to fully engage with priorities that matter most to you. A well-timed "no" isn't just about declining - it's about protecting your "best yes" for the things that truly deserve it. What might change in your life if you gave yourself permission to be more deliberate with your "yeses" and more prompt with your "nos"?

February 8th

"Finding a good woman to share your life with is so rare these days, so if you are lucky enough to find one, you will feel like the rest of your life is not long enough to appreciate what she brings to your life."

— Gary Hardy

This is a truth about deep, meaningful partnerships. It goes beyond just finding someone to share life with - it speaks to that rare sense of having found a connection so enriching that time itself feels too short to fully appreciate it. It's about recognising the extraordinary in what might seem ordinary to others.

The phrase "rest of your life is not long enough" captures that feeling when appreciation deepens rather than diminishes with time. It's like having an endless gift that keeps revealing new layers of value and meaning as the years pass.

For today, if you're in such a relationship, I'd suggest taking a moment to identify one specific quality about your partner that continues to amaze you - something you might take for granted in the daily rush of life. Then, share this observation with them, not just saying "I appreciate you" but naming that specific quality and how it enriches your life. If you're still searching for this kind of connection, let this quote guide you in recognising what truly matters - not just surface compatibility, but the kind of presence that makes life feel richer and more meaningful.

There's wisdom here about both gratitude and discernment - it reminds us to truly value these rare connections when we find them, while also understanding that such profound partnerships aren't commonplace. It's about recognising real treasure when you find it.

February 9th

"Is it possible for a home to be a person and not a place?"

— Stephanie Perkins

What a beautiful question Perkins poses here. It touches something deep about the nature of belonging and what truly makes us feel "at home" in this world.

We often think of home in terms of walls and roofs, addresses and furniture. But haven't we all experienced that feeling of complete "at-homeness" when with certain people or one special person? That sense that regardless of where we are physically, we've found our place of belonging simply by being in their presence?

Today, consider the person in your life who feel like home to you - those rare souls who make you feel completely yourself, totally safe to be vulnerable, fully accepted. Maybe it's a parent whose hug still makes everything feel okay, a friend whose kitchen table has heard all your stories, or a partner whose presence alone brings peace.

Remember, sometimes our truest sense of home isn't found in a specific place but in the connections we forge with others. Home becomes portable when it lives in the heart of our relationships rather than in brick and mortar.

Perhaps take a moment today to reach out to someone who feels like home to you. Let them know what their presence means in your life. After all, sometimes the most important address isn't a street number - it's the place we hold in each other's hearts.

February 10th

"Dream lofty dreams, and as you dream, so you shall become. Your vision is the promise of what you shall one day be; your ideal is the prophecy of what you shall at last unveil."

— James Allen

I love how Allen weaves together dreams and destiny here, suggesting that our visions aren't just idle fantasies but blueprints for our future selves. There's something deeply empowering about the idea that our dreams are actually glimpses of our potential. In our practical, fast-paced world, it's easy to dismiss "lofty dreams" as unrealistic or childish. But Allen reminds us that these visions serve a vital purpose - they're like spiritual compasses, pointing us towards who we're meant to become. The dream you hold in your heart today might just be tomorrow's reality taking shape.

Today, consider taking a quiet moment to reconnect with your loftiest dream - not the practical, scaled-down version you might share at a job interview, but the one that makes your heart beat faster when you dare to imagine it. What does that dream tell you about who you're capable of becoming?

Remember, every great achievement, every transformation, every leap forward in human history started as someone's "lofty dream." Your dreams aren't separate from your reality - they're the seeds of it. The key is to nurture them while taking small, consistent steps in their direction. What part of your dream could you take one tiny step towards today, knowing that each step helps unveil the person you're meant to be?

February 11th

"Whoever abandoned you in the middle of the ocean has no right to know what the sharks did to you or how you managed it to the shore."

— Unknown

This quote speaks deeply to the journey of healing and personal sovereignty after betrayal. When someone walks away from us during our darkest moments, they forfeit their right to know our story of survival. The pain of abandonment can feel like being left alone in vast waters, but our journey to shore – our path to healing and rebuilding – belongs to us alone.

Today, remember that you don't owe anyone an explanation of how you overcame their absence. Your strength, your scars, and your victories are yours to share only if and when you choose. Focus instead on celebrating how far you've come. Take a moment to acknowledge the resilience that brought you to where you are now. Whether you swam, floated, or found an unexpected lifeboat, your survival is a testament to your inner strength.

Ask yourself: Am I still giving emotional energy to people who weren't there during my struggles? Perhaps it's time to redirect that energy towards those who prove themselves worthy of your story – including, most importantly, yourself.

February 12th

"Everything you're thinking doesn't need to be said, out loud or on the internet."

— Tiffany Haddish

This is a powerful reminder about the value of discernment in our hyperconnected world. Tiffany Haddish captures a fundamental wisdom that's becoming increasingly rare – the art of holding our thoughts with discretion.

Today, before sharing your thoughts either verbally or online, pause and ask yourself three simple questions: "Does this need to be said? Will it add value? Is this the right moment?" Not every thought that crosses our mind requires expression. Sometimes, our greatest power lies in what we choose to keep to ourselves.

Consider practicing the art of selective sharing. When you feel that urgent push to post something or speak out, take a breath and let the thought sit with you for a few minutes. You might find that some thoughts are better kept as personal reflections, while others truly deserve to be shared. This isn't about suppression – it's about mindful expression.

Remember: Your inner dialogue is yours to curate, and not every thought needs an audience. In cultivating this awareness, you'll likely find yourself feeling more at peace and in control of your narrative.

February 13th

"Resilience can only form if we face, and learn how to be better equipped to manage, our problems."

— Jo Frost

This is a profound truth about personal growth and resilience. Jo Frost captures something essential here – resilience isn't about avoiding difficulties, but about actively engaging with our challenges to become stronger.

Today, instead of turning away from a problem you're facing, try to sit with it mindfully. What is this challenge teaching you? What tools or skills might help you handle similar situations better in the future? Think of each obstacle as a training ground rather than a roadblock.

Remember that becoming resilient is like building a muscle – it requires regular "exercise" through facing difficulties head-on. When you encounter a challenge today, rather than immediately seeking an escape route, pause and ask yourself: "What can I learn from this? How might this experience make me stronger?"

This isn't about seeking out hardship, but about approaching inevitable difficulties with a growth mindset. Whether it's a difficult conversation you need to have, a task you've been avoiding, or an emotion you've been suppressing – engaging with it thoughtfully today will help you build the emotional strength you'll need tomorrow.

February 14th

"Instead of expecting, try accepting. Life is so much less complicated and drama free when you expect nothing from people, and accept that you are going to allow them to show you exactly who they are."

— Gary Hardy

Here I have spoken about something fundamental in human relationships and peace of mind. I've noticed how much suffering comes from the gap between who we expect people to be and who they actually are.

When we carry around these expectations - that our friend should always be available, that our partner should somehow know what we need without being told, that everyone should operate according to our personal values - we're setting ourselves up for constant disappointment. More than that, we're not really seeing people for who they truly are.

Today, I'd invite you to practice something challenging but liberating: Notice when you're imposing expectations on others and try gently letting them go. This doesn't mean lowering your standards or accepting mistreatment. Rather, it's about seeing people clearly, without the fog of your expectations clouding your vision.

Think about someone in your life who often disappoints you. Are you trying to make them fit into a role they never agreed to play? What would it feel like to simply observe and accept who they actually are, rather than who you wish they would be?

There's such freedom in this approach. When we accept people as they are, we can make clearer decisions about our relationships. We can choose who to keep close and who to create boundaries with, based on who they've shown themselves to be - not who we hope they'll become.

Remember, accepting people as they are doesn't mean you have to keep them in your life. It just means you're dealing with reality rather than fiction. And reality, though sometimes uncomfortable, is always easier to navigate than illusion.

February 15th

"You're overthinking because you really care what happens next—you don't want to fail, and you don't want to let people down. But no amount of planning, worrying, or over-analysing can give you control over what happens next. Breathe. Loosen your grip. Experience life as it comes."

— Michell C. Clark

This quote beautifully captures the struggle so many of us face with anxiety and perfectionism. Clark understands that overthinking often comes from a place of deep caring and responsibility – it's not a flaw, but rather a sign of how much we invest in our lives and relationships.

Today, notice when you start spiralling into overthinking. Remember that your analytical mind is trying to protect you, but it's overworking itself. When you catch yourself in an overthinking loop, try this simple practice: Take three deep breaths and name one thing you can see, hear, and feel right now. This grounds you in the present moment, where life is actually happening. Consider the idea that some of the best moments in your life weren't meticulously planned – they simply unfolded. Could you allow today to unfold with a bit more trust? When you feel the urge to control every detail, gently remind yourself that life's beauty often lies in its unpredictability.

The invitation here isn't to stop caring or planning altogether, but to find a balance between preparation and presence. Today, try to catch yourself when you're gripping too tightly to outcomes, and practice loosening that grip just a little. Notice how this small shift might actually help you experience life more fully and authentically.

February 16th

"Life is a dream for the wise, a game for the fool, a comedy for the rich, a tragedy for the poor."

— Norman Mailer

This quote from Mailer offers a profound reflection on how differently life can be experienced based on our circumstances and perspectives. Let me share a slightly different take on it that might be helpful for daily living.

Today, consider how your own perspective shapes your experience of life. While Mailer's quote highlights social and economic realities, it also reminds us that we have some agency in how we view our journey. The "wise" he mentions aren't necessarily the most educated or wealthy – they're often those who can find meaning and beauty even in difficult circumstances. Ask yourself: Regardless of your current situation, what aspects of your life could you view differently? Perhaps there are moments you're taking too seriously that could be approached with more playfulness, or challenges you're dismissing that deserve more thoughtful consideration.

The real wisdom might lie in being able to hold multiple perspectives at once – to acknowledge life's hardships while still remaining open to its moments of joy and wonder. Whether your current circumstances are comfortable or challenging, there's value in developing the ability to see both the dream and the game, the comedy and the tragedy in your daily experiences. Remember, our perspective isn't fixed – we can choose to shift how we view our circumstances, even if we can't always change them immediately.

February 17th

"I am just a human being trying to make it in a world that is rapidly losing its understanding of being human."

— John Trudell

Wow, this quote really resonates deeply with our current moment, doesn't it? Despite being written years ago, it feels especially relevant in our increasingly digital, fast-paced world. There's something both vulnerable and defiant in Trudell's words - this simple declaration of being human in a world that sometimes seems to be moving away from human connection and understanding.

For today's reflection, I'd invite you to consider what being "human" means to you. In a world of productivity metrics, social media personas, and artificial interactions, maybe we need to intentionally create space for our messy, imperfect humanity. Think about the moments when you feel most authentically human - perhaps it's sharing a laugh with a friend, feeling moved by music, or simply sitting quietly with your thoughts.

Try this today: Take a moment to engage in something purely human. Maybe it's having a face-to-face conversation without checking your phone, expressing an emotion without filtering it, or simply taking time to feel whatever you're feeling without trying to optimise or improve it. Sometimes just acknowledging our basic humanity - our needs for connection, rest, or understanding - can be revolutionary in a world that often expects us to function like machines.

Remember, being human isn't about being perfect or even particularly extraordinary. It's about being present, being authentic, and connecting with others in meaningful ways. Perhaps understanding this is the first step in preserving our humanity in an increasingly complex world.

What makes you feel most authentically human in your daily life?

February 18th

"Grudges are a terribly heavy burden to carry through your life."

— Michael Lipsey

This is such a gentle yet powerful reminder about the weight we choose to carry when we hold onto resentment. Lipsey touches on a profound truth – holding grudges often hurts us more than the person we're holding them against.

Today, take a moment to notice if you're carrying any grudges, big or small. Feel their weight – how they might be affecting your peace of mind, your relationships, or even your physical well-being. Ask yourself: "Who am I really punishing by holding onto this anger or hurt?"

Remember that letting go of a grudge doesn't mean excusing what happened or inviting that person back into your life. Instead, it's about freeing yourself from the burden of carrying that pain day after day. Consider releasing just one small grudge today – perhaps something minor like a forgotten slight or an old misunderstanding. Notice how much lighter you feel when you consciously choose to set down that weight.

Think of forgiveness not as a gift to others, but as a gift to yourself. Each grudge we release creates more space for joy, peace, and new possibilities in our lives.

February 19th

"I opened my mouth, almost said something. Almost. The rest of my life might have turned out differently if I had. But I didn't."

— Khaled Hosseini

This haunting quote from Hosseini captures one of life's most poignant moments – the weight of words unsaid and paths not taken. It speaks to those pivotal moments where silence shapes our future as powerfully as speech.

Today, pay attention to those moments when you feel the urge to speak but hesitate. What holds you back? Is it fear, pride, or uncertainty? While not every thought needs to be voiced, consider whether your silence serves you or constrains you.

Try this: Choose one important thing you've been holding back from saying. It might be "I love you," "I'm sorry," "I need help," or even "This isn't working for me." Write it down first if you need to. Then ask yourself – what's the real risk in saying it? Often, we find the fear of speaking up is more damaging than any potential consequence.

Remember that while we can't change yesterday's silences, we can choose to speak today. Your words – especially the difficult ones – might be exactly what someone needs to hear, or what you need to say for your own growth and peace. Life rarely gives us perfect moments to speak. Sometimes courage means saying what needs to be said, even if your voice shakes, even if the moment isn't perfect.

February 20th

"I'm going to tell you a secret: You don't have to believe every thought that pops into your head."

— B. Dave Walters

This quote from Walters offers such liberating wisdom about our relationship with our own minds. It's a gentle reminder that we are not our thoughts – we're the awareness that observes them.

Today, try to catch yourself when you're automatically believing your thoughts, especially the self-critical ones. Notice how many thoughts pass through your mind like clouds in the sky – some dark and stormy, others light and peaceful. You don't have to grab onto every one. Practice watching your thoughts with curiosity rather than immediately accepting them as truth. When a difficult thought appears – maybe "I'm not good enough" or "I'll never figure this out" – try asking yourself: "Is this actually true? Do I need to believe this right now?" Often, you'll find these thoughts are just old patterns or temporary fears, not facts.

Remember that having a thought doesn't make it real or true. Just as you wouldn't believe everything someone else tells you without question, you can learn to be discerning with your own mental chatter. This isn't about suppressing thoughts, but about choosing which ones deserve your attention and energy. Consider treating your thoughts like suggestions rather than commands – you can acknowledge them, thank them for their input, and then decide whether to take them seriously or let them float by.

February 21st

"Don't keep staring at the way things are. It keeps you stuck. Look for how they can become. It moves you forwards."

— Jerry Corstens

This beautiful quote from Corstens speaks to the transformative power of vision and possibility thinking. It reminds us that focusing too intently on current circumstances can become its own form of limitation.

Today, when you encounter something that feels stuck or unchangeable in your life, pause and practice shifting your perspective. Instead of dwelling on "what is," try asking yourself "what could be?" This isn't about denial or toxic positivity – it's about expanding your field of vision to include possibilities you might not see when focused solely on current challenges.

Try this simple practice: Take one situation that's been frustrating you. First, acknowledge how it is right now without judgement. Then, allow yourself to imagine three different ways it could evolve or improve. They don't have to be immediate solutions – even small shifts in perspective can start moving you in a new direction.

Remember that every major change, invention, or breakthrough started with someone looking beyond "what is" to "what could be." Your circumstances might be your current reality, but they don't have to be your permanent story. Sometimes the first step forward is simply lifting your eyes from the ground where you stand to the horizon ahead of you.

February 22nd

"If you want to make your dreams come true, the first thing you have to do is wake up."

— J.M. Power

This quote beautifully balances inspiration with practicality. Power reminds us that dreams require more than just dreaming – they demand our conscious, awakened engagement with reality.

Today, consider how you can take one small but concrete step towards a dream you've been holding. Dreams have their place – they inspire us and show us what's possible. But true transformation happens in those awake moments when we actively work towards our vision.

Ask yourself: What dream have you been carrying while sleeping through the opportunities to act on it? Maybe it's a creative project you've been thinking about but not starting, a relationship you want to improve but haven't taken steps towards, or a change you've been hoping for but not actively pursuing.

Remember that "waking up" means different things: It might mean facing reality about what it truly takes to achieve your dreams. It could mean recognising that some dreams need updating. Or it might simply mean acknowledging that now – this very moment – is the time to begin. Consider this: Between dreaming and achieving lies the critical step of waking up to take action. What's one thing you could do today, fully awake and present, to move towards your dream?

February 23rd

"If you have no excuse, admit it, rather than coming up with a bad one."

— Gary Hardy

This quote strikes at the heart of personal integrity and growth. When we mess up or fall short (and we all do!), there's often this instinctive urge to craft an excuse, even when we know it's flimsy. But there's something deeply liberating about simply saying "I made a mistake" or "This one's on me."

Today, pay attention to those moments when you feel that familiar urge to make an excuse. Maybe you're running late to a meeting or haven't completed something you promised. Instead of scrambling for a justification, try taking a deep breath and owning it.

You might find that people respect you more for your honesty, and more importantly, you'll respect yourself more. This simple practice of radical honesty, even in small situations, builds trust and personal character in ways that can transform your relationships and self-image over time.

Remember - true strength isn't in being perfect; it's in being real. Ready to try it today?

February 24th

"You did nothing wrong removing toxic people from your life and choosing yourself. Your gentle heart had enough!"

— Sibel Terhaar

This quote really touches on something profound about self-preservation and emotional well-being. So often, especially if we have kind hearts, we feel guilty about setting boundaries or walking away from relationships that drain us. But Sibel Terhaar captures an essential truth here - choosing yourself isn't selfish, it's necessary.

Take a moment today to check in with your emotional energy. Are there relationships in your life that consistently leave you feeling depleted rather than uplifted? Sometimes we keep toxic connections because we feel obligated, or because we hope things will change. Remember that your gentle heart - your capacity for kindness and empathy - is precious. It needs and deserves protection. Setting boundaries or stepping away isn't about being mean or unforgiving; it's about honouring your own well-being.

Consider this: just as you wouldn't keep drinking from a poisoned well, you don't need to keep drawing from relationships that poison your spirit. Your gentleness is a strength, not a reason to endure harm. Today, give yourself permission to prioritise your peace. Sometimes the most loving thing you can do - both for yourself and ultimately for others - is to create healthy distance where it's needed.

February 25th

"I have come to believe that caring for myself is not self-indulgent. Caring for myself is an act of survival."

— Audre Lorde

Audre Lorde's words carry such profound wisdom, especially in a world that often makes us feel guilty for taking care of ourselves. She understood that self-care isn't about luxury spa days or indulgence - it's about maintaining our fundamental well-being, our ability to keep going, to stay whole.

Today, I encourage you to reframe how you think about taking care of yourself. When you feel that twinge of guilt about setting aside time for rest, or saying no to demands on your energy, remember: you're not being selfish - you're practicing survival. Like a car needs fuel to run, or a plant needs water to grow, you need to replenish your physical, emotional, and mental resources.

Think about what true self-care looks like for you today. Maybe it's taking a proper lunch break instead of working through it. Perhaps it's going to bed early rather than pushing through another episode. It could be simply sitting quietly for five minutes to breathe and check in with yourself. Whatever it is, do it with the understanding that you're not just treating yourself - you're maintaining your capacity to face life's challenges and show up fully in your relationships and responsibilities. Remember: You can't pour from an empty cup, and you can't light the way for others if your own flame has gone out. Your well-being isn't a luxury - it's a necessity.

February 26th

"Until you value yourself, you won't value your time. Until you value your time, you will not do anything with it."

— M. Scott Peck

This quote from M. Scott Peck cuts straight to the heart of how self-worth connects to everything we do - or don't do - with our lives. It's like a chain reaction: when we don't value ourselves, we treat our time as if it were worthless, and our days slip away without purpose.

Today, try looking at how you spend your time through the lens of self-worth. When you say "yes" to things you don't really want to do, or when you scroll mindlessly through social media instead of pursuing your dreams, ask yourself: "What is this behaviour saying about how I value myself?"

Start small. Pick one hour today and treat it as precious - because it is. Maybe use it to work on that project you've been putting off, or to take that first step towards a goal you've been dreaming about. Notice how it feels to act as if your time matters, because you matter.

Remember: Every time you treat your time as valuable, you're making a powerful statement about your own worth. Your hours are the building blocks of your life - and you deserve to fill them with things that reflect your true value. What will you do with your next hour that shows you value yourself?

February 27th

"Meditation is not about stopping thoughts, but recognising that we are more than our thoughts and our feelings."

— Arianna Huffington

What a clarifying insight from Arianna Huffington. So many people get frustrated with meditation because they think they're "failing" when thoughts keep coming. But she captures something essential here - the real power isn't in achieving some thought-free state, but in discovering that there's a deeper part of us that watches those thoughts float by.

Today, try this simple perspective shift: instead of fighting your thoughts during quiet moments, imagine yourself as the sky, and your thoughts as clouds passing through. The sky isn't defined by the clouds - it's the vast space that holds them. Similarly, you're not your worried thoughts about that work project, or your excited plans for the weekend, or your memories of yesterday. You're the awareness that notices all of these.

Take just five minutes today to sit quietly and practice this. When you notice yourself getting caught up in a thought (and you will - that's normal!), gently remind yourself: "I am noticing this thought." This simple practice can help you develop a healthier relationship with your mental chatter and find more peace, even in the midst of a busy mind. Remember: The goal isn't to empty your mind, but to recognise that you are larger than the contents of your thoughts. Can you feel the spaciousness in that truth?

February 28th

"The only way to make sense out of change is to plunge into it, move with it, and join the dance."

— Rebecca McCallum

This quote beautifully captures the fluid nature of life and how we can best navigate it. Often we try to control change, to resist it, or to understand it completely before we're willing to embrace it. But Rebecca McCallum reminds us that change is more like a dance than a problem to be solved.

Today, notice where you might be resisting changes in your life - big or small. Are you trying to think your way through something instead of experiencing it? Sometimes we get so caught up in analysing and planning that we forget to simply move with the rhythm of what's happening.

Try approaching one change in your life today with this dancing spirit. Instead of asking "Why is this happening?" or "How can I control this?", ask yourself "How can I move with this?" Maybe it's an unexpected shift at work, a change in plans, or even just a shift in your mood. Rather than bracing against it, see if you can find some grace in flowing with it.

Remember: A good dancer doesn't fight the music - they let it guide their movements. Similarly, when we stop resisting change and start moving with it, we often find ourselves exactly where we need to be. What change are you ready to dance with today?

February 29th

"Another day, another day...!"

— Walter Scott

Ah, what beautiful wisdom we can find in Walter Scott's simple words when we shift our perspective! This isn't just about an extra day on a leap year or the passing of time - it's a celebration of being given another precious gift of 24 hours to experience this magnificent adventure called life.

Today, let's embrace the gift of waking up to a new sunrise. While we're here, breathing and feeling our hearts beat, we have another chance to hold our loved ones close, to hear their laughter, to share in their joys and sorrows. We have another opportunity to taste our morning coffee, feel the warmth of sunlight on our skin, or watch the clouds dance across the sky.

Think about it - each "another day" means another chance to tell someone "I love you," another opportunity to chase our dreams, another moment to simply marvel at being alive. It's not just another box on the calendar - it's another collection of moments where we can experience the full spectrum of what it means to be human.

Remember: Every heartbeat, every breath, every "another day" is a gift that not everyone received this morning. How beautiful is it that we get to be here, right now, experiencing this moment? What will you do with this precious gift of another day?

March 1st

"Our life is March weather, savage and serene in one hour."

— *Ralph Waldo Emerson*

What a vivid metaphor from Emerson that captures the unpredictable nature of life! Just like March weather, with its sudden shifts between winter storms and spring sunshine, our lives can transform from challenging moments to peaceful ones in the blink of an eye.

This month, consider embracing both the "savage" and "serene" moments in your life, understanding that both are natural and necessary parts of your journey. When you're in the middle of a personal storm, remember that like March weather, it will pass, making way for calmer skies. And during peaceful moments, savour them fully while accepting that new challenges may arise.

Try this: Instead of resisting the changing weather of your life, practice acknowledging each state as it comes. When facing difficulties, remind yourself "This too shall pass." When experiencing peace, breathe it in deeply. This acceptance of life's dual nature can help you stay grounded through both the storms and the sunshine.

Remember: Just as March serves as the bridge between winter and spring, our challenging moments often lead us to growth and renewal. Can you find strength in knowing that both the storms and the calm are shaping you into who you're becoming?

March 2nd

"Having a child that is wise beyond their years is a blessing, you will notice that they have a wisdom and a knowing that will surprise you."

— Gary Hardy

This quote really touches on something special. As someone who's seen many parents navigate their relationships with their children, I've noticed how some kids just seem to have this incredible depth to them - like old souls in young bodies. They pick up on things that even adults miss sometimes, and they have this natural wisdom that can stop you in your tracks.

What I love about this observation is that it reminds us to really listen to our children, or to the young people in our lives. Sometimes we get caught up in thinking we always know better because we're older, but wisdom doesn't always correlate with age.

Here's something practical you could try today: The next time you're talking with a young person - whether it's your child, niece, nephew, or a student - try approaching the conversation with genuine curiosity. Instead of jumping to give advice, ask them what they think about a situation. You might be amazed by their perspective, and it could open up some really meaningful conversations. Sometimes the most profound insights come from the most unexpected sources.

March 3rd

"You are a happy parent when you have strong, kind and funny children, their laughter is the most beautiful sound in the world."

— Gary Hardy

This one hits right at the heart, doesn't it? In all my conversations about parenting, I've noticed that nothing quite lights up a parent's face like talking about their child's laughter or witnessing their authentic personality shine through. Hardy captures something really profound here - it's not just about having children, but about having children who embody these wonderful qualities that make life richer.

What I find particularly meaningful is how he combines strength, kindness, and humour. In today's world, that's such a powerful combination. Strong enough to face life's challenges, kind enough to make the world better, and funny enough to find joy along the way. And that bit about laughter being the most beautiful sound - any parent who's heard their child's genuine belly laugh knows exactly what he means. It's like pure joy made audible.

Here's a simple suggestion for today: Try to create a moment specifically designed to laugh with your children or the young people in your life. Maybe share a silly story from your own childhood, start an impromptu dance party, or play their favourite game. These moments might seem small, but they're actually building something incredibly precious - they're strengthening bonds and creating memories that celebrate your children's wonderful qualities.

March 4th

"Maybe that's worse, not letting ourselves be loved. Because we're too afraid of giving ourselves to someone we might lose."

— Mitch Albom

This quote from Albom touches on one of the deepest human paradoxes – how fear of loss can keep us from experiencing love. It reveals the often unconscious way we might sabotage our own happiness by trying to protect ourselves from pain.

Today, notice if you're holding back in your relationships – whether with family, friends, or romantic partners – because of fear. Are there moments when you create distance not because you want to, but because you're afraid of being vulnerable? Perhaps there are walls you've built so gradually you barely noticed them going up.

Consider taking one small risk today in letting someone see the real you. It doesn't have to be dramatic – maybe it's sharing a genuine fear, expressing appreciation you normally keep to yourself, or allowing someone to help you when you'd usually insist on handling things alone.

Remember that while protecting ourselves from loss might feel safer, it also protects us from the very experiences that make life rich and meaningful. Yes, love always carries the risk of loss – but a life without deep connection might be the greater loss.

The courage to love despite uncertainty isn't about being fearless; it's about being brave enough to let love in even when we're afraid.

March 5th

"The kindest thing you can do for yourself is to let people go when they want to go. No chasing. No begging. Let it hurt, then let it heal."

— Parm K.C

This quote touches on one of life's most challenging but important lessons. As someone who has witnessed many people struggle with letting go, I can tell you that holding on too tightly to those who wish to leave only prolongs our own suffering. Think about it - when we chase after someone who has chosen to walk away, we're not just disrespecting their choice, we're also diminishing our own worth. It's like telling ourselves that our happiness depends on convincing someone to stay who has already decided to go. That's a heavy burden to carry, and it rarely leads to the outcome we hope for.

Today, I invite you to consider: Is there someone or something you're holding onto too tightly? Are you spending emotional energy trying to keep someone in your life who has shown they want to leave? Remember, letting go isn't a sign of weakness - it's an act of self-respect and courage.

Yes, it will hurt. That's natural and even necessary. But like any wound, it can only truly heal when we stop reopening it. Sometimes the kindest thing we can do for ourselves is to simply say "I understand you want to go, and I'm going to respect that" - both to the person leaving and to ourselves. The healing comes not from the absence of pain, but from our willingness to face it and move through it with dignity and self-compassion.

March 6th

"You can never articulate to others what you feel in your bones because you rarely understand it yourself."

— Connor Franta

That's a powerful quote that really speaks to the depths of human experience. As someone who has spent a lot of time reflecting on personal growth, I find this captures something profound about our inner lives.

Those moments when you feel something so deeply - maybe it's a gut instinct about a decision, or an inexplicable connection to a piece of music, or just a sense that something in your life needs to change - but when someone asks you to explain it, the words just aren't there? That's exactly what Franta is touching on. Some of our deepest truths resist being put into neat little boxes of language.

Today, I'd encourage you to sit with those unexplainable feelings instead of dismissing them because you can't articulate them perfectly. Maybe it's that nagging feeling about your job, or that inexplicable pull towards a new path, or even just an emotion you can't quite name. Instead of forcing yourself to explain it or justify it to others, try just acknowledging it and asking yourself: "What might this feeling be trying to tell me?"

Sometimes our bones know things before our minds can catch up. Learning to trust and honour those deep instincts, even when we can't explain them, can be a powerful guide in living a more authentic life.

March 7th

"You are confined only by the walls you build yourself."

— Andrew Murphy

This quote really cuts to the heart of how we often become our own biggest obstacles. I've seen this play out countless times - we create these invisible barriers around ourselves, built from fears, self-doubt, and limiting beliefs we've collected over the years. Think about it - how many times have you stopped yourself from trying something new because you decided in advance that you "couldn't do it" or "weren't good enough"? These walls we build can feel so real and solid, but they're often just constructions of our own making.

For today's reflection, I'd encourage you to pause and notice: What walls have you built around yourself? Maybe it's the belief that you're "not creative enough" to start that project you've been dreaming about. Or perhaps it's the assumption that you're "too old" to learn something new. Once you identify these self-imposed limitations, ask yourself: "Who would I be without these walls?"

Remember, acknowledging these walls doesn't mean they'll instantly crumble. But awareness is the first step to dismantling them. Try challenging just one of these limitations today - take one small step beyond your comfortable boundaries. It could be as simple as speaking up in a meeting if you usually stay quiet, or learning the first few words of a new language if you've told yourself you're "bad at languages." The truth is that most of these walls exist only in our minds. And just as we built them, we have the power to take them down, one brick at a time.

March 8th

"It's okay to be sad. You don't owe anyone a performance of being okay when you feel like you're falling apart."

— Daniell Koepke

This quote really touches something deep and true about our relationship with difficult emotions. The world often pushes us to "stay positive" and "keep smiling," there's something profoundly liberating about giving ourselves permission to simply... not be okay.

As someone who has had my own and also sat with many people through their darkest moments, I can tell you that trying to maintain a facade of happiness when you're hurting inside is like trying to hold a beach ball underwater - it takes so much energy, and eventually, it's going to burst up to the surface anyway.

Today, I want you to consider this: What would it feel like to release yourself from the obligation to perform "okayness" for others? Maybe you're going through something difficult right now - a loss, a disappointment, or just one of those periods where life feels heavy. Instead of forcing yourself to put on a brave face, try giving yourself permission to simply acknowledge: "I'm not okay right now, and that's okay."

This doesn't mean you need to broadcast your pain to everyone you meet. But it does mean creating space for your authentic emotions, even the uncomfortable ones. Sometimes, being honest about not being okay is the first step towards actually being okay again.

Remember, your feelings aren't an inconvenience to be hidden away - they're valid signals from your inner self that deserve to be acknowledged and honoured. Healing doesn't come from pretending we're not hurt; it comes from allowing ourselves to feel what we feel, without judgement.

March 9th

"Without courage, wisdom bears no fruit."

— Baltasar Gracian

This is a profound observation about the relationship between knowing what's right and actually doing it. I've seen many people - myself included - who understand exactly what they should do, but that final step of taking action? That's where courage comes in, and that's often where we hesitate. Think about it - wisdom without action is like having a map but never starting the journey. You might know exactly where you need to go, but unless you have the courage to take that first step, to risk being wrong, to face potential failure... well, that wisdom just sits there, unrealised.

Today, I encourage you to look at the areas in your life where you "know better" but haven't taken action. Maybe you know you should have that difficult conversation with someone you care about. Perhaps you understand that you need to make a career change. Or maybe you're clear that a particular relationship or situation isn't serving you anymore.

Ask yourself: What's one piece of wisdom you're holding onto that needs courage to bring to life? Then consider taking just one small brave step towards acting on that wisdom today. Remember, courage doesn't mean not being afraid - it means acting despite that fear. The fruit of wisdom only grows when we nurture it with brave actions, no matter how small they might seem. Sometimes, the quietest acts of courage yield the sweetest fruit.

March 10th

"Damaged people are dangerous. They know they can survive."

— Josephine Hart

This quote resonates with me personally, I recognise it as a truth about human resilience that often gets overlooked. When I reflect on this, I see it not as a warning, but as a testament to the incredible strength that emerges from adversity.

Think about it - people who have weathered serious storms in life develop a kind of unshakeable knowledge about their own capacity to endure. They've been through the fire and emerged on the other side. This makes them "dangerous" not in a harmful way, but in the sense that they're no longer bound by the fear of "what if things go wrong?" They already know they can handle it when things do go wrong.

For today's reflection, I invite you to consider: How have your own struggles shaped your strength? Those difficult experiences you've survived - they're not just scars, they're evidence of your resilience. Maybe you've lived through loss, failure, heartbreak, or betrayal. Each of these experiences has taught you something invaluable about your own strength.

The "danger" in being damaged and surviving isn't about being destructive - it's about having the confidence to take risks others might shy away from, to speak truths others might keep quiet, to stand up when others might stay down. You know you can weather the storm because you've done it before.

Remember, your wounds aren't just memories of pain - they're proof of your ability to heal, to persist, to survive. That knowledge is indeed powerful, and yes, maybe even a little dangerous - in the most empowering way possible.

March 11th

"To me, losing all hope was freedom."

— Chuck Palahniuk

This quote from Palahniuk carries a profound paradox that speaks to a deeper truth about liberation. Sometimes our hopes - especially rigid expectations about how things "should" be - can actually become prisons that keep us from accepting and embracing what is.

Today, consider what hopes you might be clinging to that are actually causing you suffering. Sometimes when we release our grip on specific outcomes or expectations, we find an unexpected freedom. It's like finally exhaling a breath we didn't know we were holding.

This isn't about becoming cynical or giving up on dreams. Rather, it's about finding freedom in accepting reality as it is, not as we desperately hope it to be. When we stop struggling against what is, we often find new possibilities we couldn't see before.

Remember: Sometimes our greatest breakthroughs come when we let go of our preconceived notions of how things must be.

What hope might you need to release today to find a deeper freedom? What new possibilities might emerge when you stop forcing life to fit your expectations?

March 12th

"Never take anyone you love in your life for granted, you never know when a simple twist of fate means that they may no longer be here."

— Gary Hardy

This quote touches something deep and universal about the fragility of life and our relationships. It's one of those truths we all know intellectually, but it's so easy to forget in the daily rush of life - how precious and uncertain our time is with those we love. It reminds me of how we often treat time with loved ones like an unlimited resource, postponing calls, delaying visits, leaving things unsaid. We fall into routines and assumptions, thinking there will always be another chance, another tomorrow. But life has a way of reminding us that nothing is guaranteed.

Here's something meaningful you could do today: Choose one person you care about and reach out to them in a way that shows you truly value them. It doesn't have to be grand - maybe it's sending a voice message sharing a specific memory you cherish with them, writing a note expressing what they mean to you, or making that call you've been putting off. The key is to make it genuine and specific, not just a routine "hey, how are you?"

The beauty of this awareness isn't that it should make us anxious, but rather that it can help us live more fully and love more openly while we have the chance. Each interaction becomes more precious when we remember it's not guaranteed. When was the last time you told someone important to you exactly what they mean to you?

March 13th

"In breaking away from the familiar and the expected, you'll be forced and privileged to face greater challenges, learn harder lessons, and really get to know yourself."

— Kelly Cutrone

As someone who has watched many people navigate major life changes, I can tell you that our most significant moments of growth often come when we step away from our comfort zones. Think about it - when everything is familiar and predictable, we can operate on autopilot. We don't have to question our assumptions, test our capabilities, or discover new aspects of ourselves. It's comfortable, yes, but comfort rarely leads to profound self-discovery.

For today's reflection, I'd encourage you to consider: What familiar patterns or situations might you be clinging to out of habit rather than genuine fulfilment? Maybe it's a job that no longer challenges you, relationships that have become stagnant, or daily routines that have lost their purpose.

The word "privileged" in this quote is particularly striking - it reframes challenges as opportunities rather than burdens. Yes, breaking away from the familiar is scary. Yes, it often means facing uncertainty and difficulty. But these challenges are actually gifts that help us uncover strengths we never knew we had. Remember, getting to know yourself isn't always comfortable, but it's always valuable. Maybe today is the day to take one small step away from the expected - not because you have to, but because that's where the real adventure of self-discovery begins.

March 14th

"You can knock on a deaf man's door forever."

— Nikos Kazantzakis

This quote carries a truth about human communication and effort. It speaks to those moments when we keep trying the same approach over and over, even though it's clearly not working. Think about times you've tried to convince someone who simply wasn't ready or willing to hear your message - it's like knocking on that deaf man's door, isn't it?

Here's a practical way to apply this wisdom today: Take a moment to reflect on a situation where you feel like you're hitting a wall with someone - maybe at work, in a relationship, or with a personal goal. Ask yourself: "Am I just knocking on a deaf man's door?" If you are, perhaps it's time to either find a different "door" (change your approach) or recognise that this particular door might not be meant to open right now.

Sometimes the wisest thing we can do is step back and save our energy for opportunities where our efforts can actually make a difference. After all, the real waste isn't in giving up on an impossible task - it's in persisting with a method that simply cannot work.

This isn't about giving up on important goals, but rather about being smart enough to recognise when we need to change our strategy or redirect our energy to more receptive paths.

March 15th

"Keep your dreams alive. Understand to achieve anything requires faith and belief in yourself, vision, hard work, determination, and dedication. Remember all things are possible for those who believe."

— Gail Devers

As someone who has witnessed many people's journeys towards their goals, I've seen how each element Devers mentions plays a crucial role.

Faith and belief in yourself - that's really the foundation. Without it, even the most talented people can falter. But it's fascinating how this self-belief often grows stronger through action, through those small daily steps we take towards our vision. It's like building a muscle - the more you exercise it, the stronger it becomes.

Today, I'd encourage you to examine your own dreams and the beliefs you hold about them. Are there places where your self-doubt is creating unnecessary obstacles? Remember, believing in yourself isn't about being certain of success - it's about being certain that you're worthy of trying.

Think about one dream you're holding close to your heart right now. How can you align your daily actions with that vision? Maybe it's dedicating 30 minutes each morning to work on a project, or taking one small step towards a bigger goal. The key is making sure your hard work, determination, and dedication are pointing in the direction of your dreams.

Remember, believing doesn't mean it will be easy - it means believing it's worth it even when it's hard. Your dreams deserve that kind of dedication. And yes, there will be obstacles and doubts along the way, but as Devers suggests, when you combine genuine belief with consistent action, you create a powerful force for making the impossible possible.

March 16th

"Do not be afraid to walk the path that you must go just because you cannot see the end. The path becomes clearer as you continue to go on."

— Tracy Allen

As someone who has walked many unclear paths and guided others through their own journeys, I can tell you that the fog of uncertainty often lifts only after we've taken those first brave steps. Think about it like walking through the woods at dawn - you might only be able to see a few steps ahead, but as you move forward, more of the path gradually reveals itself. The key is having the courage to take those first steps even when you can't see the whole journey laid out before you.

Today, I invite you to consider: What path are you hesitating to walk because you can't see its end? Maybe it's a career change, starting a creative project, or making a significant life decision. Remember, most meaningful journeys in life don't come with a detailed roadmap.

Try focusing just on the next step ahead of you rather than straining to see the entire path. What's one small action you can take today towards that unclear destination? Sometimes simply starting the journey provides the clarity we've been seeking all along. Remember, clarity often comes from movement, not contemplation. Each step you take not only brings you closer to your destination but also helps illuminate the path ahead. The courage isn't in knowing where you'll end up - it's in being willing to begin even when you don't.

March 17th

"I guess each of us, at some time, finds one person with whom we are compelled towards absolute honesty, one person whose good opinion of us becomes a substitute for the broader opinion of the world."

— Glen Cook

In our daily lives we often wear different masks - being professional at work, casual with friends, formal in certain settings. But there's usually that one special person - maybe a best friend, a partner, or even a parent - where all those masks just fall away. With them, we can simply be... ourselves. The thing is that when we find this person who truly sees and accepts us, their faith in us can become like an anchor. Their belief in our goodness and potential often gives us the strength to face challenges that might otherwise feel overwhelming. It's as if their opinion matters more than all the others combined, not because we're seeking approval, but because they see us with such clarity and compassion.

Today, I'd encourage you to think about who this person might be in your life. If you have someone like this, perhaps take a moment to appreciate the gift of being able to be completely honest with them. And if you haven't found this person yet, consider opening yourself up to that possibility - sometimes being the first to show vulnerability can create space for deep, authentic connections. The real magic happens when we can translate this experience into greater self-acceptance. Because ultimately, while having someone who believes in us completely is powerful, learning to be that person for ourselves is transformative.

March 18th

"I am a complicated person with a simple life."

— Charlotte Eriksson

That's a wonderfully introspective quote that captures something many of us feel but struggle to express. I find there's something beautifully honest about acknowledging this duality in ourselves - the rich inner landscape of thoughts, feelings, and complexities that exists alongside our often routine daily lives. It reminds me of how we can be filled with dreams, fears, memories, and contradictions, yet our days might consist of simple routines like making coffee, going to work, or taking care of basic responsibilities. We contain multitudes, as Walt Whitman would say, even when our external lives follow predictable patterns.

Today, I'd invite you to embrace both aspects of yourself. Rather than seeing it as a contradiction, consider how your complex inner world enriches even the simplest moments of your day. Maybe it's finding deeper meaning in a morning walk, or appreciating how your unique perspective colours ordinary interactions.

There's something freeing about accepting this contrast - recognising that having a simple life doesn't mean we have to be simple people, and being complicated doesn't mean we need complicated circumstances to feel fulfilled. Sometimes the simplest life provides the perfect canvas for our complex selves to flourish. What aspects of your complex inner world do you find most enriching in your daily life?

March 19th

"To find the universal elements enough; to find the air and the water exhilarating; to be refreshed by a morning walk or an evening saunter ... to be thrilled by the stars at night; to be elated over a bird's nest, or over a wild flower in spring—these are some of the rewards of the simple life."

— John Burroughs

In our rush to find excitement or meaning in big moments, we sometimes miss the quiet magic that surrounds us every single day. Burroughs reminds us that true richness in life often comes from developing an almost childlike appreciation for the basic elements of our world - the crisp morning air that fills our lungs during a walk, the way stars pierce through the darkness on a clear night, the unexpected discovery of a bird carefully crafting its home.

Today, I'd encourage you to practice what I like to call "intentional wonder." Choose one simple element of your day - maybe it's your morning coffee, the feeling of sunlight on your face, or the sound of rain against your window. Really allow yourself to experience it fully, as if you're encountering it for the first time. Notice how this small shift in attention can transform an ordinary moment into something remarkable.

These moments of awareness are always available to us. They don't cost anything, they don't require special circumstances, and they can't be taken away. They're like little doorways to contentment that we can choose to walk through at any time. What simple element of your daily life might you see differently if you looked at it with fresh eyes?

March 20th

"Be careful who you trust, remember, the devil was once an angel."

— Dean Winchester

It's interesting how Dean's quote uses religious imagery to convey a universal truth about the complexity of people and relationships. The message isn't about being cynical or distrustful, but rather about exercising wisdom in how we open ourselves to others.

Today, I'd encourage thinking about trust as something that's earned gradually rather than given immediately. Just like building a house, strong relationships need a foundation that's laid carefully, one brick at a time. This doesn't mean living in fear or suspicion, but rather developing healthy boundaries and paying attention to people's actions over time, not just their initial presentation.

Consider taking a moment today to reflect on your own relationships and boundaries. Are there areas where you might benefit from being more discerning? Or perhaps situations where past experiences have made you overly cautious? The goal isn't to wall ourselves off from connections, but to build meaningful relationships that are grounded in genuine trust and understanding.

Remember, wisdom in relationships often comes from finding that balance between being open to connections while still protecting your wellbeing. It's about being hopeful but mindful, trusting but observant. How do you currently balance openness with appropriate caution in your relationships?

March 21st

"I'd spent so long trying to fit in, trying to be someone I wasn't, that I had no idea who I was any more."

— Dorothy Koomson

Many of us have experienced that moment when we realise we've lost touch with our authentic selves in the pursuit of acceptance. This often happens so gradually that we don't notice until we're already feeling hollow inside.

Today, I'd invite you to pause and consider: What parts of yourself have you perhaps tucked away to fit someone else's mould? It might be a passion you've downplayed, a quirky habit you've hidden, or even opinions you've learned to keep quiet. Sometimes we adapt so much to please others or meet expectations that we become more of an amalgamation of what others want than who we truly are.

Try this today: Take a few quiet moments to remember something you genuinely loved doing or being before you started worrying about fitting in. Maybe it was singing out loud, wearing bold colours, pursuing an unconventional hobby, or expressing an unpopular opinion. Consider taking one small step to reclaim that part of yourself.

The journey back to authenticity doesn't have to be dramatic - it can start with tiny moments of choosing to be true to yourself. Remember, the world doesn't need another perfect copy of someone else; it needs your unique voice and perspective. What small part of your authentic self might you be ready to rediscover today?

March 22nd

"But I have seen the best of you and the worst of you, and I choose both."

— Sarah Kay and Phil Kaye

This quote beautifully captures the essence of deep, unconditional love and acceptance. There's something incredibly powerful about being seen completely - both our light and our shadows - and being chosen anyway. It's not about ignoring the flaws or only celebrating the victories, but embracing the whole person.

Today, I'd encourage you to think about both self-acceptance and how we love others. Often, we're our own harshest critics, accepting others' imperfections more readily than our own. Consider taking a moment today to practice this kind of complete acceptance with yourself first - acknowledging both your achievements and your struggles, your strengths and your growing edges.

This perspective can transform our relationships too. When we truly accept someone - not despite their flaws but including them - we create space for genuine growth and connection. It's like saying "I see all of you, and I'm choosing to stay." This kind of acceptance doesn't mean enabling harmful behaviour; rather, it's about acknowledging our shared humanity.

Try practicing this dual vision today: Can you hold space for both the best and the challenging parts of yourself and those closest to you? Sometimes, just acknowledging this complexity can deepen our capacity for compassion and authentic connection. What might change in your relationships if you consciously chose to accept both the light and shadow in yourself and others?

March 23rd

"The most basic of all human needs is the need to understand and be understood."

— Ralph Nichols

In all our rushing around seeking success, achievement, or material comfort, we sometimes forget that at our core, what we're really seeking is this human connection - to truly understand and be understood by others.

Today, I'd encourage you to think about both sides of this equation. Understanding others requires us to truly listen - not just waiting for our turn to speak, but really being present with someone else's experience. And being understood... well, that requires the courage to be vulnerable, to share our authentic thoughts and feelings, even when it feels risky.

Try something today: In your next conversation, practice what I call "whole person listening." This means setting aside your phone, your mental to-do list, and even your desire to offer solutions. Just be fully present with someone else's words, their tone, their body language. Notice how this simple act of deep attention might change the quality of your connection.

And perhaps more challengingly, consider sharing something authentic about yourself with someone you trust. It doesn't have to be a deep secret - maybe just an honest feeling about your day or a hope you've been holding close. Sometimes these small moments of vulnerability create space for deeper understanding to grow.

Remember, in a world that often feels increasingly disconnected, every moment of genuine understanding we create ripples outward, touching not just our own lives but the lives of those around us.

What might change in your relationships if you made understanding - both giving and receiving it - your primary focus today?

March 24th

"I'm about to make a wild, extreme and severe relationship rule: the word busy is a load of crap and is most often used by assholes. The word "busy" is the relationship Weapon of Mass Destruction. It seems like a good excuse, but in fact in every silo you uncover, all you're going to find is a man who didn't care enough to call. Remember men are never too busy to get what they want."

— Greg Behrendt

This quote hits hard with its raw honesty about how we often use "busy" as a shield in relationships. While Behrendt focuses specifically on men in dating relationships, I think this speaks to a broader truth about human connection - when something or someone truly matters to us, we make time, period.

For today's reflection, I'd encourage you to think about both sides of this dynamic. First, examine where you might be using "busy" as a gentle letdown or an avoidance tactic in your own life. Are there relationships or commitments where you're saying you're too busy, when really you're just not prioritising them? That kind of honesty with ourselves can be uncomfortable but enlightening.

Then, consider where you're accepting "busy" as an answer from others. Sometimes we hold onto hope when someone says they're busy, rather than accepting the deeper message their actions are sending about our place in their priorities. As painful as it might be, recognising when someone's "busy" really means "not interested" can save us from prolonged disappointment and help us invest our emotional energy where it's truly valued.

Try this today: When you find yourself about to say "I'm busy," pause and consider what you really mean. Could you be more honest with yourself and others about your priorities? And when someone tells you they're busy, listen to their actions more than their words. Are they consistently making time for the things and people that matter to them?

What might change in your relationships if you replaced "I'm busy" with more honest communication about your priorities?

March 25th

"Express your creativity in the manner that you choose. Not in a way that is meant to appease others. Their discomfort is not your burden to bear."

— Robin S. Baker

There's something powerful about giving ourselves permission to create without the weight of others' expectations or judgements. It's like finally taking off a costume we've been wearing to please an audience we never actually signed up to perform for.

Today, I'd encourage you to think about where in your life you might be dimming your creative light to make others more comfortable. Maybe you're holding back from wearing that bold outfit, pursuing that unconventional project, or expressing that unique viewpoint because you're worried about what others might think.

Try this today: Choose one small way to express yourself authentically, regardless of potential judgement. It doesn't have to be grand - maybe it's writing that poem you've kept hidden, sharing that idea you've been sitting on, or simply allowing yourself to laugh freely without worrying if it's too loud. Notice how it feels to create or express yourself purely for your own satisfaction.

Remember, your creativity is your voice in the world. When we shape it to fit others' comfort zones, we're not just compromising our expression - we're denying the world something unique that only we can offer. Your authentic creative voice might make some people uncomfortable, and that's okay. Those who resonate with your true expression will find their way to you.

What aspect of your creativity have you been holding back that might be ready to be shared with the world?

March 26th

"I am an introvert. I'm not mad, or depressed, or antisocial. I just need to not talk to anyone for a while. And that's OK."

— Unknown

There's this wonderful self-acceptance in acknowledging that needing solitude isn't a flaw or a social deficiency - it's simply part of how some of us recharge and maintain our wellbeing.

Today, I'd encourage you to think about how you honour your own need for solitude, especially in a world that often celebrates constant connectivity and social interaction. There's no need to apologise for requiring quiet time to replenish your energy. Just as we wouldn't expect a phone to work without charging, we shouldn't expect ourselves to function well without the downtime we need.

Try this today: Set aside some intentional solitude time - even if it's just 15 minutes. Maybe it's a quiet morning coffee before the day begins, a lunch break spent reading alone, or an evening walk without your phone. Notice how this time affects your energy levels and overall wellbeing. Pay attention to how it feels to give yourself this gift without guilt.

Remember, explaining your need for alone time to others isn't always necessary. Just as some people need to socialise to recharge, you need your quiet time. It's not about being antisocial - it's about knowing and honouring what you need to be your best self. When you start viewing your introversion as a natural part of who you are rather than something to overcome, how might that change your relationship with yourself and others?

March 27th

"Remember that the happiest people are not those getting more, but those giving more."

— H. Jackson Brown Jr

Think about those moments when you've given something meaningful to someone else - maybe it was your time, a helping hand, or just your full attention. That warm feeling that spreads through your chest? That's real happiness, and science actually backs this up.

It's interesting how we often chase happiness through acquiring things - a new phone, a bigger house, more likes on social media. But that kind of happiness tends to fade quickly. When you give, though, whether it's volunteering at a local shelter, mentoring someone at work, or simply being there for a friend in need, that feeling stays with you and grows deeper.

Today, I'd encourage you to try this: Find one small way to give to someone else. It doesn't have to be grand - maybe send that encouraging message you've been meaning to write, help a coworker with a task, or spend fifteen minutes really listening to someone who needs to talk. Pay attention to how it makes you feel. I think you'll notice that in giving, you'll actually receive something far more valuable - a genuine sense of purpose and joy.

Remember, we all have something to give, even on days when we feel we have little. Sometimes the most precious gift is simply our presence and care.

March 28th

"I don't think that anything happens by coincidence... No one is here by accident... Everyone who crosses our path has a message for us. Otherwise they would have taken another path, or left earlier or later. The fact that these people are here means that they are here for some reason."

— James Redfield

As someone who's spent a lot of time reflecting on human interactions, I find this idea particularly compelling. It invites us to look at every encounter – even the seemingly random ones – as potentially meaningful.

Think about it: that person who sat next to you on the bus and shared an unexpected insight, or that old friend who called out of the blue just when you needed someone to talk to. While we might not believe in a predetermined script for our lives, there's something powerful about approaching our interactions with this level of mindfulness and curiosity.

Today, I'd suggest paying closer attention to your encounters, especially the ones that seem insignificant. Maybe that colleague who keeps bringing up a certain topic is actually highlighting something you need to learn. Or perhaps that challenging person in your life is teaching you patience or boundary-setting – lessons you didn't even know you needed.

Try this: Instead of rushing through your interactions today, pause and ask yourself, "What might I learn from this person? What message or lesson could be hidden in this moment?" You might be surprised by the insights that emerge when you view your connections through this lens.

The beauty of this perspective isn't about believing in fate – it's about staying open to the wisdom that can come from unexpected sources and recognising that every interaction has the potential to teach us something valuable about ourselves and the world around us.

March 29th

"Happiness is not how many things you do, but how well you do them. More is not better. Happiness is not experiencing something else; it's continually experiencing what you already have in new and different ways."

— Brianna Wiest

This resonates deeply with the challenge many of us face in today's world, where we're constantly pushed to do more, achieve more, and experience more. But Wiest touches on something really profound here about the quality of our engagement with life rather than the quantity of our experiences.

I've noticed how easy it is to fall into the trap of thinking "I'll be happy when..." – when I travel to more places, when I accomplish the next big thing, when I expand my experiences. But this quote reminds us that true contentment often lies in deepening our appreciation for what's already in front of us.

Today, I'd encourage you to try this: Pick just one routine activity – it could be your morning coffee, your walk to work, or even a conversation with a family member – and approach it with completely fresh eyes. Notice the details you usually miss. Maybe it's the way the sunlight catches your coffee mug, or the subtle changes in your neighbourhood's trees, or the unique expressions on your loved one's face when they talk.

The magic isn't in adding more to your plate – it's in bringing your full presence to what's already there. When we slow down and truly savour our experiences, even the most ordinary moments can become extraordinary. This isn't about lowering our ambitions; it's about finding depth and richness in what we already have.

Remember, sometimes the path to greater happiness isn't about changing what we do, but about changing how we do it.

March 30th

"When you have nothing, you are open to limitless possibilities. You can be anything. You can do anything."

— Nimish Dayalu

This is such a liberating perspective that challenges how we typically view having "nothing." We often see starting from zero as a disadvantage, but there's a profound truth here about the freedom that comes with a clean slate.

Think of it like being an artist facing a blank canvas. While some might find that emptiness intimidating, it actually represents pure potential – every colour, every stroke, every possibility is still available to you. When we're unburdened by preconceptions, established patterns, or others' expectations, we're truly free to reimagine who we can become.

For today's reflection, I'd invite you to experiment with this mindset: Think of an area in your life where you feel like you're starting from scratch or where you feel you have "nothing." Instead of seeing this as a deficit, try viewing it as a space of pure possibility. Maybe you're starting a new career, learning a new skill, or rebuilding after a setback.

Try this: Write down three completely different paths you could take from this point – even ones that seem improbable. The key isn't necessarily to pursue all of them, but to recognise that starting from zero means you're not constrained by past investments or established ways of doing things.

Remember, some of the most innovative companies started in garages, and many great artists found their voice only after losing everything they thought they needed. Having "nothing" means having no limits on what you can imagine for yourself.

The beauty of this perspective is that it transforms our relationship with fresh starts and setbacks – they become doorways to possibilities rather than obstacles to overcome.

March 31st

"Don't fight uphill battles, it's not worth it, because even if you win, you'll be tired."

— Gary Hardy

This practical piece of wisdom speaks to something many of us struggle with – knowing which battles to pick in life. I've seen so many people, including myself at times, exhaust themselves fighting against situations that ultimately weren't worth the energy they demanded.

Think about it like climbing a mountain – sure, you might eventually reach the top of that steep face you've chosen, but what if there's an easier path around the side that leads to the same summit? The key isn't about avoiding all challenges, but about being strategic with our energy and choosing our paths wisely.

Today, I'd suggest taking a moment to examine the current "battles" in your life. Ask yourself: Which situations am I pushing against that maybe I should walk away from? What am I fighting simply because I've already invested time in it, rather than because it truly matters?

Try this: List one situation that's draining your energy right now. Then ask yourself three questions: Is this battle aligned with my core values and long-term goals? Is there an easier way to achieve the same result? If I succeed, will the victory be worth the cost of the climb?

Remember, conserving your energy for the battles that truly matter isn't giving up – it's wisdom. Life presents us with enough necessary challenges; we don't need to create additional ones by fighting every uphill battle that comes our way. Sometimes, the most powerful thing we can do is simply choose a different path.

April 1st

"April is a reminder that life is a beautiful, ever-renewing cycle."

— E.E. Cummings

I really connect with how E.E. Cummings captures April's essence – it's not just about spring flowers and rain showers, but about the deeper message nature sends us during this time. In April, we witness one of life's most hopeful displays as everything around us demonstrates the power of renewal.

Think about it – even after the harshest winter, April faithfully arrives with its green shoots and new buds, showing us that nothing stays dormant forever. It's nature's way of reminding us that setbacks and difficult seasons in our lives aren't permanent either. There's always potential for new growth, no matter how long our personal winter has been.

Here's something practical you might try today: Take a short walk outside and find one sign of new growth – maybe a tiny leaf, a flower bud, or even a bird building a nest. Let that be your tangible reminder that renewal is always possible in your own life too. Then, identify one area of your life where you feel stagnant and take one small action towards growth, just as those plants are doing. It could be as simple as sending that email you've been putting off, or finally opening that book you've meant to read. The beauty of April is that it doesn't rush its renewal – each bud opens in its own time. We can take that same gentle, patient approach with our own growth too.

April 2nd

"Standing alone is better than standing with someone who doesn't value you."

— Unknown

It's interesting how often we stay in situations – whether friendships, romantic relationships, or even work environments – where we're not truly valued, simply because we fear being alone.

I've seen many people, myself included at times, who rationalise staying in unfulfilling relationships or situations because the thought of solitude seems more daunting than the pain of being undervalued. But here's the thing: when we stand alone, we actually create space for growth and for the right people to enter our lives.

Today, I'd encourage you to examine your current relationships and situations honestly. Are you staying somewhere not because it serves your highest good, but because you're afraid of the alternative? Remember, choosing to stand alone isn't about isolation – it's about having the courage to honour your worth.

Try this: Think of one situation in your life where you might be compromising your value for the sake of not being alone. Ask yourself: If I knew with absolute certainty that something better would come along, would I still stay? Sometimes just acknowledging where we're settling can be the first step towards positive change.

Remember, the temporary discomfort of standing alone is far better than the permanent pain of diminishing yourself to fit into spaces where you're not truly valued. Your worth isn't determined by who stands with you – it's intrinsic, and sometimes standing alone is the most powerful way to honour that truth.

April 3rd

"Don't let mental blocks control you. Set yourself free. Confront your fear and turn the mental blocks into building blocks."

— Dr Roopleen

This is such a powerful perspective on how we can transform our internal obstacles into foundations for growth. As someone who's witnessed many transformations, I can tell you that our biggest mental blocks often contain the seeds of our greatest breakthroughs.

Think of it like this: every time you encounter a mental block – whether it's self-doubt, fear of failure, or limiting beliefs – you're actually facing an opportunity to build something new. These blocks aren't walls meant to stop you; they're raw materials waiting to be reshaped into something that serves your growth.

Today, I'd encourage you to identify one mental block that's been holding you back. Maybe it's the thought "I'm not qualified enough" or "I could never do that." Instead of trying to push it away or ignore it, examine it closely. What is this fear or doubt trying to teach you? What strength might you develop by working through it?

Try this: Take that mental block and literally rewrite it as a building block. For example, if your block is "I'm afraid of failing," transform it into "Each attempt teaches me something valuable, regardless of the outcome." Notice how the energy shifts from something that stops you to something that supports you.

Remember, freedom doesn't come from avoiding our mental blocks – it comes from engaging with them consciously and learning to use their energy differently. Every time you transform a mental block into a building block, you're not just solving a problem – you're developing emotional muscle that will serve you in future challenges.

April 4th

"Our greatest glory is not in never falling, but in rising every time we fall."

— Oliver Goldsmith

I've noticed how often we beat ourselves up for failing or falling, when actually, those moments are setting the stage for our most meaningful comebacks.

Think about any significant achievement in your life – chances are, if you're similar to me, it came after some setbacks, right? What makes the journey powerful isn't the absence of falls, but the strength and wisdom we gather each time we pick ourselves up. It's like learning to ride a bike – those falls are part of mastering the skill, not evidence that we shouldn't be riding.

Today, I'd encourage you to shift your perspective on failure. Instead of seeing your falls as something to be ashamed of, try viewing them as proof of your courage to try and your resilience to continue. After all, you can't fall unless you're moving forward, taking risks, attempting something meaningful.

Try this: Think about a recent setback or "fall" in your life. Rather than focusing on the fall itself, write down what you learned when you got back up. What strength did you discover? What wisdom did you gain? Sometimes our greatest insights come not from the fall, but from the rising.

Remember, every time you get back up, you're not just returning to where you were – you're rising with new knowledge, greater strength, and deeper understanding. That's where the true glory lies – not in being perfect, but in being perfectly resilient.

April 5th

"Just be you...'cause that's good enough for me!"

— Cory Monteith

As someone who's seen the transformative power of self-acceptance, I find this message particularly meaningful. We often spend so much energy trying to be what we think others want us to be – more successful, more outgoing, more accomplished – when sometimes the most powerful thing we can do is simply be ourselves. The beauty of this quote lies in its reminder that real connection and love don't require us to be anything other than who we are.

Today, I'd invite you to practice radical self-acceptance. Notice the moments when you're trying to edit yourself to fit others' expectations. Are you dimming your enthusiasm? Hiding your quirks? Downplaying your interests?

Try this: For just one day, consciously choose to be fully yourself in each interaction. Not a perfect version of you, not an improved version – just you, exactly as you are right now. Pay attention to how it feels to release the exhausting work of constantly trying to be "better" or "different."

Remember, when someone tells you that being yourself is enough, they're offering you one of the most precious gifts possible – the freedom to exist without pretence. It's not just about self-acceptance; it's about creating space for authentic connections where we can all just be who we are.

April 6th

"When someone tells me "no," it doesn't mean I can't do it, it simply means I can't do it with them."

— Karen E. Quinones Miller

This is such an empowering way to reframe rejection. I've seen how a single "no" can sometimes make people question their entire journey, when really, it's just one door closing – not the end of the path.

Think about it like this: every "no" you receive is actually clarifying something important. It's not telling you to stop; it's simply showing you who isn't aligned with your vision. Sometimes these "nos" are actually gifts, steering us away from partnerships or paths that wouldn't have served our highest good anyway.

Today, I'd encourage you to look at a recent "no" you've received. Instead of seeing it as a rejection of your worth or abilities, view it as information about compatibility. Maybe it's a job application, a creative project, or a personal relationship – whatever it is, the "no" isn't about your capability, it's about finding the right fit.

Try this: Take one goal you're working toward and write down three alternative paths to achieve it. If one person or opportunity says "no," what other routes could you take? Who else might say "yes"? Sometimes the most beautiful opportunities come after someone tells us "no," because it forces us to find a path that's actually better suited to who we are.

Remember, successful people aren't the ones who never hear "no" – they're the ones who understand that "no" just means "not this way" or "not with me." Your dreams don't depend on any single person's approval or participation. They depend on your persistence in finding the right path and the right people who see your vision.

April 7th

"Let your hopes, not your hurts, shape your future."

— Robert H. Schuller

As someone who has seen many people transform their lives, I've noticed how our response to hurt can either limit us or launch us towards something better.

Think of it like tending a garden – we can either focus on the plants that didn't survive last season, letting that discourage us from planting anything new, or we can use those experiences to learn and dream up an even more beautiful garden for the future. Our hopes are like seeds of possibility, while our hurts can be the compost that helps new growth flourish – but only if we choose to use them that way.

Today, I'd suggest taking a moment to notice where past hurts might be shaping your decisions. Are you holding back from new relationships because of old heartbreaks? Hesitating to pursue a dream because of past failures? Then, try this: For each hurt you identify, consciously plant a hope in its place. Not to deny the pain, but to give your future something more inspiring to grow towards.

Remember, your hurts are part of your story, but they don't have to be the author of your future. Every time you choose to let hope guide your next step, you're not just moving forward – you're creating a path that others might find the courage to follow. Your hopes have the power to heal not just your own heart, but to inspire healing in others too.

April 8th

"The key to life is your attitude. Whether you're single or married or have kids or don't have kids, it's how you look at your life, what you make of it. It's about making the best of your life wherever you are in life."

— Candace Bushnell

This quote really speaks to something fundamental about happiness and fulfilment. I love how it cuts through all the external circumstances we often get caught up in – relationship status, family situation, career stage – and points to something much more powerful: our perspective.

Think about it – we all know people who seem to have "everything" but are miserable, and others who face real challenges yet maintain a sense of joy and purpose. The difference often comes down to how they view and engage with their lives.

Today, I'd encourage you to pause and notice your own mental habits. When you encounter a challenge or something that isn't "perfect" in your life, do you automatically focus on what's missing or wrong? Try this: Pick one situation you've been viewing negatively and consciously look for three positive aspects or opportunities within it. It could be as simple as a busy day at work becoming a chance to prove your capabilities, or a quiet evening alone becoming precious time for self-care and reflection.

This isn't about forced positivity – it's about developing the skill of finding meaning and possibility in whatever circumstances you find yourself in. That's where real empowerment lies. What area of your life could benefit from this shift in perspective today?

April 9th

"Today I'll be my own hero...I promise you today...Today I will begin to save me."

— Elizabeth Tapp

I find this quote deeply moving as it captures a profound truth about personal growth and self-reliance. It speaks to that pivotal moment when we realise that while support from others is valuable, the most important step in healing and growth must come from within.

Today, I'd encourage you to think about what being your own hero actually means in practice. It's not about rejecting help or going it alone – rather, it's about taking responsibility for your own wellbeing and happiness. Consider starting your day by asking: "What is one small act of self-advocacy I can do today?"

This might mean:

Setting a boundary that you've been hesitating to establish, taking that first step towards a goal you've been putting off, speaking up for yourself in a situation where you usually stay quiet, making time for self-care even when your schedule feels overwhelming

Remember, becoming your own hero doesn't happen in one dramatic moment – it's built through small, consistent actions of self-respect and self-care. Start with something manageable today, and let that success build your confidence for bigger steps tomorrow.

What one small act of being your own hero could you commit to today?

April 10th

"It's not stress that kills us, it is our reaction to it."

— Hans Selye

As someone who has experienced and thought deeply about stress and its impact, I find this quote reveals a powerful truth: while we can't always control what life throws at us, we have more control over our response than we often realise.

Today, I'd invite you to notice your stress responses. When something challenging happens, do you immediately tense up? Does your mind race to worst-case scenarios? These reactions, while natural, often cause more harm than the stressor itself. When you feel stress arising, pause for just three breaths before reacting. In that small space, ask yourself: "How can I respond to this situation in a way that serves my wellbeing?" Sometimes, just that brief pause can transform a knee-jerk stress reaction into a thoughtful response.

This might look like when a work deadline feels overwhelming, instead of spiralling into panic, taking a moment to break the task into smaller steps. When stuck in traffic, rather than gripping the wheel tighter, using the time to listen to a favourite podcast or practice deep breathing. When facing conflict, stepping back to consider if this will matter in a week, a month, or a year

Remember, the goal isn't to eliminate stress – that's impossible and even undesirable. Instead, it's about developing a relationship with stress that doesn't amplify its impact on your life.

What different choice could you make today in how you respond to stress?

April 11th

"The world is difficult, and we are all breakable. So just be kind."

— Caitlin Moran

This simple yet profound quote touches something deep in our shared human experience. It reminds me that beneath our different exteriors, we all carry our own burdens, face our own struggles, and have moments when we feel like we might break.

Today, I'd encourage you to carry this awareness with you. The person who seemed short with you at the coffee shop, the colleague who missed a deadline, the family member who forgot to call – each one is navigating their own difficult path, just like you are.

Try this today: In each interaction, pause to remember that everyone you meet is fighting some kind of battle you know nothing about. Let this awareness guide your responses. Maybe that means: Offering a genuine smile to someone who seems frustrated. Taking an extra moment to thank someone for their effort, even if the result wasn't perfect. Extending patience when your first impulse might be irritation. Being gentle with yourself when you make a mistake

The beauty of kindness is that it serves both the giver and receiver. When we acknowledge our shared vulnerability and choose gentleness, we create small pockets of peace in a chaotic world.

What one act of unexpected kindness could you offer today – to others, or perhaps to yourself?

April 12th

"People tend to complicate their own lives, as if living weren't already complicated enough."

— Carlos Ruiz Zafón

We often create additional layers of complexity in our lives without even realising it. I've seen how this plays out in so many ways, from overthinking simple decisions to creating elaborate stories about what others might be thinking.

Today, I'd encourage you to notice where you might be adding unnecessary complications to your life. Are you turning a straightforward situation into something more complex? Perhaps you're spending hours researching the "perfect" option when a good enough choice would suffice, creating elaborate explanations for why you can't take action on something important, maintaining relationships or commitments that no longer serve you simply because you feel obligated, or making decisions more difficult by considering too many "what-if" scenarios.

Try this today: Pick one area of your life that feels unnecessarily complex and ask yourself, "What would this look like if it were simple?" Sometimes, the most powerful thing we can do is give ourselves permission to take the straightforward path. Remember, life will present enough genuine challenges on its own – we don't need to create additional ones. What could you simplify in your life today? This is about making conscious choices to reduce the noise and focus on what truly matters. After all, often the best solutions are the simplest ones.

April 13th

"Forgiveness is letting go of the past, and is therefore the means for correcting our misperceptions."

— Gerald Jampolsky

When we hold onto past hurts, they become like coloured lenses through which we view everything else in our lives, distorting our perception of the present and even shaping our expectations of the future.

Today, I invite you to consider how past experiences might be colouring your current perceptions. Perhaps you're carrying old wounds that make it hard to trust, or past disappointments that make you hesitant to try again. When we refuse to forgive, we often end up seeing the world through the lens of our past pain rather than seeing it as it truly is. Think of one situation or person you've been struggling to forgive. Notice how holding onto this affects your daily life, your relationships, your decisions. Forgiveness doesn't mean condoning what happened or even reconciling with someone who hurt you. Instead, it's about freeing yourself from the weight of carrying that past moment into every present one.

The real power of forgiveness lies in its ability to clear our vision. When we release our grip on past hurts, we begin to see possibilities we couldn't see before. We start to recognise that people and situations in our present don't have to be defined by our past experiences. What perspective might open up for you today if you chose to let go of just one thing you've been holding onto?

April 14th

"If someone thinks you're being dramatic or selfish, then they obviously haven't walked a mile in your shoes. It's not important for you to explain yourself. You get a pass here. Don't let anyone else try to saddle you with guilt or shame. If you need your space, take it."

— Sarah Newman

This quote carries such deep wisdom about self-validation and personal boundaries. It speaks to that universal experience of having our feelings dismissed or minimised by others who haven't lived our experiences or felt our pain.

Today, I want you to really sit with this permission to honour your own experience without needing to justify it to anyone else. Your feelings, your struggles, your needs – they're valid simply because they're yours. You don't need to make them smaller or more palatable for others to understand.

Think about this: How often do you find yourself explaining or apologising for your feelings? How many times have you pushed aside your own needs because someone else thought you were "too much"? Your emotional experience is uniquely yours, shaped by every moment that brought you to where you are now.

Try something different today: When you feel the urge to explain or justify your feelings, pause and remind yourself that you don't owe anyone an explanation for your emotional reality. If you need to step back, rest, or create space for yourself, that's not selfishness – it's self-preservation.

Remember, taking space isn't about pushing others away – it's about creating room to honour your own experience and heal in your own way, at your own pace. What kind of space do you need to give yourself today?

The most profound act of self-care sometimes lies in simply giving yourself permission to feel what you feel, without apology or explanation.

April 15th

"Fitness isn't about building a better body. It's about building a better life."

— Jillian Michaels

This quote beautifully captures the deeper meaning of what fitness and wellness truly represent. It's not just about the physical transformations we can see, but about how taking care of our bodies ripples out into every aspect of our lives.

For today's reflection, I invite you to think beyond the numbers on a scale or the size of your clothes. Consider how moving your body and taking care of your health affects your energy, your mood, your confidence, and your ability to show up fully in your life. When we commit to our physical wellbeing, we often find improvements in our sleep, our stress management, our mental clarity, and even our relationships.

Try this today: Instead of focusing on how exercise might change your appearance, notice how it makes you feel. Perhaps you have more patience with your loved ones after a walk, or better focus at work after a morning stretch, or more emotional resilience after a workout. These are the true measures of fitness success – the ways it enhances your daily life experience.

Remember, every step you take towards better physical health is really a step towards a more vibrant, energetic, and capable version of yourself. The strength you build in your body becomes strength you can draw on in all areas of your life.

What small action could you take today that would make you feel more alive and energised in your body? The journey to fitness isn't about punishment or restriction – it's about creating a life that feels good to live in.

April 16th

"You have to love and respect yourself enough to not let people use and abuse you. You have to set boundaries and keep them, let people clearly know how you won't tolerate to be treated, and let them know how you expect to be treated."

— Jeanette Coron

This quote touches on something so essential to our wellbeing – the courage to establish and maintain healthy boundaries. It's not just about saying "no" or pushing people away; it's about having enough self-respect to create the conditions where genuine, healthy relationships can flourish.

Today, I want you to consider how you often feel after interactions with different people in your life. Do you feel drained, taken for granted, or like your needs are constantly pushed aside? These feelings are often signals that your boundaries need strengthening. Self-respect isn't selfish – it's the foundation for all healthy relationships, including the one with yourself.

Try this today: Notice moments when you feel that subtle internal resistance, that quiet voice saying "this doesn't feel right." Instead of pushing that feeling aside, honour it. Your discomfort is often wisdom trying to protect you. When someone crosses a line, practice saying something as simple as "I'm not comfortable with that" or "This doesn't work for me."

Remember, setting boundaries isn't about controlling others – it's about taking responsibility for your own wellbeing. People will treat you the way you teach them to treat you. When you clearly communicate your limits and expectations, you create space for relationships built on mutual respect rather than convenience or habit.

What small boundary could you establish or reinforce today that would help you feel more respected and valued? Sometimes, the most loving thing we can do for ourselves and others is to be clear about what we will and won't accept in our lives.

April 17th

"Don't allow yourself to be defeated by negative thoughts, believe the opposite of what they are whispering to you."

— Gary Hardy

So often, our greatest obstacles aren't external circumstances but the whispers of our own negative thoughts.

Today, I want you to think about how frequently we accept negative thoughts as truth without questioning them. These thoughts might tell you "you're not good enough," "you'll never succeed," or "you don't deserve better." But here's the powerful insight – just because your mind suggests something doesn't mean it's true.

Try this today: When you catch a negative thought creeping in, pause and consciously flip it around. If your mind whispers "you'll probably fail at this," respond with "I have the capability to succeed." If it suggests "no one values your input," counter with "my perspective is unique and worthwhile." This isn't about empty positive thinking – it's about challenging the automatic negative assumptions we've learned to accept.

Remember, your negative thoughts are not prophecies – they're often just old patterns, fears, or echoes of past difficulties. Every time you choose to believe in possibility rather than limitation, you're rewiring these patterns and creating new neural pathways of hope and resilience.

What negative thought could you challenge and transform today? Sometimes, the simple act of questioning our inner critic can open up whole new worlds of possibility.

April 18th

"I can't think of anything more disheartening than living a life without a clear purpose."

— Daniel Willey

This quote touches something deep in the human experience – that universal longing for meaning and direction in our lives. It speaks to that hollow feeling we sometimes get when we're just going through the motions, living day to day without a greater sense of why.

Today, I invite you to consider that finding purpose isn't always about grand gestures or dramatic life changes. Sometimes it's about recognising the meaning that already exists in your daily actions and relationships. Purpose can be found in the way you show up for others, in the care you put into your work, or in the small ways you make your corner of the world a little better.

Try this today: Take a moment to reflect on the moments when you feel most alive, most useful, or most connected. These moments often point towards your natural sense of purpose. Perhaps you feel it when helping others learn, when creating something with your hands, when solving complex problems, or when nurturing relationships. These aren't just activities – they're clues to what gives your life meaning.

Remember, purpose isn't always a single, clear destination – it can evolve and shift throughout our lives. The key is to stay curious and open to discovering what truly matters to you, not what others think should matter.

What small action could you take today that aligns with what you value most? Sometimes, purpose reveals itself not in the big questions, but in the daily choices we make to live according to our deepest values.

April 19th

"That's how you can tell that you're filling yourself with the wrong things. You use a lot of energy, and in the end, you feel emptier and less comfortable than ever."

— Glennon Doyle Melton

I've observed in life how we often chase things that seem fulfilling but actually drain us. Think about those times when you've scrolled social media for hours, or shopped for things you didn't need, or maybe tried to please everyone around you at your own expense. These activities consume so much of our energy, yet somehow leave us feeling hollow.

Today, I'd encourage you to pause and ask yourself: "What activities or relationships in my life truly fill my cup, and which ones drain it?" Maybe spend 5 minutes writing down two columns - one for things that genuinely energise you (perhaps reading a good book, taking a walk in nature, or having a deep conversation with a close friend), and another for things that leave you feeling depleted despite consuming lots of your time and energy.

The beauty of this awareness is that it empowers you to make different choices. You don't need to drastically change everything at once, but you can start making small shifts - perhaps spending 15 minutes less on social media and using that time to do something that genuinely nourishes your soul. Remember, true fulfilment often comes from the simplest things that align with your authentic self.

April 20th

"You deserve to need me, not to have me."

— Augusten Burroughs

This is a profound observation about healthy relationships and self-worth. There's a crucial distinction between "needing" and "having" someone - when we say someone "has" us, it can suggest possession or dependency, while "needing" someone speaks to genuine connection and mutual value.

For today's reflection, consider examining your relationships - both romantic and platonic. Are you allowing yourself to be vulnerable enough to need others while maintaining your independence? Sometimes we build walls because we're afraid of needing people, or we swing to the opposite extreme and become possessive. The sweet spot is acknowledging that it's beautiful and human to need connection while understanding that no one can truly "have" another person.

Try this today: Express genuine appreciation to someone you need in your life - not because they belong to you, but because their presence makes your life richer. Maybe it's telling a friend "I'm grateful for your perspective in my life" or letting a family member know specifically how they've impacted you. This helps shift our mindset from possession to appreciation, from having to needing, and ultimately leads to more authentic connections.

Remember, healthy relationships are about mutual support and respect, not ownership. You deserve to be both needed and free.

April 21st

"The pain of yesterday is the strength of today."

— Per Petterson

This is one of those powerful truths about the human experience that I've seen play out countless times. That pain we carry from our past - whether it's from heartbreak, failure, loss, or difficult challenges - it isn't just hurt that we endured. It's also the foundation of our resilience.

Today, I'd encourage you to look at a past difficulty that you've overcome. Instead of focusing on the pain itself, notice how that experience has equipped you with wisdom, understanding, or strength you didn't have before. Maybe a failed relationship taught you what you truly need in a partner. Perhaps a professional setback helped you develop persistence you never knew you had.

Try this simple practice today: When a challenging moment arises, pause and ask yourself, "How might my past difficulties actually be helping me handle this situation better?" You might be surprised to discover that your hardest moments have given you tools you use every day - whether it's patience, empathy, resilience, or wisdom.

The beauty of this perspective is that it doesn't diminish your past pain or suggest it was "worth it" - rather, it acknowledges that you've found ways to transform that pain into something meaningful. Your struggles haven't just made you stronger; they've made you deeper, more compassionate, and more equipped to face whatever comes next.

April 22nd

"Empathy begins with understanding life from another person's perspective. Nobody has an objective experience of reality. It's all through our own individual prisms."

— Sterling K. Brown

As someone who has spent time observing and thinking about how people relate to each other, I find there's profound wisdom in recognising that each person's reality is uniquely their own.

Today, I invite you to practice what I call "perspective pause" - when you find yourself in disagreement with someone or feeling frustrated by their actions, take a moment to imagine what their "prism" might look like. What experiences have shaped their view? What might be happening in their life that you can't see?

Try this simple exercise today: In your next conversation, especially if it's with someone whose viewpoint differs from yours, focus first on understanding rather than responding. Ask questions like "What led you to think that way?" or "Can you help me understand your perspective?" Notice how this shifts the energy of your interactions.

The beautiful thing about cultivating empathy is that it's like a muscle - the more you practice looking through others' prisms, the more natural it becomes. And paradoxically, by truly understanding others' perspectives, we often gain greater clarity about our own. This doesn't mean you have to agree with everyone, but understanding where they're coming from can transform conflicts into conversations and barriers into bridges.

Remember, every person you meet is navigating life through their own unique lens, shaped by their joys, sorrows, fears, and hopes. When we approach each other with this awareness, we create space for deeper understanding and genuine connection.

April 23rd

"Finding your purpose does not have to be about your career. Your purpose is about your soul. It is about how you engage life."

— S Mcnutt

This is such a liberating perspective on purpose, and one I find deeply meaningful. So often, we get caught up in thinking our purpose must be tied to our job title or career achievements, when really, purpose is woven into the very way we move through each day.

For today's reflection, I'd invite you to shift your focus from "what do I do?" to "how do I do it?" Think about the moments in your life when you feel most alive, most connected, most like yourself - whether that's in how you listen to a friend in need, the way you notice beauty in everyday moments, or how you bring your unique energy to simple interactions.

Try this today: Pay attention to three moments where you feel genuinely engaged with life - it could be as simple as how you make your morning coffee, the way you greet your neighbour, or how you approach a challenge at work. Notice what these moments have in common. Is its presence? Creativity? Kindness? Care? These patterns often reveal more about your purpose than any job description could.

Remember, your purpose isn't waiting for you in some future achievement or role - it's alive right now in how you choose to engage with each moment, each person, each challenge and joy. Your soul's purpose might express itself in how you make others feel seen, how you bring peace to tense situations, or how you share your unique perspective with the world. These qualities can infuse everything you do, regardless of your profession or position.

April 24th

"Don't hang out with people who don't love you. Don't try to impress people who aren't worth it. Don't try to win people over who aren't worth it ... Focus on the people who are really awesome and who love you."

— Beth Ditto

This quote hits at something so fundamentally important for our wellbeing. I've seen so many people - myself included in moments of reflection - exhaust themselves trying to win approval from those who simply don't value them for who they are.

Today, I'd encourage you to think about your energy investments in relationships. Notice where you might be performing rather than being authentic, or where you're constantly trying to prove your worth. These are often signs that you're spending precious life energy on connections that don't truly nourish you.

Try this simple exercise today: Make a conscious choice to direct your attention towards someone who already appreciates you for exactly who you are. Instead of spending energy trying to win someone over, invest that same energy in deepening a connection with someone who already sees your worth. Maybe send a message to a supportive friend, spend quality time with a family member who gets you, or plan something special with people who make you feel at home in your own skin.

The beautiful thing about focusing on those who already love us is that it creates a positive cycle - when we spend time with people who appreciate us, we naturally become more confident and authentic, which in turn attracts more genuine connections. It's not about closing ourselves off from new relationships, but rather about being selective with our emotional energy and choosing to nurture the connections that help us thrive.

Remember, your energy is precious, and you deserve to spend it in places where it multiplies rather than diminishes.

April 25th

"Listening closely is one of the most valuable gifts we can give to another human being."

— Dave Isay

This quote touches something so fundamental about human connection. I've noticed that in our fast-paced world, truly listening has become increasingly rare - and therefore, increasingly precious.

Today, I'd encourage you to notice the difference between hearing and listening. When we truly listen, we're not just waiting for our turn to speak or planning our response - we're fully present with another person's words, emotions, and experience. It's like creating a sacred space where another person can feel truly seen and understood. In your next conversation, focus entirely on listening without planning your response. Notice the speaker's tone, their pauses, what lights them up, what makes them hesitate. You might be surprised by how much more you perceive when you're not mentally preparing what to say next. Watch how people respond when they feel truly heard - there's often a visible shift in their energy, a deepening of trust.

Remember, some of the most healing moments in life don't come from someone solving our problems, but from someone simply being present enough to truly hear us. When you give someone your complete attention, you're not just hearing their words - you're honouring their experience, their perspective, their humanity. In a world full of distractions, this kind of presence is indeed one of the most meaningful gifts we can offer.

April 26th

"Loving someone is taking a constant risk with your emotions. When you find the right person, the one you know you want to be with, that person becomes worth the risk."

— Monica Murphy

This quote beautifully captures both the vulnerability and courage involved in deep love. It acknowledges something I've observed to be profoundly true - that real love requires us to be brave enough to risk getting hurt, yet also wise enough to choose who's worth that risk.

Today, consider how this balance plays out in your own life. Perhaps you've been hurt before and built walls to protect yourself - that's natural and understandable. But notice if those same walls might be keeping out the genuine connections that could enrich your life. Or maybe you tend to give your heart too freely, and need to be more discerning about who you open up to.

Try this today: Take a moment to appreciate the people in your life (romantic or otherwise) who have proven themselves worthy of your emotional investment. Notice what makes them trustworthy - is it their consistency? Their honesty? Their willingness to be vulnerable themselves? Understanding these qualities can help us make wiser choices about who we let into our inner circle.

Remember, taking emotional risks doesn't mean being reckless with your heart. It means being brave enough to remain open to genuine connection while being wise enough to recognise who has earned that trust. When you find those people who consistently show up, who handle your vulnerability with care, who make you feel both safe and free to be yourself - those are the relationships worth risking your heart for.

April 27th

"People's opinions of us will always change, but how we see ourselves will stay with us forever."

— Ralph Smart

What a powerful insight about the relationship between external validation and self-perception. In my experience working with others, I've seen how chasing others' approval can be like trying to catch the wind - constantly shifting and ultimately exhausting.

For today's reflection, I invite you to explore how much of your self-image is built on others' opinions versus your own deep knowing of who you are. Think about the times you feel most centred and at peace - are those moments when you're seeking approval, or when you're simply being authentic to your own values and truth?

Try this meaningful practice today: When you catch yourself wondering what others think about a choice you're making or something you're doing, pause and ask yourself, "How do I feel about this? What does my inner wisdom say?" Start building the habit of checking in with yourself first, before looking outward for validation.

Remember, others' opinions are often more about them than about you - they're viewing you through their own filters, fears, and experiences. While feedback can be valuable, your relationship with yourself is the one constant throughout your life. Nurturing a strong, compassionate self-image gives you an anchor that remains steady even when others' views shift like the weather.

The beautiful thing is, when you develop a solid foundation of self-knowledge and self-respect, you become less reactive to others' changing opinions and more responsive to your own inner guidance. This isn't about ignoring feedback entirely - it's about knowing which voice matters most in defining who you are.

April 28th

"Gossip needn't be false to be evil - there's a lot of truth that shouldn't be passed around. Gossip is the opiate of the oppressed. It is just as cowardly to judge an absent person as it is wicked to strike a defenceless one."

— Frank A Clark

This quote reaches deep into something I find both fascinating and troubling about human nature - how we can justify causing harm by claiming we're "just telling the truth." It reveals an important distinction between what's true and what's right to share.

Think about the power you hold in conversations. Even when something is true, sharing it isn't always harmless. Consider this: Are you passing along information because it genuinely helps someone, or is it serving a different purpose - perhaps making you feel more connected, important, or in-the-know? Today, before sharing information about someone who isn't present, pause and ask yourself three questions: Why am I really sharing this? Would I say this if they were here? Does sharing this information help or heal anything?"

Remember, having information about others is a form of power, and like all power, it comes with responsibility. When we share details about others' lives - even true ones - we're making choices about their privacy, their dignity, and their right to control their own story. Sometimes the most courageous thing we can do is choose not to pass along information, even when we know it to be true. The beautiful thing is, when we start being more mindful about what we share about others, we often find our conversations becoming richer and more meaningful, focused on ideas and experiences rather than people's private lives.

April 29th

"We are not the same persons this year as last; nor are those we love. It is a happy chance if we, changing, continue to love a changed person."

— W. Somerset Maugham

This is one of those profound observations that gets deeper the more you sit with it. It speaks to something I find both challenging and beautiful about love and relationships - the constant dance of growth, change, and acceptance.

Today, consider how both you and your loved ones have evolved over time. Maybe you've developed new interests, shifted perspectives, or changed priorities. The magic isn't in staying exactly the same - it's in choosing to grow together, or at least growing in ways that still allow your paths to intertwine.

Try this thoughtful exercise today: Think about someone close to you who you've known for years. Rather than focusing on how they've changed in ways that might challenge you, notice how their evolution has enriched your life or helped you grow. Maybe their new perspectives have broadened your own, or their personal growth has inspired yours.

Remember, when we love someone, we're not just loving who they are in this moment - we're also loving who they're becoming. True love isn't about keeping someone in a familiar box; it's about creating space for both people to evolve while maintaining the core connection that brought them together. It's like tending a garden - the plants will grow and change, but with care and attention, they can grow in harmony.

The real gift isn't in finding someone who never changes - it's in finding someone who makes you feel safe enough to change and grow yourself, and who you can support in their own evolution.

April 30th

"The problem with human attraction is not knowing if it will be returned."

— Becca Fitzpatrick

This quote touches on one of the most vulnerable aspects of being human - that heart-fluttering uncertainty when we feel drawn to someone. I find it fascinating how this fundamental tension between hope and fear shapes so many of our relationships.

Today, I'd encourage you to consider how this uncertainty might actually serve a deeper purpose. While it can feel uncomfortable, even painful at times, this not-knowing often pushes us to be more authentic, to show up more fully, to take those brave steps towards meaningful connection.

Try this perspective shift today: Instead of seeing unreturned attraction as just a source of anxiety, notice how it might be teaching you something valuable about yourself. What does your response to uncertainty reveal about your own needs, fears, and capacity for courage? Sometimes our strongest growth comes from these vulnerable spaces.

Remember, feeling attracted to someone - whether romantically, intellectually, or as a potential friend - is a sign that your heart is still open, still capable of being moved by others. While we can't control whether others return our interest, we can honour our own capacity to feel deeply and take mindful risks in pursuit of genuine connection.

The beauty isn't in knowing for certain - it's in being brave enough to stay open to possibility while remaining grounded in your own worth, regardless of the outcome. After all, every meaningful connection started with someone being willing to step into that uncertainty.

May 1st

"The world's favourite season is the spring. All things seem possible in May."

— Edwin Way Teale

Ah, what a beautiful quote that captures something so fundamentally human - our natural attraction to new beginnings and possibility. Spring really is nature's way of showing us that fresh starts are always available to us, just like those first tender shoots breaking through the soil or buds unfurling on branches. I find it fascinating how Teale connects this physical renewal we see in nature to our own sense of potential. It's true, isn't it? There's something about spring that makes us feel like anything is possible - whether it's starting that project we've been putting off, rekindling old friendships, or making positive changes in our lives.

This month, take moments to embrace that "spring energy" in your own life, regardless of the actual season. What's one small seed of possibility you could plant this month? It doesn't have to be May for you to tap into that feeling of renewal and potential. Maybe it's as simple as trying a new route to work, reaching out to someone you've been meaning to contact, or taking the first step towards a goal you've been contemplating.

Remember, just like spring doesn't transform the world overnight, you don't need to make dramatic changes all at once. Nature teaches us that growth happens gradually, one small unfurling at a time. What matters is that first step, that initial moment when you decide to let something new begin.

May 2nd

"Appreciation can make a day, even change a life. Your willingness to put it all into words is all that is necessary."

— Margaret Cousins

What a profound reminder of the simple yet transformative power of expressing gratitude. In our fast-paced world, we often underestimate just how much a few heartfelt words of appreciation can mean to someone.

Think about a time when someone took a moment to genuinely thank you or acknowledge your impact - how did that make you feel? Often, these moments stay with us for years, sometimes even shaping how we see ourselves and our worth in the world.

Today, I'd suggest this: Take a moment to think about someone who has positively influenced your life - maybe it's a teacher who believed in you, a friend who was there during tough times, or even a stranger who showed unexpected kindness. Now, instead of just feeling that gratitude silently, consider putting it into words. It doesn't have to be elaborate or poetic - authenticity matters more than perfection.

Write that email you've been meaning to send, make that phone call, or pen that note. Don't wait for a special occasion. The beauty of appreciation is that it creates its own perfect moment. And remember - while your words might take just a few minutes to express, their impact could last a lifetime in someone's heart.

What's particularly powerful about this practice is that it creates a beautiful ripple effect - when we express genuine appreciation, we not only lift others but also become more attuned to the goodness in our own lives. It's a simple act that can transform both the giver and receiver.

May 3rd

"When someone you love dies, and you're not expecting it, you don't lose her all at once; you lose her in pieces over a long time—the way the mail stops coming, and her scent fades from the pillows and even from the clothes in her closet and drawers. Gradually, you accumulate the parts of her that are gone. Just when the day comes—when there's a particular missing part that overwhelms you with the feeling that she's gone, forever—there comes another day, and another specifically missing part."

— John Irving

This quote deeply resonates with me. It captures something that most people never tell you about grief. When my wife passed away from Leukaemia at 36, I discovered that grief isn't what the world often portrays it to be. Everyone expects that crushing moment of the initial loss, the funeral, the first night alone. Yes, those moments shatter you - but they're just the beginning of a much longer journey.

What I've learned, what I needed to share, is that you don't lose someone all at once. Instead, you lose them gradually, in quiet moments that ambush you when you least expect it. It's finding her hair tie in a drawer months later. It's realising her name has stopped appearing on junk mail. It's the day you notice you can't quite remember the exact sound of her laugh anymore. Each discovery feels like losing her all over again, a fresh reminder that your world has irreversibly changed.

The strangest, smallest things catch you off guard - the way her closet slowly loses her scent, the empty space on the bathroom counter where her toothbrush used to be, the gradual disappearance of her fingerprints from the windows she used to keep spotless. Each of these moments becomes its own kind of goodbye, teaching you anew what it means to live in a world without someone who was woven into the very fabric of your daily life.

Just when you think you've experienced every possible way of missing them, something new emerges - another "specifically missing part" you hadn't prepared for. Maybe it's seeing their favourite flowers bloom in spring and not being able to bring them home, or reaching for your phone to share exciting news before remembering you can't.

I've come to understand that grief doesn't follow any timeline or pattern. Each little loss is simultaneously a reminder of the love that was there and, in some ways, still is. It's painful, yes, but it's also a testament to how deeply that person mattered, how fully they lived in our world, and how many different ways they were loved.

Today, I want to acknowledge that this isn't the kind of quote that leads to simple action steps or easy solutions. Instead, it invites us to be more gentle with ourselves and others who are grieving. Understanding that grief unfolds this way - in these small, unexpected moments - can help us be more patient with our own healing process or more understanding of others who are going through loss.

If you're experiencing grief, remember that it's okay to feel these little losses freshly, even long after the initial shock. There's no timeline for when you should be "over it.

I wrote this not just to express my own loss, but to reach out to others walking this same path. To tell them that these small moments of grief are valid, that they're not alone in experiencing loss this way, and that each of these little goodbyes honours the beauty of the love we shared. Because ultimately, grief isn't just about loss - it's about love that was real, love that mattered, love that continues to shape us even in absence.

May 4th

"It is an absolute human certainty that no one can know his own beauty or perceive a sense of his own worth until it has been reflected back to him in the mirror of another loving, caring human being."

— John Joseph Powell

This quote captures something I've observed countless times - we often struggle to see our own light until someone else helps us recognise it. Powell touches on a fundamental truth about human connection and self-worth.

Think about it - haven't you noticed how a genuine compliment from someone who truly sees you can change your entire day, or even your self-perception? It's because we're social beings, and our understanding of ourselves is deeply intertwined with our relationships with others.

Today, take a moment to be that "mirror" for someone in your life. Choose one person - maybe your partner, a friend, family member, or colleague - and share something specific you genuinely appreciate about them. Not just "you're nice" but something like "I admire how you always make time to listen when others need you" or "I'm inspired by your dedication to learning new things." This practice serves two purposes - it helps others see their worth (which is valuable in itself), and it often leads to deeper, more meaningful connections that ultimately help us better understand our own value. Plus, when we regularly acknowledge the beauty in others, we tend to become more aware of our own positive qualities too.

May 5th

"Happiness is in simplicity. To be happy, always try to have happy thoughts."

— Debasish Mridha

This quote speaks to a profound yet often overlooked truth about happiness. In our complex modern world, we tend to overcomplicate our pursuit of happiness, chasing after external achievements or material goals. But Mridha reminds us that happiness can be found in something as simple as our own thoughts.

Today, set aside 5 minutes, perhaps during your morning coffee or tea, to deliberately focus on happy thoughts. Think about simple pleasures - the warmth of sunlight on your face, the sound of birds chirping, a child's laughter, or the comfort of your favourite chair. These aren't grand or complicated things, but they're genuinely uplifting moments that we often rush past.

What's powerful about this approach is that it's always available to us. We can't always control our circumstances, but we can practice directing our thoughts towards what brings us joy. It's like exercising a muscle - the more we practice finding happiness in simple things, the more naturally it comes to us.

Think of it as creating small pockets of contentment throughout your day. Would you be willing to try this 5-minute practice tomorrow morning?

May 6th

"Words are singularly the most powerful force available to humanity. We can choose to use this force constructively with words of encouragement, or destructively using words of despair. Words have energy and power with the ability to help, to heal, to hinder, to hurt, to harm, to humiliate and to humble."

— Yehuda Berg

This quote deeply resonates with me as it captures the profound impact our words can have on both ourselves and others. Think of words as seeds we plant - they can grow into either beautiful gardens of support and connection, or thorny barriers that wound and divide.

Berg brilliantly points out that we have this incredible power at our disposal every single day, in every interaction. What's fascinating is that often we don't fully realise the ripple effects our words create - a single kind comment can lift someone's entire day, while a harsh word might echo in someone's mind for years.

Today, before each significant conversation or interaction, take a brief three-second pause. In that moment, ask yourself: "Will my next words build up or break down?" This tiny pause can be transformative. It's like installing a gentle filter between your thoughts and your speech.

You might be surprised how this small practice starts changing your relationships. Maybe you'll catch yourself before making that sarcastic comment to your colleague, or you'll find the right words to encourage your friend who's struggling. It's not about being perfect - it's about being more conscious of this incredible tool we all possess.

Think of it like having a superpower that you're learning to use more wisely. After all, very few things in life give us such immediate ability to impact our world as our choice of words.

Has there been a moment when someone's words particularly impacted you? Sometimes reflecting on such experiences helps us better understand the power we hold in our own words.

May 7th

"Just don't give up trying to do what you really want to do. Where there is love and inspiration, I don't think you can go wrong."

— Ella Jane Fitzgerald

What I love about this quote from Ella Fitzgerald is how it weaves together three essential elements of a fulfilling life: persistence, passion, and purpose. Coming from someone who faced numerous obstacles yet became one of the most celebrated jazz vocalists in history, these words carry special weight. The beauty of this wisdom lies in its focus on internal guidance rather than external validation. When our actions are driven by genuine love for what we do and sparked by real inspiration, we're already successful in a profound way, regardless of conventional measures of achievement.

Today, take 10 minutes to reconnect with something you truly love doing but may have put aside due to doubts, busy schedules, or perceived obstacles. It could be as simple as sketching, writing poetry, playing an instrument, or working on that business idea you've been dreaming about. Don't worry about doing it perfectly - just engage with it purely for the joy of it.

This small step can reignite that spark of inspiration Fitzgerald talks about. Sometimes we get so caught up in the "how" and "what if" that we forget the "why" - the love that drew us to something in the first place. Remember, even small steps in the direction of your true desires count as progress. What activity or dream would you like to reconnect with today?

May 8th

"I think there are pieces of yourself that you will always guard."

— Kiera Cass

This is such an intimate observation about human nature and self-preservation. What Cass captures here is the beautiful complexity of being human - how even in our closest relationships and most vulnerable moments, there are still parts of ourselves we keep protected, like precious jewels in a velvet box. And you know what? That's not just okay - it's healthy. These guarded pieces often represent our deepest sensitivities, our most profound experiences, or parts of ourselves we're still trying to understand. They're not walls, but rather sacred spaces within us that we honour by choosing when and with whom to share them.

Today, take a quiet moment to acknowledge these protected parts of yourself without trying to change or expose them. Maybe write in a private journal about one of these guarded pieces - not to share, but simply to honour its existence and understand its purpose in your life. This practice can help you feel more at peace with the natural boundaries you maintain.

Think of these guarded pieces not as barriers to connection, but as proof of your self-respect and emotional wisdom. Just as we wouldn't leave our front door unlocked all the time, we don't need to bare every corner of our soul to be authentic or caring. Reflect on how these carefully guarded pieces have served to protect and preserve important aspects of who you are?

May 9th

"The 'what ifs' and 'should haves' will eat your brain."

— John O Callaghan

This quote hits at something so fundamentally human - our tendency to get trapped in cycles of regret and hypothetical scenarios. You know that feeling when your mind starts spinning with thoughts like "What if I had taken that job?" or "I should have said something different"? It's like being caught in a mental maze where every turn leads to more self-doubt.

Today, when you catch yourself in a "what if" spiral, try this 30-second reset. Take a deep breath and say to yourself: "This is where I am now, and this is what I can do from here." Then immediately take one small action in the present moment - even if it's just sending that email you've been putting off or taking a short walk.

The power of this practice lies in shifting from paralysis to movement. Those "what ifs" and "should haves" drain our energy precisely because they're focused on things we can't change. But we always have power in the present moment.

I've noticed that people who find peace and success aren't the ones who never make mistakes or always make perfect choices - they're the ones who get skilled at redirecting their energy from past scenarios to present possibilities.

What kind of "what if" thoughts tend to catch you most often? Sometimes just naming them can help reduce their power over us.

May 10th

"Only you can take inner freedom away from yourself, or give it to yourself. Nobody else can."

— Michael A. Singer

This quote from Singer touches on something truly profound about personal power and freedom. What's fascinating is how it flips the script on how most people think about freedom - instead of focusing on external circumstances, it points directly to our internal world, where the real power lies. Think about it - how often do we give away our inner peace and freedom by letting our reactions to others' opinions, past hurts, or future worries control us? It's like we hand over the keys to our emotional home to everyone except ourselves.

Today, when you feel yourself becoming reactive or losing your sense of inner freedom, pause for a moment and ask: "Am I choosing to give away my peace right now?" Then take three slow breaths and consciously choose to reclaim your inner space. You might say to yourself: "This is my inner world, and I choose to remain free here."

This isn't about ignoring real challenges or dismissing valid emotions. Rather, it's about recognising that even in difficult circumstances, we have the power to maintain our inner sovereignty. It's like having an internal sanctuary that remains yours, no matter what's happening outside.

I'm curious - can you think of a recent situation where you might have unconsciously given away your inner freedom? Understanding these moments can be the first step to reclaiming our power.

May 11th

"The hardest thing is to take less when you can get more."

— Frank McKinney Hubbard

This observation by Hubbard cuts straight to the heart of human nature and wisdom. As someone who's witnessed the subtle power of "enough," I can tell you that this seemingly simple idea touches on one of life's most challenging lessons.

Knowing when to stop – whether it's with food, work, possessions, or even information – often requires more strength than pushing for more. In a world that constantly broadcasts "more is better," choosing less can feel like swimming upstream.

Today, practice the art of "purposeful restraint." Choose one area of your life where you typically default to taking more, and experiment with taking less. It might be: Leaving a little food on your plate when you're satisfied but could eat more. Ending a meeting 5 minutes early when everything important has been covered. Buying one quality item instead of several cheaper alternatives. Taking on fewer commitments even when you could squeeze in more. Pay attention to how it feels. Often, there's an initial discomfort, followed by a subtle sense of freedom. Notice if taking less in one area creates more space for something else valuable in your life.

Remember, this isn't about deprivation – it's about finding your personal "sweet spot" where having less actually gives you more: more peace, more time, more satisfaction. Sometimes the most abundant life comes from knowing when to say "enough."

May 12th

"People make mistakes, mess up, make wrong decisions that will hurt you, some may even do it on purpose. Bad things are going to happen in your life, for your own good, the best thing to do is to not use it as an excuse to hurt them back."

— Gary Hardy

This is one of life's hardest but most important lessons. When someone hurts us – whether it's intentional or not – our first instinct is often to want to hurt them back. It's natural, it's human. But choosing revenge or retaliation usually just creates more pain, both for others and ourselves. It's like drinking poison and expecting the other person to get sick. I've seen this play out countless times in life, both in my own experiences and others'. When we hold onto hurt and use it as justification to harm others, we're actually giving that initial pain power over us, letting it shape who we become. The real strength lies in breaking that cycle.

Here's something practical you might try today: When someone frustrates or disappoints you (even in a small way), pause for a moment before reacting. Take a deep breath and ask yourself, "Will responding with negativity actually make my life better?" Usually, you'll find that letting go – while still maintaining healthy boundaries – leaves you feeling more at peace than any revenge could. This isn't about being a doormat or pretending you weren't hurt. It's about choosing your own path forward rather than letting others' actions dictate your behaviour. Sometimes the bravest thing we can do is refuse to let someone else's darkness dim our own light.

May 13th

"Wisdom is the reward you get for a lifetime of listening when you'd have preferred to talk."

— Doug Larson

We all love to share our thoughts and opinions. There is a natural impulse to want to be heard, to prove what we know. But the real gems of wisdom often come when we quiet that impulse and truly listen to others.

Think about the wisest people you've met in your life. Chances are, they're also excellent listeners. They've learned that every person they meet – whether younger, older, more or less educated – has something valuable to teach them. It's not always comfortable to listen when we're bursting to speak, but that's often when we learn the most.

Today, in your next conversation, try practicing what I call "complete listening." When someone is speaking, put aside that voice in your head that's planning what you'll say next. Just focus entirely on understanding their perspective. You might be amazed at what you learn when you're not waiting for your turn to talk.

This isn't just about collecting information – it's about developing empathy, understanding different viewpoints, and gradually building the kind of deep wisdom that comes from truly hearing others' experiences and insights. Remember, everyone you meet knows something you don't.

May 14th

"Relax, Recharge and Reflect. Sometimes it's OK to do nothing."

— Izey Victoria Odiase

We are always under pressure to be productive, to always be doing something "worthwhile." But sometimes, the most valuable thing we can do is absolutely nothing.

I've noticed that many people – myself included at times – feel guilty about taking genuine downtime. We've somehow convinced ourselves that rest is laziness, that recharging is a luxury rather than a necessity. But think about it: even your phone needs time to recharge, right? Why would we expect any less from our minds and bodies?

Today, set aside 15 minutes – just 15 minutes – where you give yourself permission to do absolutely nothing. No scrolling on your phone, no TV, no planning your next task. Just sit or lie down quietly. Notice your breathing. Let your mind wander. If you feel that familiar guilt creeping in about "wasting time," remind yourself that this nothingness is actually something very important – it's maintenance for your well-being and self care.

This kind of intentional pause isn't just about rest; it's about giving yourself space to process your experiences, let your mind make new connections, and return to your activities with renewed energy and clarity. Sometimes, doing nothing is actually doing something very powerful for yourself.

May 15th

"In the end, our choices make us who we are."

— Kristen Iversen

It's easy to think our lives are shaped mainly by circumstances or what happens to us. But the truth is, while we can't control everything that comes our way, we absolutely control how we respond to it. Each choice we make – whether big or small – adds up to create the person we become.

I've seen this play out countless times: two people face similar challenges, but their different choices lead them down entirely different paths. It's not just about the major life decisions either. Sometimes it's those small, daily choices that really define us – choosing kindness when we're frustrated, choosing effort when we're tired, choosing honesty when it would be easier to cut corners.

Today, before making any decision, pause for a moment and ask yourself, "What kind of person do I want to be, and does this choice align with that?" It could be as simple as choosing whether to hit snooze again or deciding how to respond to a difficult email.

Remember, we're not just choosing what to do – we're choosing who to become. Every time you make a conscious choice that aligns with your values, you're building the foundation of who you'll be tomorrow. It's empowering when you think about it – we're all constantly crafting ourselves through these moments of choice.

May 16th

"A break from social media isn't missing out; it's gaining time for what truly fulfils you."

— Unknown

This really hits on something crucial about modern life. It's fascinating how we've developed this fear of missing out – this anxiety that if we're not constantly connected, we're somehow falling behind or losing touch. But there's a beautiful irony here: often, what we're actually missing out on is real life happening right in front of us.

I've noticed how social media can create this illusion of connection while actually disconnecting us from deeper, more meaningful experiences. It's like we're so busy documenting and scrolling through life that we forget to actually live it.

Here's a simple challenge for today: Choose one specific time period – maybe your first hour after waking up or your last hour before bed – and make it a social media-free zone. Use that time to do something that truly feeds your soul, whether that's reading a book, having an uninterrupted conversation with someone you love, or just sitting quietly with your morning coffee. Don't even keep your phone nearby – let yourself be fully present in that moment.

The interesting thing is, you might find that what you gain isn't just time – it's clarity, peace of mind, and a stronger connection to what really matters to you. Sometimes we need to create a little space to remember what truly fills us up, rather than what just fills our time.

May 17th

"Times will change for the better when you change."

— Maxwell Maltz

This hits on such a fundamental truth about personal growth. You know how sometimes we sit around waiting for circumstances to improve, for other people to change, or for luck to turn in our favour? But real transformation usually starts from within. It's like that old saying about being the change you want to see – it's not just a nice quote, it's actually how life tends to work.

I've seen this play out countless times: when someone shifts their mindset or behaviour, suddenly their whole world seems to shift with them. It's not that everything around them magically changes – it's that they start responding differently, making different choices, seeing new opportunities they might have missed before.

Today, pick one small thing you wish was different in your life. Instead of focusing on external factors, ask yourself, "How might I need to change to create this difference?" Maybe it's being more patient, more proactive, or more honest with yourself. Then take one tiny step in that direction.

Remember, this isn't about blaming yourself for circumstances beyond your control. It's about recognising where you do have power to create change. When you shift, even slightly, you might be amazed at how the world around you begins to respond differently. The best part is, you don't have to wait for anyone's permission to start.

May 18th

"The hardest battles you fight, are the ones you battle in silence."

— Gary Hardy

We often celebrate the visible victories in life – getting that promotion, running that marathon, achieving those goals everyone can see. But some of our most challenging and important battles happen where no one else can witness them. These silent battles – whether they're with anxiety, self-doubt, loneliness, or past trauma – can feel especially heavy because they're carried alone. Sometimes the hardest part isn't even the struggle itself, but feeling like you have to maintain a brave face while fighting it.

Here's a gentle suggestion for today: Give yourself permission to acknowledge your silent battles. Maybe take a quiet moment to write down what you're really dealing with – not for anyone else to see, just for you to recognise your own strength in facing it. Sometimes simply acknowledging our internal struggles makes them feel a little less overwhelming.

Remember, fighting battles in silence doesn't mean you have to face them alone. While not everyone needs to know your struggles, consider sharing with just one trusted person. Often, just having someone who knows what you're going through can make that silent battle feel a little less lonely. There's incredible strength in continuing to show up each day while carrying these invisible weights. Your battles may be silent, but that doesn't make them – or your courage in facing them – any less real.

May 19th

"I am a big believer in visualisation. I run through my races mentally so that I feel even more prepared."

— Allyson Felix

This really speaks to the power of mental preparation and how our minds can shape our performance. It's fascinating how elite athletes like Allyson Felix use visualisation not just as a nice add-on, but as a crucial part of their success strategy. What they understand is that our brains can't always tell the difference between a vividly imagined experience and a real one – both create similar neural patterns.

Today, before any important event – whether it's a presentation, a difficult conversation, or even just your morning routine – take five minutes to mentally walk through it. Close your eyes and really see yourself going through each step successfully. Feel the confidence in your body, imagine the positive responses, visualise yourself handling any challenges with grace.

The key is to make it as detailed and sensory-rich as possible. Don't just see it – feel it, hear it, experience it fully in your mind. Include small details like what you'll wear, the words you'll use, how you'll carry yourself. This isn't just daydreaming – it's mental rehearsal that builds neural pathways for success.

I've seen this work wonders not just in sports, but in all areas of life. When you've already "experienced" success in your mind, your body and brain are better prepared to create it in reality. It's like giving yourself a preview of your own potential.

May 20th

"Life goes on whether you choose to move on and take a chance in the unknown or stay behind, locked in the past, thinking of what could've been. I don't want to live in the past anymore. I'm so lonely here, there's nothing for me here anymore."

— Stephanie Smith

This quote touches on how we can sometimes get stuck in the limbo of "what-ifs" and missed opportunities. It's natural to feel the pull of the past – those memories, relationships, or paths we didn't take. But sometimes holding on to what was (or what could have been) becomes its own kind of prison.

I've seen how this paralysis of looking backward can create a self-fulfilling prophecy. When we're so focused on what we've lost or what could have been, we literally can't see the new doors opening around us. It's like trying to drive a car while only looking in the rearview mirror – not only do you miss what's ahead, but it's actually dangerous.

Today, take a piece of paper and write down one thing from your past that you keep revisiting. Then, right next to it, write down one small, concrete step you could take towards something new. It doesn't have to be huge – maybe it's joining a local group, taking a class, or even just exploring a different part of town. The key is to actively create forward motion, no matter how small.

Remember, moving forward doesn't mean the past didn't matter or that those feelings weren't valid. It's about acknowledging that while that chapter was important, it doesn't have to be the whole story. Life really does keep moving, and you deserve to move with it – to discover new possibilities, new connections, new versions of yourself.

Sometimes the bravest thing we can do is simply take that first step into the unknown, trusting that while we don't know exactly what's ahead, it has to be better than staying stuck in a place that no longer serves us.

May 21st

"When someone loves you, the way they talk about you is different. You feel safe and comfortable."

— Jess C. Scott

This quote touches on something so true about genuine love – it's not just in the big gestures, but in those subtle ways someone carries you in their words and thoughts. You know how you can sometimes tell the difference between when someone is just talking about a person versus when they're talking about someone they truly care about? There's a warmth there, a careful attention to how they present that person to the world.

When someone truly loves you, they become a sort of guardian of your story. They tend to highlight your strengths, explain your quirks with affection, and even when discussing your struggles, there's this underlying tone of understanding and protection. It creates this invisible safety net that you can feel even when they're just talking about you to others.

Here's a small suggestion for today: Pay attention to how you talk about the people you care about when they're not around. Are you creating that sense of safety for them? Sometimes we forget that how we speak about our loved ones to others is also a form of caretaking – it's protecting and nurturing the relationship even in those moments when they're not present.

And if you're wondering about the authenticity of love in your own life, listen not just to what people say to you, but how they represent you to others. That feeling of safety, of being held with care even in conversation – it's one of those quiet but profound indicators of genuine love.

Remember, true love isn't just about feeling butterflies or grand declarations – it's about feeling like you can fully exhale, knowing that you're safe in someone's words and thoughts even when you're not there to hear them.

May 22nd

"Don't play for safety. It's the most dangerous thing in the world."

— Hugh Walpole

I've observed in life how playing it "safe" can actually be the riskiest choice of all. You know what's fascinating? Often, when people choose the seemingly safe path – staying in that comfortable but unfulfilling job, not speaking up, avoiding change – they're actually risking something far more precious: their potential, their dreams, their chance at genuine fulfilment. I've seen how this "safety first" mindset can become a kind of slow-motion risk, where years pass and suddenly you realise that by trying to avoid all risks, you've actually risked everything. It's like holding your breath to stay safe – eventually, you have to exhale and take in fresh air to truly live.

Today think of one thing you've been avoiding because it feels "safer" not to try. Maybe it's sharing an idea in a meeting, starting that creative project, or having that conversation you've been putting off. Take one small step towards it – not recklessly, but thoughtfully. Remember, courage isn't about not feeling fear; it's about not letting fear make your choices for you. The irony is that when we dare to step out of our comfort zones, we often discover new strengths and capabilities we never knew we had. Sometimes what feels like a risk is actually an investment in yourself, in your growth, in your future. The biggest risk might just be never taking any risks at all.

May 23rd

"If you're always worrying about what other people think, you'll never get any tougher."

— Kanae Minato

I have seen this hold back so many people. When we're constantly looking over our shoulder, wondering what others think of our choices, our clothes, our career moves – we stay stuck in this fragile state. It's like we're asking for permission to be ourselves.

Building mental toughness is a lot like building physical strength – it requires pushing through discomfort and accepting that not everyone will cheer you on. Sometimes, the most important growth happens when you make decisions that others might not understand at first.

Here's a simple but powerful thing you could try today: Make one small decision purely based on what you want, not what others expect. Maybe it's wearing that outfit you love but have been hesitant about, or speaking up in a meeting with an idea you've been sitting on. Notice how it feels to act from your own truth rather than others' expectations. Yes, you might feel uncomfortable at first – that's exactly where the toughness begins to build.

Remember, the goal isn't to stop caring about others completely – it's about finding the balance between being considerate and being true to yourself. Would you like to share what kind of situations make you most conscious of others' opinions?

May 24th

"The poison leaves bit by bit, not all at once. Be patient. You are healing."

— Yasmin Mogahed

This quote beautifully captures the reality of healing from emotional wounds, traumas, or difficult experiences. Just as how physical toxins need time to leave our system, emotional pain and hurt follow a similar pattern – they fade gradually, almost imperceptibly at times.

Sometimes we get frustrated when we're still carrying pain or negative feelings from past experiences, thinking "I should be over this by now." But healing isn't a race or a linear journey. Some days you might feel like you've made huge progress, and other days old feelings might resurface. That's completely normal and part of the process.

Today, start a small healing journal. When you notice even the tiniest positive change or moment where you felt lighter – maybe you thought about a painful situation and it stung a little less, or you went a whole day without that anxious thought that usually bothers you – write it down. These small victories are your "poison leaving bit by bit." Looking back at these entries can remind you that you're making progress, even on days when it doesn't feel like it.

Healing is a lot like watching a garden grow. You don't see the changes day to day, but when you look back after a few months, you can see how far you've come. Would you like to share what kind of healing journey you're on right now?

May 25th

"I need to learn how to stop destroying myself, stop being hard on myself, and be nice to myself."

— Daul Kim

This quote really touches on something so many of us struggle with – that inner voice that can be our harshest critic. It's powerful because it recognises both the problem and the solution: we often know we're being too hard on ourselves, but changing that pattern takes real effort and conscious learning.

Treating ourselves kindly isn't just about positive thinking – it's about developing a whole new relationship with ourselves. Think about how you'd treat a close friend who's going through a tough time. You wouldn't berate them for their mistakes or constantly point out their flaws. Yet somehow, we often think it's okay to do this to ourselves.

Today, start a "self-kindness pause." When you catch yourself in self-criticism (maybe after a mistake or when looking in the mirror), pause for just 10 seconds. Take a breath and ask yourself: "Would I say this to someone I love?" If the answer is no, try to rephrase your thought with the same gentleness you'd offer a friend. For example, instead of "I'm so stupid for making that mistake," try "I'm learning and doing my best."

Remember, being kind to yourself isn't self-indulgent – it's essential for your wellbeing and growth. When we're gentler with ourselves, we actually become more capable of making positive changes in our lives. Sometimes the strongest thing we can do is put down the weapons we've been using against ourselves. Have you noticed particular situations that tend to trigger your harshest self-criticism?

May 26th

"Eye contact is a dangerous, dangerous thing. But lovely. God, so lovely."

— Hedonist Poet

There's something so profound about this observation – how it captures both the vulnerability and beauty of truly connecting with another person through eye contact. It's fascinating how this simple act can feel like both a risk and a reward at the same time. It's interesting how many of us have learned to avoid sustained eye contact in our daily lives, often hiding behind screens or quick glances. Yet those moments when we truly look into someone's eyes – whether it's a loved one, a friend, or even a stranger – can create some of the deepest feelings of human connection we experience.

Here's something transformative you could try today: During one conversation, practice mindful eye contact. Not in an intense or uncomfortable way, but with genuine presence. Maybe it's while listening to a friend share a story, or while thanking the barista for your coffee. Notice how it feels, how it might change the quality of the interaction. Notice if you feel the urge to look away – that's the "dangerous" part the poet mentions – but see if you can stay present just a moment longer. The beauty of eye contact is that it creates a moment of genuine vulnerability and connection in a world where those moments are becoming increasingly rare.

When we look into someone's eyes, we're saying "I see you, and I'm willing to let you see me too." It's like a wordless conversation that can sometimes say more than words ever could.

May 27th

"Most people need love and acceptance a lot more than they need advice."

— Bob Goff

This quote really hits at something fundamental about human nature. It's funny – often when someone comes to us with a problem, our first instinct is to jump in with solutions and suggestions. But what Bob Goff captures here is that deeper human need that often lies beneath the surface of every conversation, every shared struggle.

Sometimes the most powerful thing we can do for someone isn't to fix their problems or offer wisdom – it's simply to be there, to listen without judgement, and to make them feel truly seen and accepted for who they are. Think about times in your own life when you were going through something difficult. While advice might have been helpful, wasn't it the people who just sat with you, who made you feel loved despite your struggles, who made the biggest difference?

Here's something meaningful you could try today: When someone shares a problem or struggle with you, practice just listening and showing acceptance first. Instead of immediately offering advice, try saying something like "That sounds really difficult. I'm here with you." Watch how this small shift might deepen your connections and allow others to feel safer being vulnerable with you.

This approach isn't just about helping others – it's also about recognising this need in ourselves. Sometimes we get so caught up in trying to improve, fix, or change ourselves that we forget to simply accept and love who we are in this moment.

Have you noticed how different it feels when someone offers you acceptance versus when they jump straight to giving advice?

May 28th

"And now here is my secret, a very simple secret: It is only with the heart that one can see rightly; what is essential is invisible to the eye."

— Antoine de Saint-Exupéry

This quote from "The Little Prince" touches on one of life's most profound truths. In our world that's so focused on appearances, achievements, and tangible metrics, Saint-Exupéry reminds us that the most meaningful aspects of life often can't be seen or measured. When we learn to "see with our heart," we start noticing things our eyes might miss – the unspoken kindness in a gesture, the deeper story behind someone's actions, or the true value of a simple moment of connection. It's about developing emotional intelligence and intuition that goes beyond surface-level judgements.

Here's something transformative you could try today: In each interaction, practice looking for what's invisible. Maybe it's understanding what someone is really saying beneath their words, or noticing the feeling in a room rather than just the physical space. When you meet someone new, try to sense their story rather than just seeing their appearance. During a conversation, tune into the emotions being shared rather than just the words being spoken. This kind of heart-sight is like a muscle – the more we use it, the stronger it gets. When we lead with our hearts in understanding situations and people, we often make wiser, more compassionate choices. It helps us value what truly matters in life: the relationships we build, the love we share, and the impact we have on others' lives.

May 29th

"Showing your emotions to people is like bleeding next to a shark."

— Unknown

This is quite a vivid and powerful metaphor that speaks to the vulnerability we feel when showing our true emotions. It captures that raw fear of emotional exposure – how sharing our feelings can sometimes make us feel like we're risking everything. While this quote reflects a very real fear many people have, it's worth considering that not every situation is as dangerous as it feels. Yes, there are certainly "sharks" out there who might take advantage of our vulnerability, but there are also countless people who respond to emotional openness with empathy and understanding.

Today, start building an "emotional safety map." Take a moment to identify one or two people in your life who have consistently shown themselves to be trustworthy with your feelings – the "safe harbour's" rather than the "sharks." These might be people who've never used your vulnerabilities against you, who listen without judgement, or who share their own emotions honestly with you.

The key isn't to never show emotion – that would be like never entering the ocean at all – but rather to be discerning about where and with whom we choose to be vulnerable. Just as a skilled swimmer knows when and where it's safe to enter the water, we can learn to recognise the difference between situations that call for emotional guardedness and those that allow for safe emotional expression. Have you found certain ways to identify the people you can safely be emotionally open with?

May 30th

"Embody what you most want to impart, and keep your mouth shut."

— Jon Kabat-Zinn

This quote really hits at a fundamental truth about personal influence and leadership. It reminds me of that old saying "actions speak louder than words," but takes it to a deeper level – it's about becoming the very change or wisdom you wish to share with others. There's something powerful about silent teaching through example. When we lecture or preach, people often put up walls. But when we quietly live our values, practice what we believe in, and let our actions do the talking, we create a different kind of impact – one that invites others to learn through observation rather than instruction.

Here's something transformative you could try today: Choose one value or quality you often find yourself advising others about – maybe it's patience, kindness, or self-discipline. Instead of talking about it, focus entirely on embodying it yourself. Notice how different it feels to simply live it rather than speak about it. Pay attention to how others respond to this silent demonstration.

It's like being a lighthouse – you don't shout at ships to follow your beam; you simply shine, consistently and steadily. Your presence and actions become the teaching. This approach often creates more lasting change than any amount of verbal instruction could achieve. Have you ever noticed how someone's quiet example has influenced you more deeply than their words could have?

May 31st

"At the end of your life, you will never regret not having passed one more test, not winning one more verdict, or not closing one more deal. You will regret time not spent with a husband, a friend, a child, a parent."

— Barbara Bush

This is a reminder about what truly matters in life. Barbara Bush captures something profound here – how we often get caught up in the rat race of achievements and milestones, while the real richness of life quietly slips by in the moments we're too busy to notice. It's interesting how our society pushes us to constantly chase the next professional accomplishment, yet when people look back on their lives or face difficult times, it's rarely their career achievements they reach for – it's the memories of connections, of love shared, of time spent with those who matter most.

Today, take a "relationship audit." Look at your calendar for the past week and notice how you've allocated your time. Then, choose one important relationship in your life and create what I call a "non-negotiable moment" – even if it's just 30 minutes of completely undistracted time with that person. No phones, no multitasking, just presence. Maybe it's having coffee with your parent, playing with your child, or taking a walk with your partner. The beauty of this quote is that it's not asking us to abandon our professional goals – it's simply reminding us to maintain perspective. Success means little if we sacrifice all our meaningful connections to achieve it. Sometimes the most important "deal" we can close is the gap between ourselves and those we love.

June 1st

"June is the time for being in the world in new ways, for throwing off the cold and dark spots of life."

— Joan D. Chittister

What a beautiful perspective on the transformative nature of June! This quote captures the spirit of renewal and emergence that comes with early summer. There's something so hopeful about how Chittister frames this time as an opportunity for personal reinvention and shedding what weighs us down. While she's speaking literally about the season, there's a deeper wisdom here about creating our own personal "June moments" – times when we consciously choose to step into the world differently and leave behind what's been holding us back. Just as nature sheds its winter coat in June, we too can choose to release our old patterns and dark thoughts.

Here's something enriching you could try this month: Create your own symbolic "June cleanse." Choose one "cold or dark spot" in your life – maybe it's a negative thought pattern, a draining habit, or a weight you've been carrying – and consciously decide to begin letting it go. Then, choose one new way to be "in the world" this month. Perhaps it's going for a daily walk and really noticing the summer blooms, starting your day with five minutes of sunshine on your face, or reaching out to someone you've been meaning to connect with. Think of it as spring cleaning for your spirit – a gentle but intentional shift towards lightness and renewal. Just as June marks a natural transition point in the year, we can use this energy to mark our own transitions towards growth and light. Have you felt this urge for renewal lately? What "cold and dark spots" are you ready to throw off?

June 2nd

"There isn't a someday. There never was. No one has ever been to the future that you keep putting your life on hold for. All we ever have is now. And if you continually put your life on hold for what your life will be like tomorrow, or the next year, or when you finally lose the weight, you won't recognise that you already have what you want because you will have spent years training yourself to want, not have."

— Geneen Roth

We often live in a perpetual state of "waiting" for our real life to begin. It hits at something deeply human – our tendency to put conditions on our happiness and fulfilment, always pushing it into some imagined future.

It's almost like we create these invisible barriers between ourselves and our present life. We say things like "I'll start living fully when..." or "I'll be happy once..." – but as Roth points out so beautifully, that "when" or "once" never actually arrives. We're like traveler's always packing for a journey that never begins, missing the scenery that's right in front of us.

Here's something meaningful you could try today: Choose one thing you've been "saving" for someday – maybe it's wearing that special outfit, using those nice dishes, starting that project, or expressing that feeling – and do it now. Not because you've reached some goal or milestone, but simply because this moment, this "now," is where your life is actually happening.

The most profound part of this quote is how it reveals that constant wanting can become a habit that blinds us to what we already have. It's like having a beautiful garden but never enjoying it because you're too busy planning how it will look next season. The irony is that when we finally learn to inhabit our present moment fully, we often discover that many of the things we were waiting for were already here.

June 3rd

"I have the choice of being constantly active and happy or introspectively passive and sad. Or I can go mad by ricocheting in between."

— Sylvia Plath

This quote from Sylvia Plath really speaks to something I've observed about the human experience. She captures that internal struggle we all face between action and reflection, but I think she presents a false dichotomy. Life isn't actually about choosing between being constantly active or completely passive - it's about finding a meaningful balance. When Plath talks about "ricocheting in between," she's describing what happens when we swing between extremes: exhausting ourselves with constant activity or getting lost in our thoughts. I've seen how this can leave people feeling unstable and drained.

Today, set aside 15 minutes for what I call "active reflection." Find a quiet spot and write down what you're doing in your life that energises you and what tends to drain you. Don't just think about it - actually write it down. Then choose one small action that combines both movement and meaning. It could be as simple as taking a walk while processing your thoughts, or working on a creative project that allows you to be both productive and contemplative.

The key isn't to avoid either action or introspection, but to weave them together in a way that serves your wellbeing. This helps prevent that exhausting ricocheting effect Plath describes and creates a more sustainable way of living.

June 4th

"We are born in one day. We die in one day. We can change in one day. And we can fall in love in one day. Anything can happen in just one day."

— Gayle Forman

Too often, we get caught up thinking meaningful change requires months or years, but some of life's most significant moments happen in the span of 24 hours.

Think about it - we all know how a single day can completely alter our life's trajectory. Maybe it was the day you met someone special, received life-changing news, or made a decision that set you on a new path. The beauty of Forman's words lies in their reminder that each day holds infinite potential.

Today, try approaching this day as if it's significant - because it is. Instead of going through your routine on autopilot, pause occasionally and ask yourself, "What could make today meaningful?" It doesn't have to be dramatic. Maybe it's finally sending that message you've been putting off, starting that project you've been dreaming about, or simply being fully present with someone you care about.

By being mindful of each day's potential, we open ourselves to possibilities we might otherwise miss. After all, while we can't control everything that happens in a day, we can control how present and receptive we are to its opportunities.

June 5th

"There is love in holding and there is love in letting go."

— Elizabeth Berg

This simple yet profound quote touches on one of life's most challenging paradoxes. Berg captures something I've come to understand deeply about love - that it manifests both in the moments we hold close and in those times when we must open our hands and release.

Think about how a parent loves their child. There's love in holding them when they're small, in keeping them safe and close. But there's also profound love in letting them go off to school, move away to college, or build their own life. Or consider how we sometimes need to let go of relationships that no longer serve us, not out of lack of love, but because love sometimes means allowing both ourselves and others the freedom to grow separately.

Here's a gentle suggestion for today: Identify one thing you might be holding too tightly - whether it's a worry, a relationship, an expectation, or even a dream. Take a moment to consider if some form of "letting go" might actually be an act of love - either for yourself or someone else. Maybe it's as simple as letting go of the need to control every outcome, or releasing yourself from an unrealistic standard you've set.

Remember, letting go doesn't mean you didn't love deeply. Sometimes it's proof that you did.

June 6th

"If you can love the wrong one so much, just imagine how much you can love the right one."

— Brandon Stanton

This quote touches something deep in our understanding of love and growth. It's fascinating how we often look back at past relationships with regret or see them as "mistakes," but Stanton flips this perspective beautifully. He suggests that our capacity to love deeply, even when it wasn't the right person, is actually evidence of something quite remarkable about ourselves. Think about it - if you can invest so much heart, so much care, so much genuine love into a relationship that ultimately wasn't right for you, that's not a weakness. It's proof of your incredible capacity for love. It's like having a superpower and using it on the wrong mission - the power itself is still amazing.

Here's a thoughtful suggestion for today: Rather than carrying past relationships as wounds or failures, try to see them as evidence of your heart's capacity. Write down three things you learned about love from a past relationship - not the painful lessons, but the beautiful ones about what you're capable of giving. Maybe it's your ability to be patient, to be deeply supportive, or to see the best in someone.

This perspective helps transform what might feel like wasted love into preparation - preparation for when you meet someone who can match and return that remarkable capacity for love you've already demonstrated. After all, love is not a limited resource that gets used up - it's a skill that grows stronger with practice.

June 7th

"Strange about learning; the farther I go the more I see that I never knew even existed. A short while ago I foolishly thought I could learn everything – all the knowledge in the world. Now I hope only to be able to know of its existence, and to understand one grain of it. Is there time?"

— Daniel Keyes

This reminds me of that moment when you first realise just how vast knowledge truly is - it's both humbling and exhilarating. Keyes captures that beautiful transition from the confidence of youth to the wisdom of understanding our own limitations.

What I find particularly moving is how he describes that shift from wanting to "learn everything" to hoping just to understand "one grain" deeply. It's like standing on a beach and initially thinking you could count all the sand, then realising that understanding even a single grain thoroughly would take a lifetime of study. Yet there's something deeply beautiful about that realisation - it means we never have to stop growing, never have to stop being amazed by what we discover.

Here's a suggestion for today: Choose one thing you think you know well - maybe it's your profession, a hobby, or even a relationship - and spend 15 minutes exploring just one small aspect of it that you've never really thought about before. Don't try to master it; just let yourself be curious about it. Maybe it's wondering about the origin of a word you use every day, or questioning why you do something in a particular way.

The beauty isn't in racing to learn everything - it's in maintaining that sense of wonder about how much there is still to discover. And to answer Keyes' question - yes, there is time. There's always time to learn something new, to understand one more grain of sand in this vast beach of knowledge.

June 8th

"You can knock on a deaf man's door forever."

— Nikos Kazantzakis

This seemingly simple quote carries a powerful truth about effort, receptiveness, and futility. You see, Kazantzakis captures something profound about human interaction and the importance of recognising when our efforts are meeting an immovable barrier.

The image of knocking endlessly on a deaf man's door illustrates those moments in life when we persist in actions that simply cannot produce our desired result - not because we aren't trying hard enough, but because the very nature of the situation makes success impossible. It's like trying to fill a bucket with a hole in it, or attempting to convince someone who has completely closed their mind to new ideas.

Here's a thoughtful suggestion for today: Take a moment to reflect on where in your life you might be "knocking on a deaf man's door." Is there a situation where you're expending energy but the other party simply cannot or will not receive your message? Maybe it's a relationship where you're the only one putting in effort, or a goal you're pursuing through methods that fundamentally can't work. Consider if it's time to find a different door to knock on, or perhaps a different way to communicate entirely.

Remember, recognising when to stop knocking isn't giving up - it's wisdom. Sometimes the most productive thing we can do is redirect our energy towards more receptive pathways.

June 9th

"You are absolutely capable of creating the life you can't stop thinking about."

— Unknown

I find this quote particularly potent because it connects two powerful forces: our persistent thoughts and our innate capabilities. It's fascinating how our minds often fixate on the life we dream of - whether it's a career change, a creative pursuit, or a different way of living. Those recurring thoughts aren't just daydreams; they're often signals pointing us towards our authentic path.

But what makes this quote especially meaningful is how it challenges the common narrative of "wishful thinking." Instead of dismissing these persistent thoughts as mere fantasy, it reframes them as evidence of our hidden potential. After all, why would your mind keep returning to something if there wasn't some part of you ready to make it real?

Today, take five minutes to write down what life you "can't stop thinking about." Be specific - not just "a better job" but what exactly about that different life keeps pulling at your thoughts. Then choose one small, concrete step you can take today towards that vision. Maybe it's sending one email, doing 15 minutes of research, or having one conversation that moves you closer to that life.

Remember, capability isn't about having everything figured out from the start. It's about recognising that those persistent thoughts might be your inner compass pointing towards what's possible for you.

June 10th

"I realise, for the first time, how very lonely I've been, and how comforting the presence of another human being can be."

— Suzanne Collins

This quote touches something deeply human about our need for connection. It's fascinating how we sometimes don't recognise our own loneliness until we experience its opposite - that warming presence of another person. Collins captures that moment of revelation beautifully, that instant when we suddenly understand what we've been missing.

It reminds me of how we can get so caught up in being independent, in handling everything ourselves, that we forget how fundamentally nourishing simple human presence can be. It's not always about conversation or doing things together - sometimes it's just about sharing space, knowing another heart beats nearby.

Today, create a moment of genuine presence with someone. It doesn't need to be elaborate. Maybe it's sitting with a friend in comfortable silence, calling someone you care about just to hear their voice, or even acknowledging the cashier at your local store with real attention rather than automatic politeness. If you're feeling particularly lonely, remember that reaching out isn't weakness - it's recognising our shared human need for connection. The beauty of this realisation that Collins describes isn't in the loneliness itself, but in how it awakens us to the incredible gift of human connection - something we all have the power to both give and receive.

June 11th

"Because with the right person, sometimes kissing feels like healing."

— Lisa McMann

This is such a tender observation about intimacy and human connection. McMann captures something profound here about how the right kind of love can be restorative. It's not just about the physical act of kissing - it's about that rare, beautiful moment when vulnerability meets acceptance and creates healing.

It's interesting how she uses the word "healing," suggesting that perhaps we all carry wounds of some kind - past hurts, insecurities, or emotional scars. But with the right person, those moments of intimate connection can feel like gentle medicine for our hearts. It's about being seen, being accepted, being cherished exactly as you are.

Here's a thoughtful suggestion for today: Whether you're in a relationship or not, take a moment to reflect on what "healing love" means to you. What kind of connection makes you feel whole? Maybe it's about feeling safe enough to be vulnerable, or being accepted without judgement. Write down these qualities - they can serve as a compass for recognising and nurturing healing connections in your life, romantic or otherwise.

Remember, healing love isn't just about romantic kisses - it's about any deep connection that helps mend our hearts and restore our faith in human connection.

June 12th

"I can't give you a sure-fire formula for success, but I can give you a formula for failure: try to please everybody all the time."

— Herbert Bayard Swope

It's fascinating how many of us fall into the trap of trying to shape ourselves into whoever we think others want us to be. Swope brilliantly points out that this people-pleasing instinct, which often feels like a path to success, is actually a guaranteed route to failure.

Think about it - when we try to please everyone, we end up pleasing no one, including ourselves. It's like trying to be a chameleon that changes colours so frequently it loses its own true shade. Not only is it exhausting, but it's also impossible - because different people want different, often contradictory things from us.

Here's a practical suggestion for today: Choose one decision you need to make - big or small - and make it based solely on what feels right to you, not what you think others expect. Maybe it's as simple as ordering what you actually want for lunch instead of what others might approve of, or expressing an opinion you usually keep to yourself. Notice how it feels to choose for yourself rather than for others' approval.

Remember, success isn't about making everyone happy - it's about being true to your own values and purpose, even if that means some people won't approve. After all, the most successful people in history often faced significant criticism along their path - but they stayed true to their vision anyway.

June 13th

"Rejection, though--it could make the loss of someone you weren't even that crazy about feel gut wrenching and world ending."

— Deb Caletti

This is such an insightful observation about human nature and our complex relationship with rejection. It's fascinating how rejection can magnify feelings we didn't even know were that significant. Caletti touches on something really profound here - how it's often not the loss of the person that hurts most, but the sting of being the one who wasn't chosen.

It's like when you're not particularly interested in a job, but getting that rejection email still feels like a punch to the gut. Or when someone you've been casually dating ends things first, and suddenly you're questioning your whole worth - even though last week you were wondering if you were that into them anyway. It's not really about them; it's about what the rejection says to our deeper insecurities.

Today, when you feel the sting of any kind of rejection, try this perspective shift - ask yourself "Am I hurt because I truly value what I lost, or am I hurt because I was rejected?" Write down your honest answer. This simple act of self-reflection can help separate genuine loss from wounded pride, making it easier to process the feelings and move forward.

Remember, sometimes rejection hurts not because we lost something precious, but because it triggers our deep-seated fears about being unworthy. Recognising this difference can be the first step in healing from rejection more genuinely and completely.

June 14th

"Yesterday's the past, tomorrow's the future, but today is a gift. That's why it's called the present."

— Bil Keane

This quote has such a beautiful way of reminding us about the power of the present moment. While it might seem playful with its wordplay on "present," it actually touches on something profound about how we experience time and life itself.

I think what makes this perspective especially valuable is how it gently redirects us from two common human tendencies - either dwelling in the past, which we can't change, or anxiously anticipating the future, which hasn't arrived yet. Instead, it reminds us that right now, this moment, is literally a gift we're being given.

Here's a meaningful suggestion for today: Set a few "presence alarms" on your phone - maybe three throughout the day. When each one goes off, take 30 seconds to fully notice your present moment. What can you hear? Feel? See? What's good about this exact moment? It's amazing how these brief pauses can transform an ordinary day into a series of small gifts we might otherwise miss.

Remember, while we can learn from yesterday and plan for tomorrow, the only moment we can actually experience and influence is this one, right now. And just like a gift, each present moment comes with the opportunity to either fully appreciate it or let it pass by unopened.

June 15th

"One thing people need to understand about extremely kind, nice, and loving people, is that their other side is just as extreme. It's the hell they survive that makes them gentle. Don't mistake their self-control for weakness. The beast in them is sleeping, not dead."

— Unknown

This quote really resonates with me. It speaks to a profound truth about human nature - that often, the kindest and gentlest souls have weathered the fiercest storms. Their compassion isn't born from naivety, but from a deep understanding of pain and struggle. They choose kindness not because they're weak, but because they know both the light and the shadow within themselves. Think about someone you know who's consistently kind and patient. Chances are, they've faced significant challenges that taught them the value of gentleness. They don't react harshly to situations not because they can't, but because they've learned the wisdom of restraint.

Here's a practical suggestion for today: When you encounter someone who's being particularly difficult, pause and remember this quote. Instead of matching their energy or dismissing them as weak if they respond with kindness, consider what experiences might have shaped their approach to conflict. Try responding with deliberate gentleness - not because you can't fight back, but because you're choosing a more powerful path. This mindset shift can transform your daily interactions. It reminds us that true strength often manifests as kindness, and that our past struggles can become the foundation for our greatest gifts to others.

June 16th

"You're only one workout away from a good mood."

— Maria Marlowe

This quote captures a powerful truth about the mind-body connection. As someone who understands both the science and lived experience behind this, I can tell you that exercise really is like a reset button for your mental state.

When you work out, your brain releases endorphins, dopamine, and serotonin - essentially nature's mood enhancers. But it's more than just chemistry. There's something transformative about pushing through physical challenges that shifts your entire perspective.

Here's a practical suggestion for today: The next time you're feeling down, stressed, or stuck in a negative headspace, commit to just 10 minutes of movement. It doesn't have to be an intense gym session - a brisk walk, some jumping jacks, or even dancing in your living room can work wonders. The key is to start small and just get moving.

Don't worry about performance or doing it perfectly. The goal isn't to transform your body in that moment - it's to transform your mood. Often, those 10 minutes will naturally extend longer once you get started, but even if they don't, you'll likely find your mental state improved.

Remember: You're never more than one workout away from shifting your emotional state. Keep this in your back pocket as a reliable tool for those harder days.

June 17th

"I want you to be honest with me. Even if it hurts. Although I would prefer for it not to hurt."

— David Levithan

This quote beautifully captures the delicate dance we all do with truth and vulnerability. It reflects something deeply human - that internal conflict between wanting authentic connection and fearing the pain it might bring. What I find particularly touching is the raw honesty of that last part: "Although I would prefer for it not to hurt." It's such a genuine admission of our emotional complexity. We know we need truth in our relationships, yet we can't help wishing it could come without the sting.

Today, when you need to have an honest conversation with someone, try acknowledging both sides of this tension. You might say something like "I want to talk about something important, and while I'm committed to being honest, I also want to be caring in how we discuss this." This approach honours both the need for truth and the natural desire to minimise pain.

Remember that seeking honest communication, even while acknowledging our fear of getting hurt, isn't weakness - it's one of the bravest things we can do. It shows we're willing to risk discomfort for the sake of authentic connection. Consider using this mindset not just with others, but also in your internal dialogue. Being honest with yourself, while still being gentle about that truth, can lead to profound personal growth.

June 18th

"You do not need to know precisely what is happening, or exactly where it is all going. What you need is to recognise the possibilities and challenges offered by the present moment, and to embrace them with courage, faith and hope."

— Thomas Merton

This is such a grounding and liberating quote, especially relevant in times of uncertainty. It reminds me of how often we get caught up in trying to predict and control everything, when sometimes the wisest thing we can do is embrace the present moment with openness. What I find particularly powerful is how Merton isn't suggesting blind optimism - he acknowledges both "possibilities and challenges." It's about finding that balance between accepting uncertainty while remaining engaged and hopeful.

Today, when you find yourself overwhelmed by uncertainty about the future, try this brief exercise: Take a moment to identify three possibilities in your current situation, no matter how small. Maybe it's a chance to learn something new, strengthen a relationship, or simply practice resilience. The goal isn't to ignore challenges but to recognise that uncertainty often carries hidden opportunities. Think of it like being in a boat on the ocean - you can't control the waves, but you can adjust your sails and stay alert to changing conditions. Sometimes our greatest growth comes not from knowing exactly where we're going, but from how we navigate the journey.

Remember: Every moment, even the uncertain ones, offers us

something to work with. The key is to meet it with courage while remaining open to possibilities we might not have imagined yet.

June 19th

"My bad habits aren't my title. My strengths and my talent are my title."

— Layne Staley

This quote hits deep - it's about refusing to be defined by our struggles. Layne Staley, who battled his own demons while being one of rock's most powerful voices, really understood this truth. It's about recognising that our challenges don't diminish our worth or capabilities.

What makes this quote especially powerful is its honesty. It doesn't deny the existence of bad habits or personal struggles - it simply puts them in their place. They're part of our story, but they're not our whole story or even the most important part.

Here's a practical suggestion for today: Take a moment to write down three of your strengths or talents - things you're proud of, skills you've developed, positive qualities others see in you. Keep this list somewhere visible. The next time you find yourself fixating on a habit you're trying to break or a personal struggle, glance at this list. Let it remind you that you're so much more than your challenges.

Think of it like a book - your bad habits might be a chapter, but they're not the title. Your talents, your kindness, your resilience, your creativity - these are what truly define you. They're the essence of who you are, regardless of what habits you're working to improve.

Remember: Acknowledging our struggles while refusing to be defined by them isn't just honest - it's empowering. It gives us the space to work on ourselves while still honouring our inherent worth and capabilities.

June 20th

"It's your place in the world; it's your life. Go on and do all you can with it, and make it the life you want to live."

— Mae Jemison

What a powerful quote from Mae Jemison - and how fitting coming from someone who refused to let others define her limits as she became the first Black woman to travel in space. This quote really speaks to our personal responsibility and power to shape our own destiny.

I love how it combines both empowerment and accountability. When she says "it's your place in the world," she's acknowledging that each of us has a legitimate right to be here and make our mark. But then she follows with "do all you can with it" - that's the call to action, the reminder that having a place means we also have a responsibility to make something of it.

Here's a practical suggestion for today: Take 10 minutes to reflect on one area of your life where you might be living according to others' expectations rather than your own desires. It could be in your career, relationships, hobbies, or daily routines. Then make one small but concrete change that better aligns with your vision for your life. Maybe it's signing up for that class you've been hesitating about, or finally starting that project you've been putting off because others might not understand it.

Remember: Your life isn't a dress rehearsal, and you're not here to play a role in someone else's script. Every day you spend living according to others' expectations is a day you're not fully inhabiting your own life. Start small, but start today - because this is your life, and you're the only one who can make it what you want it to be.

June 21st

"A day without laughter is a day wasted."

— Nicolas Chamfort

This simple quote carries such a profound truth about joy and living well. There's something beautiful about how it elevates laughter from just a pleasant addition to our day to an essential ingredient of a life well-lived. I find it particularly meaningful because it doesn't demand grand achievements or major milestones - just moments of genuine joy, however small. Whether it's a silly joke with a friend, a funny video that makes you chuckle, or laughing at yourself when you make a harmless mistake, these moments add richness to our lives.

Here's a practical suggestion for today: Create a "laughter trigger" in your daily routine. Pick a regular moment in your day - maybe your morning coffee, your commute, or your lunch break - and use it as a reminder to seek out or create something that makes you laugh. It could be sharing a joke with a coworker, watching a short comedy clip, or recalling a funny memory.

The beauty of this practice is that it often has a ripple effect. When we laugh, we tend to spread that joy to others around us. And on harder days, having this intentional moment of lightness can help shift our entire perspective.

Remember: Laughter isn't frivolous - it's a vital part of a fulfilling life. It's medicine for the soul, a stress reliever, and a connection builder all wrapped into one.

June 22nd

"Find a place inside where there's joy, and the joy will burn out the pain."

— Joseph Campbell

This quote speaks to something deep about human resilience and our innate capacity for healing. Campbell understood that joy isn't just a fleeting emotion - it's a powerful internal resource we can cultivate and return to, especially in difficult times.

What I find particularly meaningful is how he describes joy as something already within us - not something we need to chase or create from scratch. It's about finding that place inside ourselves where joy naturally resides, even if it's been overshadowed by pain or hardship.

Today, take a few minutes to create what I call a "joy inventory." Think of three moments or activities that reliably bring you genuine joy - not just pleasure or entertainment, but real, soul-warming happiness. Maybe it's playing with a pet, creating something with your hands, or spending time in nature. Write these down, and commit to spending even just five minutes today engaging with one of them.

The key isn't to deny or suppress pain when it's present, but rather to strengthen our connection to joy so it can act as an internal healing force. Think of it like tending to an inner garden - the more we nurture these sources of joy, the stronger they grow, and the more naturally they can help balance our darker moments.

Remember: Your capacity for joy isn't diminished by pain or hardship. Sometimes it's just waiting to be rediscovered, like a warm light that's always burning inside you, ready to help heal and restore when you need it most.

June 23rd

"Stretching is a beautiful way to connect with your body."

— Unknown

This quote captures something wonderfully simple yet profound about self-care and mindfulness. It reframes stretching from just a physical activity into a form of connection and self-awareness.

What's particularly insightful is how it recognises that our relationship with our body isn't just about function or appearance - it's about creating moments of conscious connection. When we stretch, we're not just lengthening muscles; we're taking time to listen to our body and respond to what it needs.

Today, set aside just 5 minutes, maybe right after waking up or before bed, for what I call "mindful stretching." Choose 2-3 gentle stretches, but instead of rushing through them, really focus on how each movement feels. Notice where you hold tension, where you feel ease, how your breathing changes. Make it less about achieving perfect form and more about creating a dialogue with your body.

Think of it as a daily check-in with yourself - a moment to pause and acknowledge the body that carries you through each day. It's not about pushing or forcing; it's about gentle awareness and appreciation. Remember: In our busy lives, we often treat our bodies like machines that need to be maintained rather than partners that deserve to be listened to. Taking even a few minutes to stretch mindfully can help rebuild that essential connection.

June 24th

"An emotional wound requires the same priority attention as a physical wound."

— Melba Colgrove, Harold H. Bloomfield & Peter Williams

This quote speaks to something vital about healing that we often overlook. As someone who's worked with people through various life challenges, I've noticed how we tend to take physical injuries seriously - we clean them, bandage them, give them time to heal - but often expect emotional wounds to just disappear on their own. What I find particularly powerful about this insight is how it legitimises emotional pain. Just like you wouldn't tell someone with a broken leg to "just walk it off," emotional injuries need proper care, time, and sometimes professional help to heal properly.

Here's a practical suggestion for today: Think about an emotional wound you might be carrying - maybe it's from a recent disappointment, a harsh word from someone you care about, or an older hurt that still stings. Give it the same attention you'd give a physical injury. This might mean setting aside some quiet time to process it, talking to someone you trust about it, or even writing about it. Just like you wouldn't go running on a sprained ankle, give yourself permission to take a break from situations or relationships that might be aggravating your emotional wound. Remember, treating emotional wounds with care isn't self-indulgent - it's essential maintenance for your well-being. Just as ignored physical wounds can become infected, emotional wounds that aren't properly tended to can affect our entire life experience.

June 25th

"If you are ever tempted to look for outside validation then you have compromised your self worth."

— George Pornaris

This quote offers a powerful perspective on the relationship between self-worth and external validation. What I find particularly striking is how it doesn't just caution against seeking outside approval - it suggests that even the temptation to do so indicates we've already stepped away from our inner strength.

I especially value how direct this message is. In a world that constantly pushes us to measure ourselves through likes, comments, achievements, and others' opinions, it reminds us that true self-worth is an inside job.

Here's a practical suggestion for today: When you notice yourself about to seek validation for something - maybe before posting on social media, making a decision, or even choosing what to wear - pause and ask yourself: "What would I choose if no one else would ever know about this?" Then try making your decision based solely on your own values and preferences.

Think of your self-worth like an internal compass - when we constantly look outside for direction, we lose touch with our own sense of true north. The goal isn't to never care what others think, but to ensure our core sense of value comes from within.

Remember: Every time you resist the urge to seek external validation, you're strengthening your internal foundation. Your worth isn't determined by others' reactions or approval - it's inherent in who you are, independent of any outside assessment.

June 26th

"You will enrich your life immeasurably if you approach it with a sense of wonder and discovery, and always challenge yourself to try new things."

— Nate Berkus

This quote beautifully captures the transformative power of curiosity and openness in our lives. I love how Berkus connects personal growth not to grand achievements, but to something as simple and natural as maintaining a sense of wonder.

What makes this message particularly compelling is how it links enrichment to attitude rather than circumstance. It suggests that a rich life isn't about what happens to us, but about how we approach what's in front of us - with curiosity, openness, and willingness to step out of our comfort zone.

Here's a practical suggestion for today: Choose one routine activity and approach it with fresh eyes, like you're experiencing it for the first time. Maybe it's your morning coffee - really notice the aroma, the warmth, the taste. Or take a different route to work and notice three things you've never seen before. Then, challenge yourself to try one small new thing - it could be as simple as tasting a new food, learning one phrase in a new language, or trying a different way to organise your day.

Think of it like being an explorer in your own life. Every day holds potential discoveries if we're willing to look at things with fresh eyes and take small steps into new territory.

Remember: Wonder isn't just for children, and discovery doesn't require grand adventures. They're available to us in everyday moments if we're willing to stay curious and open to new experiences, no matter how small they might seem.

June 27th

"Losing an illusion makes you wiser than finding a truth."

— Ludwig Borne

I find this quote incredibly powerful because it speaks to how our growth often comes not from what we gain, but from what we let go of. Think about it - when we lose an illusion, we're actually shedding something that was never real to begin with, even though it might have felt comforting or familiar. It's like when you finally accept that a relationship isn't what you imagined it to be, or when you realise a long-held belief about yourself isn't actually true. That moment of disillusionment can feel painful, even devastating. But in that space of letting go, we make room for something more authentic. It's through losing these comfortable illusions that we develop a clearer, more grounded understanding of reality.

Today, take a moment to reflect on something you once firmly believed but later realised wasn't true. It could be something small, like a misconception about how something works, or something more personal, like an assumption about relationships or success. How did losing that illusion change you? What wisdom did you gain from that experience?

The beauty of this insight is that it encourages us to be less afraid of disillusionment. Instead of seeing it as a loss, we can recognise it as a doorway to deeper wisdom. Sometimes, it's the shattering of our illusions that finally allows us to see things as they truly are. What illusions have you lost that made you wiser?

June 28th

"The truth is I can stand alone, grow alone, be alone. But I do not want to have to"

— C Joybell C

This quote really cuts to the heart of something deeply human - the beautiful tension between our strength and our longing for connection. It's like acknowledging two equally true parts of ourselves. The first part is this incredible inner resilience we all have - that core strength that lets us handle life's challenges on our own. We can build our lives, pursue our dreams, and find our way through difficult times by ourselves. And there's something really empowering about knowing that about ourselves.

But then there's this other truth - that even though we *can* do it alone, there's this deep yearning for shared experiences and meaningful connections. It's not about neediness or weakness; it's about recognising that life is richer, warmer, and more meaningful when we share it with others.

Here's a small but meaningful way to honour both truths today: Tackle something challenging on your own - maybe a task you've been putting off or a small personal goal. Feel that independence and capability. Then, reach out and share your accomplishment with someone you care about. Not because you needed their help, but because sharing our victories, however small, makes them sweeter. After all, being strong enough to stand alone is admirable, but choosing to stand together - that's where the real magic of life happens.

June 29th

"If you are driven by fear, anger or pride nature will force you to compete. If you are guided by courage, awareness, tranquility and peace nature will serve you."

— Amit Ray

This is such a profound observation about how our internal state shapes our entire experience of life. I find it fascinating how Amit Ray captures the stark difference between living from a place of reactivity versus living from a place of centeredness.

Think about it - when we're caught up in fear, anger, or pride, we're constantly on edge, seeing threats and rivals everywhere. It's exhausting, isn't it? We end up trapped in a cycle of comparing, defending, and striving against others and life itself. It's like swimming upstream, constantly fighting the current.

But there's this beautiful shift that happens when we cultivate courage, awareness, and tranquility. Instead of battling life, we start flowing with it. Opportunities naturally arise, relationships deepen, and solutions present themselves. It's not that challenges disappear - they're still there - but we meet them from a completely different space.

Today, when you feel yourself getting triggered or tense, pause for just three slow breaths. During those breaths, notice if fear, anger, or pride is driving your reaction. Just that moment of awareness can help you shift from a reactive state to a more centred one. You might be surprised how often things work out more smoothly when you approach them from this calmer space.

I've seen this simple practice transform not just individual moments, but entire relationships and life paths over time. What do you think about starting with those three breaths?

June 30th

"You usually check in on family and friends, but have you checked in on yourself today? How are you? What do you need?"

— Gary Hardy

We're often so busy taking care of others - calling mum and dad, texting friends to see how they're doing, checking in on colleagues - that we completely forget to pause and turn that same caring attention inward. It's like being a good friend to everyone except yourself. And just as our loved ones need support and care, our own well-being deserves that same thoughtful attention.

Here's a simple practice I've found helpful: Set aside 5 minutes each evening - maybe while you're getting ready for bed - to ask yourself these three questions: "How am I feeling right now? What's weighing on my mind? What would help me feel more supported?" Sometimes just acknowledging what's going on inside can be surprisingly powerful. You might realise you need more rest, a quiet moment with a book, or maybe it's time to schedule that doctor's appointment you've been putting off.

The beauty of this practice is that when you regularly check in with yourself, you become better at recognising your own needs before you hit a breaking point. And ironically, by taking better care of yourself, you actually become more capable of being there for others in a meaningful way. How does this resonate with you? Have you had a chance to check in with yourself today?

July 1st

"Everything good, everything magical happens between the months of June and August."

— Jenny Han

What a wonderful quote that captures the magical essence of summer! There's something uniquely special about those warm months that seems to spark joy and possibility in many of us.

I think Jenny Han taps into a universal feeling here - that sense that summer holds a special kind of magic. It's when the days stretch longer, when spontaneous adventures feel more possible, and when even ordinary moments can take on an enchanted quality. Whether it's the way evening light lingers until late, the sound of children playing outside, or the simple pleasure of eating dinner outdoors, summer has a way of making everyday life feel a bit more extraordinary.

Here's a gentle suggestion for embracing this summer magic in your daily life: Create a small ritual that helps you pause and savour these months. Maybe it's taking your morning coffee outside to watch the sunrise, or spending 10 minutes in the evening enjoying the summers night sky. Even in busy lives, these tiny moments can help us tap into that summer enchantment that Jenny Han describes. I find it interesting though - while she focuses on June through August, this summer magic can mean different things depending on where you are in the world. Some might find their magic in different months, or different seasons entirely. What makes summer magical for you?

July 2nd

"To get back to the person I am, I had to reject so much of who I was told that I was."

— Allyson Dinneen

This quote touches on something so fundamental to personal growth - the journey of unlearning. We spend our early years absorbing messages about who we should be, how we should act, what success looks like, what happiness means... and sometimes these messages can layer over our authentic selves like coats of paint, until we can barely remember the original canvas beneath. What's powerful about Dinneen's insight is that she recognises that authentic self-discovery often requires a kind of gentle demolition. It's about carefully examining those "should be's" and "supposed to's" we've collected over the years and having the courage to question them. Sometimes finding ourselves means letting go of the version of ourselves that was carefully constructed to please others or meet external expectations.

Today, take a quiet moment and reflect on one "should" that you carry around. Maybe it's "I should always be productive" or "I should never show weakness" or "I should want what others want." Ask yourself: Is this really my truth, or is it something I absorbed from somewhere else? Just noticing these inherited beliefs is the first step towards choosing which ones truly serve your authentic self. Remember, rejecting what doesn't align with your true self isn't selfish - it's actually an act of honesty and courage. And sometimes, paradoxically, by letting go of who we were told to be, we become more capable of genuinely showing up for others.

July 3rd

"I despise the rituals of fake friendship. I wish we could just claw each other's eyes out and call it a day; instead we put on huge radiant smiles and spout compliments until our teeth hurt from the saccharine sweetness of it all."

— Jody Gehrman

This quote really cuts through the social pretence we often find ourselves trapped in, doesn't it? There's something refreshingly honest about Gehrman's frustration with the exhausting dance of superficial relationships. I think she's touching on something many of us feel but rarely express - that bone-deep weariness that comes from maintaining polite facades in relationships that lack genuine connection. It's like we're all actors in a play, exchanging scripted pleasantries while silently yearning for something more authentic.

Today, in your next social interaction, try being just a little more genuine. Not necessarily confrontational - we don't actually need to "claw each other's eyes out" - but perhaps more honest. Maybe that means acknowledging when you're having a rough day instead of saying "I'm fine," or offering a sincere observation instead of an automatic compliment.

The irony is that when we dare to drop the artificial sweetness, we often create space for real connections to form. True friendship, after all, isn't built on perfect smiles and hollow compliments - it's built on the courage to be real with each other, imperfections and all. What might change in your relationships if you allowed yourself to be a little more authentically you?

July 4th

"You can't let a woman down multiple times and expect her energy to still be the same."

— Unknown

This quote speaks to something really fundamental about human relationships and emotional investment. It's touching on that gradual erosion of spirit and enthusiasm that happens when trust or effort isn't reciprocated consistently. It reminds me of how resilience in relationships isn't an infinite resource. Each disappointment, each letdown, each moment of taking someone for granted - it's like making small withdrawals from an emotional bank account. Eventually, even the most patient and understanding person will find their energy, their hope, their willingness to invest... it just naturally shifts.

Here's something worth reflecting on today: In your important relationships, pay attention to how you're impacting the other person's energy. Are you making deposits or withdrawals in those emotional bank accounts? Sometimes we don't notice the subtle changes in someone's enthusiasm, their willingness to reach out, their joy in connecting with us - until it's significantly diminished.

The beauty of this awareness is that it works both ways. Not only can it help us be more mindful of how we treat others, but it also validates our own natural response when our energy changes after repeated disappointments. It's not about being unforgiving - it's about honouring our emotional well-being and understanding that it's natural and healthy for our energy to shift when patterns of behaviour show us where someone's priorities truly lie.

July 5th

"Take your life in your own hands, and what happens? A terrible thing: no one to blame."

— Erica Jong

This quote brilliantly captures both the empowerment and the subtle discomfort of true personal responsibility! I love how Jong uses irony to make us think about how oddly comfortable we can become with having others to blame for our circumstances. There's something both liberating and terrifying about taking full ownership of our lives. It's like finally getting the steering wheel of a car you've been a passenger in - exciting, but now every turn and destination is your choice. That "terrible thing" Jong mentions with such wonderful sarcasm - having no one to blame - is actually the doorway to real freedom, even though it can feel uncomfortable at first.

Here's a simple but powerful practice for today: When something doesn't go as planned, catch yourself before looking for someone or something to blame. Instead, ask yourself, "What part of this can I take ownership of?" and "What can I learn from this that will help me make different choices next time?"

The beautiful paradox is that when we stop spending energy finding others to blame, we suddenly have so much more energy to create the life we want. Yes, it means facing our mistakes and accepting our role in our circumstances, but it also means recognising our power to change them. What might shift in your life if you embraced this "terrible" freedom of having no one to blame but yourself?

July 6th

"Focus on making yourself better, not on thinking that you are better."

— Bohdi Sanders

What a powerful distinction Sanders makes here! This really cuts to the heart of the difference between genuine self-improvement and ego-driven comparison. There's this fascinating paradox in personal growth - the moment we start thinking we're "better" than others, we actually stop growing. It's like the difference between climbing a mountain while appreciating each step upward versus climbing just to look down on others. One path leads to continuous growth, while the other leaves us stuck on whatever plateau our ego has claimed.

Here's a simple practice you might try today: When you catch yourself in a moment of comparison or feeling superior to others, gently redirect that energy towards identifying one small way you could improve yourself instead. Maybe it's learning something new, refining a skill, or working on a personal quality you'd like to develop. The focus shifts from outward comparison to inward growth.

The beauty of making yourself better rather than thinking you're better is that it's an endless journey of discovery and improvement. There's always another step to take, another skill to master, another understanding to reach. And ironically, the more we focus on our own growth rather than our perceived status compared to others, the more naturally we tend to inspire and lift up those around us. What aspect of yourself would you like to focus on making better today?

July 7th

"What you do, the way you think, makes you beautiful."

— Scott Westerfeld

I really love how this quote reframes beauty in such a meaningful way. It's not about surface-level appearances or fitting into some predetermined mould - it's about the essence of who you are and how you move through the world.

When I reflect on this quote, I think about those people we all know who just radiate a special kind of beauty - not because of their physical features, but because of how they think and act. Maybe it's that friend who always makes time to listen when others need support, or that colleague who approaches challenges with creativity and optimism. Their beauty shines through in their actions and their way of thinking.

Today, I encourage you to consider: What are the thoughts and actions that make you uniquely beautiful? Maybe it's your ability to find humour in difficult situations, your patience with others, or your persistence in pursuing your goals. Perhaps it's the way you think deeply about problems, or how you choose to see the best in people.

Remember, beauty isn't just something you are or aren't born with - it's something you create every day through your choices, your thoughts, and your actions. Each time you choose kindness, each time you pursue understanding, each time you act with integrity - you're creating beauty in the world.

Try focusing today not on how you look, but on how you can express your inner beauty through what you do and how you think. That's the kind of beauty that truly transforms both ourselves and the world around us.

July 8th

"The only way to make sense out of change is to plunge into it, move with it, and join the dance."

— Rebecca McCallum

So often we resist change - we tense up, try to control everything, or wish things would just stay the same. But as someone who has seen both the struggles and beauty that come with change, I've learned that fighting against it only creates more suffering.

What Rebecca McCallum is suggesting here is something quite profound - instead of viewing change as an enemy, we can choose to see it as a dance partner. Think about dancing for a moment - it requires us to stay loose, to flow with the music, to trust in the movement. When we're stiff and trying to control every step, that's when we stumble.

Today, to prepare for the next time you face an unexpected change in your day - maybe a meeting gets canceled, your plans fall through, or something doesn't go as expected - take a deep breath and ask yourself "How can I dance with this moment?" Instead of immediately reacting with frustration, pause and look for the opportunity in the change. Maybe that canceled meeting gives you time to work on something you've been putting off, or maybe that change in plans leads you to an unexpected conversation or experience. It's a small shift in perspective, but practicing this "dance with change" mindset in these everyday moments helps build the resilience and adaptability we need for life's bigger changes. What do you think about trying this approach today?

July 9th

"You're beautiful because you know your own darkness and still, that alone doesn't stop you from finding your own light."

— Julia Quinn

This quote really touches on something deep about the human journey. We all carry our own shadows - past struggles, insecurities, mistakes, or painful experiences. But what makes humans truly remarkable is their capacity to acknowledge these darker parts of themselves while still choosing to grow and seek out light.

What I find most powerful about this message is that it's not about ignoring or overcoming our darkness completely - it's about coexisting with it while still believing in our capacity for light. It's that courage to keep moving forward, knowing full well our imperfections, that makes us beautiful.

Today, take 5 minutes this evening to write down one "darkness" you've faced or are facing, and right next to it, write down one way you've grown or one positive step you're taking despite that challenge. It could be as simple as "I struggle with self-doubt, but today I still spoke up in that meeting" or "I've made mistakes in relationships, but I'm learning to communicate better."

This small practice helps remind us that our struggles don't define us - they're just part of our story, and we can keep writing new chapters even while carrying them. What matters is that we keep seeking our light, however small it might feel some days.

July 10th

"If you cannot forgive yourself, you will have a hard time to believe in yourself again."

— Jyoti Patel

When we hold onto past mistakes or perceived failures too tightly, we essentially keep ourselves locked in a prison of self-doubt. It's like trying to build a house on shaky ground - without self-forgiveness as the foundation, it becomes really hard to construct genuine self-belief.

You know what's interesting? Many of us find it easier to forgive others than to forgive ourselves. We often become our own harshest critics, replaying our mistakes and beating ourselves up long after others have moved on. But holding onto that self-judgement doesn't serve us - it just keeps us stuck and afraid to try new things or take risks.

Today, take a moment to identify one thing you're still holding against yourself. It could be a mistake, a decision you regret, or something you wish you'd done differently. Now, imagine your closest friend had done the same thing and was coming to you for advice. Write down what you would say to them - I bet you'll find your words are filled with understanding and compassion. Then, try reading those same words back to yourself, allowing yourself to receive that same gentleness you'd offer a friend.

Remember, forgiving yourself isn't about excusing mistakes - it's about freeing yourself to grow and learn from them. When we can look at our past with compassion rather than condemnation, we create space for new possibilities and renewed confidence. What past experience might you be ready to start forgiving yourself for?

July 11th

"Thank you, for the heart you kept beating even when it was broken, for every answer you gave me in my gut, for loving me back even when I didn't know how to love you, for every time you recovered when I pushed you past our limits, for today, for waking up."

— Cleo Wade

This is actually a love letter to ourselves, to our own bodies and spirit that carry us through life's hardships. We often forget to acknowledge just how much inner strength we've shown simply by continuing to move forward, by getting up each morning, by healing from heartbreaks and disappointments.

What touches me deeply about this quote is how it recognises that self-love isn't always intuitive or easy. Sometimes we don't know how to be kind to ourselves, yet something deep within us - that inner wisdom, that life force - keeps believing in us, keeps us going even when we're not consciously aware of it.

Today, after you stop reading this, and before you reach for your phone, place your hand over your heart. Feel its steady beating. Take just 30 seconds to thank your body and spirit for one specific thing - maybe for healing from a past hurt, for giving you intuition that kept you safe, or simply for showing up to face another day. It might feel a bit strange at first, but this small ritual can help shift how we relate to ourselves.

This simple act of gratitude to ourselves isn't self-indulgent - it's a recognition of our resilience, our capacity to heal, and the quiet strength that has brought us this far. Sometimes the most profound healing starts with simply acknowledging how far we've already come.

July 12th

"I imagine one of the reasons people cling to their hates so stubbornly is because they sense, once hate is gone, they will be forced to deal with pain."

— James Baldwin

This is such a piercing insight from Baldwin about the human psyche. It reveals something profound about why we sometimes hold onto our anger and hatred even when we know it's hurting us - because underneath that hatred often lies a deeper, more vulnerable pain we're not ready to face. Think about it - hatred can feel energising, even powerful. It gives us something to focus on outside ourselves, a target for all our hurt and frustration. But as Baldwin suggests, it's often just a shield, a way to avoid confronting our own wounds, disappointments, or grief.

Today, when you notice yourself experiencing a strong feeling of anger or resentment towards someone or something, pause and gently ask yourself, "What pain am I protecting myself from feeling?" Don't judge whatever comes up - just observe it with curiosity. Maybe write it down. You don't have to solve or fix anything; simply acknowledging the underlying hurt is a powerful first step.

Remember, this isn't about dismissing legitimate grievances or suggesting we should never feel anger. It's about understanding that our strongest negative emotions often point to places within us that need healing and compassion. When we're ready to look beneath our hatred, we create space for real healing to begin. What emotions might you be using as a shield today?

July 13th

"Maybe we judge people too much by their looks because it's easier than seeing what's really important."

— Alex Flinn

This quote really hits home about a universal human tendency that most of us struggle with, sometimes without even realising it. Our brains are wired to make quick judgements based on what we see - it's an old survival mechanism. But in today's world, this quick-judgement tendency often leads us to miss the deeper, richer stories of the people around us. What's particularly insightful about Flinn's observation is that last part - "because it's easier." It's true, isn't it? Looking deeper, asking questions, being curious about someone's character, dreams, and struggles - that takes time and emotional energy. It makes us vulnerable. It's so much simpler to make snap judgements based on appearances and move on.

Today, in your next three interactions with people - whether it's a colleague, a barista, or someone on the street - consciously pause your initial appearance-based judgements. Instead, try to notice one thing about their behaviour or demeanour that might hint at their story. Maybe it's the gentleness in how they handle objects, the patience they show in a stressful moment, or the warmth in their voice when they talk about something they care about. This isn't about ignoring our initial impressions entirely - that's probably impossible. It's about developing the habit of looking beyond them to what's truly important: the humanity we share with each person we meet. What might you discover when you look past the surface?

July 14th

"We rise by lifting others"

— Robert Ingersoll

This simple yet profound quote captures one of life's most beautiful paradoxes. In a world that often pushes messages of competition and individual success, Ingersoll reminds us of a deeper truth - that our own growth and fulfilment are intimately connected to how we support those around us.

I've seen this play out countless times - when we help others grow, we often find ourselves growing in unexpected ways. Maybe it's the new perspectives we gain, the skills we develop while teaching, or simply the joy and purpose we find in making a positive difference in someone else's life.

Today, choose one person in your life - it could be a your partner, friend, family member or colleague - and find one specific way to lift them up. Maybe it's sending a thoughtful message acknowledging their recent efforts, offering to help with a task they're struggling with, or simply giving them your full attention when they speak. The key is to make it genuine and specific to them.

What's beautiful about this practice is that it creates a ripple effect. When we lift others, we not only elevate ourselves but also inspire those around us to do the same. Think about it - has someone's support ever inspired you to pay it forward? That's how positive change spreads through communities, one uplifting action at a time.

July 15th

"How a person reacts to your sadness says a lot about how long they're going to be in your life,"

— Salma Deera

This is a deeply perceptive observation about relationships and emotional authenticity. Our moments of sadness or struggle often serve as a kind of litmus test for the depth and quality of our connections with others. It's in these vulnerable moments that we truly see who has the capacity to sit with us in our pain, and who might feel uncomfortable or pull away. What's particularly striking about this quote is how it points to something many of us learn through experience - that the people who can hold space for our sadness, who don't try to rush us through it or dismiss it, are often the ones who build lasting bonds with us. It's not about them having perfect responses or always knowing what to say. It's about their willingness to be present with us in our difficult moments.

Today, think about how you respond to others' sadness or pain. Next time someone shares something difficult with you, try to simply be present without immediately trying to fix or solve their problem. Just listen, acknowledge their feelings, and maybe ask "What do you need right now?" or "Would you like to talk more about it?" This practice not only helps us be better friends and supporters to others, but it also helps us recognise and appreciate those who can do the same for us. What might change in your relationships if you became more conscious of how you respond to others' vulnerable moments?

July 16th

"It is not how old you are, but how you are old."

— Jules Renard

This is such a lovely perspective on aging that really shifts how we might think about growing older. Renard isn't just playing with words here - he's offering a profound insight about how our approach to aging matters more than the number of years we've lived.

I've noticed that some people seem to grow more vibrant, curious, and wise with age, while others might become rigid or resigned. The difference often lies not in their physical age, but in their attitude towards aging - how they choose to embrace or resist each new chapter of life.

Today, take a moment to think about one way you'd like to "be old" - whether you're 25 or 85. Maybe it's maintaining your sense of wonder, staying open to learning new things, or cultivating deeper connections. Then do one small thing today that aligns with that vision. It could be learning something new that interests you, sharing wisdom with someone younger, or simply approaching a familiar situation with fresh eyes.

Remember, we're aging every single day - it's not something that happens suddenly when we reach a certain number. Each day gives us a chance to shape how we grow older, to choose whether we'll age with grace, curiosity, and purpose. What kind of relationship do you want to build with your own aging process?

July 17th

"Life is full of beauty. Notice it. Notice the bumble bee, the small child, and the smiling faces. Smell the rain, and feel the wind. Live your life to the fullest potential, and fight for your dreams."

— Ashley Smith

This quote beautifully captures something so fundamental about living a rich and meaningful life - it's often in the smallest, most ordinary moments that we find extraordinary beauty. In our rush to get through our daily tasks, we sometimes forget to pause and notice these little miracles happening all around us.

What I love about Smith's words is how she weaves together both the gentle art of noticing life's small beauties and the fierce pursuit of our dreams. It's like she's reminding us that a full life needs both - the soft moments of appreciation and the bold steps towards our aspirations.

Today, set three "beauty alarms" on your phone - maybe morning, afternoon, and evening. When each alarm goes off, pause for just 30 seconds to notice something beautiful in your immediate surroundings. It could be as simple as the way sunlight plays on your coffee cup, the sound of leaves rustling, or the kindness in a stranger's smile. Then take one small action towards a dream you're nurturing.

This practice helps train our minds to stay open to life's everyday magic while keeping us connected to our deeper purposes. It's amazing how when we start actively looking for beauty, we begin to find it everywhere - even in places we least expect it. And somehow, this awareness often gives us the energy and inspiration we need to keep pursuing our bigger dreams.

July 18th

"When things are not going the way they should be going, the wisest thing you can do is stop, just stop. Then, take a step back, give yourself time to think, don't push harder, stop and think."

— Gary Hardy

When life feels like it's falling apart or when we're facing those really tough personal struggles. Sometimes, when we're dealing with broken relationships, career setbacks, health issues, or just feeling lost in life, our first instinct is to push harder, to force things to work. But as I suggest in the quote, that's often exactly when we need to do the opposite.

It's like being in quicksand - the more you struggle and fight, the deeper you sink. What's profound about this advice is that it acknowledges that sometimes the bravest thing we can do in our hardest moments isn't to keep pushing, but to have the courage to stop and create space for clarity.

Here's a gentle practice for those difficult times: When you're feeling overwhelmed by a life challenge, create what I call a "healing pause." Find a quiet spot, maybe your car, a park bench, or even your bathroom if that's all you have.

Take three deep breaths and ask yourself these questions:

- What am I struggling against right now?
- What emotions am I trying to avoid by keeping busy?
- What wisdom might emerge if I just sit with this situation for a moment?

Remember, pausing isn't weakness - it's wisdom. Sometimes we need to step back from our problems to see the path through them more clearly. Often, the solutions to our deepest struggles emerge not from constant action, but from those quiet moments of reflection when we give ourselves permission to just be with our difficulties.

What challenge in your life right now might benefit from this kind of gentle pause?

July 19th

"She did not need much, wanted very little. A kind word, sincerity, fresh air, clean water, a garden, kisses, books to read, sheltering arms, a cosy bed, and to love and be loved in return."

— Starra Neely Blade

That's such a beautiful quote that really speaks to the essence of contentment and genuine happiness. In our world of constant consumption and pressure to acquire more, this quote reminds us that true fulfilment often comes from life's simplest gifts. It resonates deeply with me because it strips away all the unnecessary complications we tend to add to our lives and focuses on what truly nourishes our souls.

What strikes me most is how attainable these desires are - they're not about expensive possessions or grand achievements, but about basic human needs and connections. The list reads like a recipe for a well-lived life: authenticity in relationships, connection with nature, the joy of reading, physical comfort, and most importantly, love.

Today, take 10 minutes this evening to write down the simple things that brought you joy throughout your day. Maybe it was the warmth of sunlight on your face, a genuine conversation with a friend, or a moment of peace with a good book. This exercise helps train your mind to notice and appreciate these small but meaningful moments, rather than always chasing after bigger, more elaborate sources of happiness. Remember, sometimes the key to a richer life isn't about adding more, but about recognising the value in what's already there.

July 20th

"It's okay to be impatient. As long as you show your patience on the outside."

— Lisa M. Cronkhite

Ah, what a nuanced perspective on the internal struggle we all face with patience! As someone who's thought deeply about this, I find this quote particularly interesting because it acknowledges something we often feel guilty about – that internal restlessness and urgency that bubbles up inside us.

There's real wisdom here about the difference between our inner experiences and how we choose to act on them. It's not about being perfect or never feeling impatient – it's about developing the emotional maturity to manage those feelings in a way that doesn't negatively impact others.

Today, or the next time you feel that surge of impatience (maybe while waiting in line, dealing with a slow website or stuck in a traffic jam), try this – acknowledge your impatient feelings internally without judgement, take a deep breath, and then consciously choose a calm external response. Think of it as building a muscle – the more you practice this pause between feeling and reaction, the stronger your emotional regulation becomes.

What's beautiful about this approach is that it's honest about our human nature while encouraging us to be our best selves in our interactions with others. It's not about suppressing our feelings, but rather about choosing how we express them.

July 21st

"The most difficult relationship I ever ended was with the damaged and broken version of myself."

— Gary Hardy

This quote touches on something deeply personal and often unspoken – that sometimes our hardest "breakup" isn't with another person, but with the wounded version of ourselves we've carried for so long. It's particularly powerful because it frames this inner work as a relationship ending, acknowledging how attached we can become to our pain and broken patterns, even when they no longer serve us.

What strikes me most is the implicit understanding that this version of ourselves was never our true self – it was a survival mechanism, a way of being that helped us get through difficult times. Yet letting go of it can feel like losing a close companion, even if that companion wasn't always healthy for us.

Here's something you could try today: Take a moment to write a brief, compassionate "goodbye letter" to a pattern or belief that you've outgrown but maybe haven't fully released. It might be people-pleasing, self-doubt, or an old story about not being enough. Thank that pattern for how it once protected you, acknowledge why it's time to let it go, and give yourself permission to move forward without it.

Remember, ending our relationship with our damaged self doesn't mean forgetting or rejecting that part of our journey. It means recognising that while that version of us was necessary for survival then, we're ready now to embrace a more whole and healed way of being.

July 22nd

"Family don't end with blood."

— Bobby Singer

This quote captures the true meaning of family, doesn't it? From my perspective, it beautifully expresses how genuine family bonds transcend biological connections. I've seen how some of the deepest, most meaningful family relationships can be with people who don't share the same blood at all.

Today, take a moment to reach out to someone who's family to you, even though they're not related by blood. Maybe it's a step mother or father who's guided you like a parent, a close friend who's been there through thick and thin. Send them a message or give them a call just to say "You're family to me" or "I'm grateful you're in my life."

These chosen family bonds often become our strongest support systems, and nurturing them consciously can enrich our lives immensely. The beauty of this perspective is that it reminds us we have the power to create and strengthen meaningful family connections throughout our lives - our capacity to build family isn't limited by genetics or circumstance.

Remember, every time you treat someone like family, you're building a bond that can be just as strong as any blood relation. Sometimes even stronger, because it's chosen.

July 23rd

"He is happiest, be he king or peasant, who finds peace in his home."

— Johann Wolfgang von Goethe

It doesn't matter if you live in a mansion or a modest flat, true contentment comes from creating a peaceful home environment.

Here's something practical you can do today to cultivate more peace at home: Take 15 minutes to create what I call a "peace corner" - it can be as simple as a comfortable chair by a window, or a small space where you can sit quietly. Remove any clutter from this area and make it a dedicated spot for moments of calm. The key isn't the size or location, but rather establishing a physical space that signals to your mind "this is where peace lives."

What makes this quote so powerful is that it reminds us that happiness isn't about what we own or our social status - it's about creating an environment where our soul can rest. Whether you're managing a corporation or working an entry-level job, coming home to a peaceful space can be the greatest luxury of all.

Remember, peace at home isn't just about physical quiet - it's about fostering an atmosphere where everyone in your household feels safe, accepted, and at ease. Sometimes the smallest changes, like establishing a no-phones-at-dinner rule or taking ten minutes to tidy up before bed, can make a significant difference in your home's emotional climate.

July 24th

"She had this way of always finding the good and believing in everything despite all she had seen. And that is what I loved the most - the pure magic of her undying hope."

— Becca Lee

This quote touches on something truly special about certain people who have this remarkable gift. It's not about being naive - it's about having the strength to maintain hope and see beauty even after experiencing life's hardships. That's a different kind of courage altogether.

Today, start what I call a "light-finder" practice. When you encounter a challenging situation, pause and deliberately look for one positive aspect or potential opportunity within it. It could be as simple as learning something new from a mistake, or noticing how a difficult moment brought people together. The goal isn't to ignore problems, but to train yourself to spot the light even in darker moments.

What makes this perspective so powerful is that it's not about blind optimism - it's about developing the emotional resilience to acknowledge both the good and the bad, while consciously choosing to nurture hope. It's like building a muscle that gets stronger with practice. Remember, maintaining hope isn't always easy - sometimes it's the bravest thing we can do. But like the person described in this quote, we can learn to hold onto that ability to see possibilities and goodness, even when life tests us. That's not just optimism - it's a kind of everyday magic that can transform how we experience our world.

July 25th

"We are all a people in need. We are not perfect. We are not machines. We make mistakes. We need grace. We need compassion. We need help at times. We need other people. And that's okay."

— Jamie Tworkowski

This quote really touches something fundamental about our shared human experience. I love how it gently reminds us that needing help and support isn't a flaw - it's simply part of being human. It's like a permission slip to be authentically imperfect.

Today, choose one thing you've been struggling with silently and share it with someone you trust. It doesn't have to be something big - maybe you're feeling overwhelmed with work, or having trouble making a decision. The act of opening up, of allowing yourself to need and receive support, is both healing for yourself and an invitation for others to do the same.

What makes this message so powerful is how it counters the pervasive myth that we should all be self-sufficient all the time. In our world of carefully curated social media images and pressure to always appear "put together," this reminder of our shared vulnerability and interdependence is refreshing and necessary. Remember, every time you allow yourself to be helped, you're not just taking care of yourself - you're also creating a more compassionate world by showing others that it's okay for them to need help too. None of us were meant to do this life thing alone, and there's a beautiful strength in acknowledging that.

July 26th

> *"If you ignore your feelings they will get your attention in other ways."*
>
> — Kathy Kalina

This hits at a profound truth about emotional health that I've seen play out so many times. It's fascinating how our feelings, when pushed down, have a way of manifesting in unexpected ways - whether through physical symptoms, sudden outbursts, or patterns in our relationships.

Here's a practical way to work with this wisdom today: Set a simple "feeling check-in" alarm on your phone for three times during the day. When it goes off, take just 30 seconds to ask yourself "What am I feeling right now?" and "Where do I feel it in my body?" Don't try to change anything - just notice. You might be surprised by what you discover when you create these small moments of emotional awareness.

What makes this quote particularly powerful is that it warns us about the cost of emotional avoidance. Those suppressed feelings don't just disappear - they often show up as anxiety, physical tension, sleep problems, or even in how we treat others. It's like trying to hold a beach ball underwater - it takes enormous energy, and eventually, it's going to pop up somewhere. Remember, acknowledging your feelings isn't the same as being controlled by them. It's about creating enough space to hear what they're trying to tell you before they have to shout to get your attention.

July 27th

"Let everything happen to you: Beauty and terror. Just keep going. No feeling is final."

— Rainer Maria Rilke

This is one of those profound pieces of wisdom that gets deeper the more life experience you gain. There's something incredibly liberating about accepting that both beauty and difficulty are natural parts of our journey, isn't there? The power lies in that last part - "No feeling is final" - it's such a comforting reminder when we're in those darker moments.

Here's a practical way to embrace this wisdom today: Start what I call a "weather journal" of your emotional life. Just like we don't expect sunny days all the time, we can learn to accept our emotional weather patterns. When you're experiencing something intense - whether wonderful or terrible - write down "This too shall pass" and note how previous difficult feelings have indeed shifted and changed. This practice helps build emotional resilience by reminding us of the temporary nature of all feelings.

What makes this perspective so powerful is that it gives us permission to fully experience life without getting stuck in any one state. It's not about trying to avoid the terror or cling to the beauty - it's about developing the courage to remain open to whatever comes, knowing that we can endure it because everything transforms eventually.

Remember, saying "just keep going" isn't about forcing yourself to push through blindly - it's about maintaining a gentle forward movement while allowing yourself to fully experience whatever arises. Sometimes that forward movement might look like simply getting out of bed or taking one small step. And that's perfectly okay.

July 28th

"Our best successes often come after our greatest disappointments."

— Henry Ward Beecher

I've seen this play out countless times in life, both personally and in the stories of others. It's like those disappointments clear the path or prepare us in ways we couldn't have imagined at the time. Think about how many successful people share stories of their biggest failures being the turning point that led to their breakthroughs.

Here's a powerful way to put this wisdom into practice today: Take your most recent disappointment and spend a few minutes writing down what it taught you and what possibilities it might have opened up. Maybe a job rejection forced you to think more creatively about your career path, or a failed project helped you discover a better approach. The key is training yourself to look for the hidden opportunities in setbacks rather than letting them define your story.

What makes this perspective so valuable is that it helps us reframe disappointments from endpoints to potential launching pads. Instead of seeing failures as final verdicts on our abilities, we can view them as necessary steps in our growth journey.

Remember, success often comes not despite our disappointments, but because of what we learn and how we grow through them. Each setback can be fertiliser for future growth if we're willing to learn from it.

July 29th

"If you have to speculate if someone loves you and wants to be with you, chances are they don't. It's not that complicated. Don't waste moments waiting and wondering. Don't throw away your time dreaming of someone who doesn't want you. No one is that amazing, and certainly not someone who would pass you up."

— Donna Lynn

This is one of those raw, honest truths that can be hard to hear but is so important for our emotional wellbeing. I find it particularly powerful because it cuts through all the rationalisations we often make when we're emotionally invested in someone who's not fully invested in us.

Here's a practical way to apply this wisdom today: Take a piece of paper and write down the situations in your life (romantic or otherwise) where you find yourself constantly questioning where you stand. Now, ask yourself: "If someone was watching my situation as a movie, what would they see?" This outside perspective can help cut through the emotional fog and see things more clearly.

What makes this quote so valuable is that it reminds us of our own worth. When someone truly wants to be in your life, they make it clear - they don't leave you wondering and waiting. It's about recognising that uncertainty in these situations usually isn't about mystery - it's about someone else's lack of commitment.

Remember, the time and emotional energy you spend wondering about someone who's lukewarm about you could be invested in either yourself or in people who are clear about wanting to be in your life. True connection doesn't require you to be a detective trying to piece together mixed signals. You deserve someone who makes their feelings for you as clear as day.

July 30th

"If you only have one smile in you, give it to the people you love."

— Maya Angelou

This beautiful quote from Maya Angelou speaks to something deeply human – how we choose to share our emotional energy, especially during tough times. I find it particularly moving because it acknowledges that sometimes we're running on empty, that there are days when we can barely muster a single smile. And that's okay. What matters is being intentional about where we direct that precious bit of warmth we have left.

Think about it – when we're exhausted or stressed, we often end up giving our best energy to strangers, customers, or colleagues, while showing our grumpier side to those closest to us. We assume our loved ones will understand and stick around anyway. But our closest relationships deserve our brightest moments, not just what's left over at the end of the day.

When you come home today, before you walk through the door, pause for just five seconds. Take a breath and consciously choose to greet your loved ones with genuine warmth – even if you've had the worst day imaginable. That brief moment of connection can transform both your mood and theirs, creating a small but meaningful ripple of positivity in your home.

July 31st

"Even with all the pain I have experienced, I still have had moments of Serendipity that gave me something valuable that I was not seeking out."

— Gary Hardy

Here I am talking about life's unexpected gifts in the midst of our struggles. This wisdom reminds me of how life sometimes works in mysterious ways - how in our darkest moments, unexpected light can find its way through.

It's fascinating how often our most meaningful discoveries come not from our careful plans, but from those surprising moments of serendipity. When we're focused on navigating our pain or challenges, life sometimes has a way of quietly slipping us a gift we didn't even know we needed.

Today, consider looking back at some of your own challenging periods. Can you spot those serendipitous moments that brought unexpected value? Maybe it was a chance encounter that led to a beautiful relationship that you never though you'd be able to find, a wrong turn that revealed a new path, or a setback that ultimately guided you towards something better.

Remember, this isn't about minimising pain or forcing a silver lining - it's about staying open to life's surprising gifts, even in difficult times. Sometimes our deepest wounds become windows through which new light can enter.

Perhaps today, even if you're going through something challenging, you might keep your heart just slightly open to the possibility of serendipity. What unexpected gift might be waiting to be discovered in your current circumstance?

August 1st

"The month of August reminds us that a fresh start is just around the corner, waiting for us to seize it."

— J.K. Rowling

This is such a meaningful perspective on August, particularly as it sits at that transitional point between seasons. I love how J.K. Rowling captures that sense of anticipation that August brings – it's like standing on the threshold of something new, even if we're not students anymore.

There's something universal about how August feels like nature's way of giving us a gentle nudge towards change. The slightly cooler mornings, the subtle shift in sunlight, all whisper that transformation is possible. It's almost like the month itself gives us permission to reinvent ourselves or take that leap we've been considering.

Here's a practical way to harness this August energy: Take 10 minutes today to write down one change you've been wanting to make in your life. It doesn't have to be massive – maybe it's reading more, calling an old friend regularly, or starting a new morning routine. Then, use August's natural momentum of renewal to take that first small step. The key is to start before September arrives, while that sense of possibility is still fresh in the air.

Remember, you don't need to wait for January 1st to begin something new. Sometimes the best fresh starts happen on ordinary August afternoons.

August 2nd

"Without circumstances, there is no change."

— Lailah Gifty Akita

We often think of change as something we need to force through sheer willpower, but this quote reminds us of a deeper truth.

Think about it - it's usually the unexpected job loss that leads us to find our true calling, or the relationship ending that helps us discover our own strength. Sometimes it's even smaller circumstances - maybe a chance conversation that shifts our perspective, or a minor setback that teaches us a valuable lesson. These circumstances, whether challenging or fortunate, are actually the catalysts that push us to grow and transform.

Today, instead of resisting the challenging circumstances in your life, try viewing them as potential doorways to change. The next time something unexpected or difficult happens, pause and ask yourself, "What might this circumstance be inviting me to change or learn?"

I've found that this shift in perspective can transform how we experience life's challenges. Rather than seeing circumstances as obstacles to overcome, we can start recognising them as the very tools life uses to shape us into who we're meant to become.

What circumstances in your life right now might be inviting you to change?

August 3rd

"You never know what is around the corner, an unexpected message, or a phone call, can completely transform your life, never give up hope that something wonderful can happen to you."

— Gary Hardy

I really appreciate the optimistic realism in this quote. It's not just blind optimism - it's rooted in the simple truth that life has this amazing way of surprising us when we least expect it. Many of us can probably think of moments when one small, unexpected thing changed everything - a chance conversation, an email we almost didn't open, or a seemingly random encounter that led to something significant.

What I find particularly meaningful here is how it encourages staying open to possibility without demanding that we manufacture positivity. It's simply saying: keep your heart open to good things, because they can arrive in the most unexpected ways and at the most unexpected times.

For today, I'd suggest something practical to embody this wisdom: Try saying "yes" to one small thing you might usually say "no" to (as long as it's safe and reasonable, of course). Maybe it's accepting an invitation you'd normally decline, taking a different route to work, or responding to someone's message that you've been putting off. Sometimes these small openings to life's possibilities are exactly where the magic sneaks in.

Remember, hoping for wonderful things isn't about passive waiting - it's about maintaining that spark of openness that allows us to recognise and embrace opportunities when they appear. Every day carries the potential for something unexpected and beautiful to unfold.

August 4th

"There will always be obstacles and challenges that stand in your way. Building mental strength will help you develop resilience to those potential hazards so you can continue on your journey to success."

— Amy Morin

As someone who's thought a lot about emotional intelligence, I find this distinction really important for understanding ourselves better.

Think of it like this: your mood is like the weather – it can shift from cloudy to sunny throughout the day. You can influence it through activities, environment changes, or conscious choices. But your feelings? They're more like the climate of your emotional landscape. They run deeper, tied to our experiences, relationships, and core values. You can't just flip a switch to change how you truly feel about something or someone meaningful in your life.

Today, I'd encourage you to practice this awareness: Notice when you're trying to force a change in your deeper feelings versus when you're working with your mood. Are you trying to talk yourself out of feeling hurt by someone's actions? Or are you simply trying to lift your spirits after a tough morning?

Try this: Next time you're experiencing difficult feelings, instead of trying to change them, just acknowledge them. "Yes, I feel this way, and that's okay." You might find that accepting your feelings while managing your mood is a more authentic way to navigate your emotional life.

Remember, it's perfectly fine to use healthy strategies to improve your mood – exercise, music, time with friends – while still honouring your deeper feelings. The wisdom lies in knowing the difference and not expecting ourselves to change our fundamental feelings as easily as we might change our playlist.

August 5th

"And you can change your mood everyday but not with your feelings."

— Abhiyanda B

As someone who's thought a lot about emotional intelligence, I find this distinction really important for understanding ourselves better.

Think of it like this: your mood is like the weather – it can shift from cloudy to sunny throughout the day. You can influence it through activities, environment changes, or conscious choices. But your feelings? They're more like the climate of your emotional landscape. They run deeper, tied to our experiences, relationships, and core values. You can't just flip a switch to change how you truly feel about something or someone meaningful in your life.

Today, I'd encourage you to practice this awareness: Notice when you're trying to force a change in your deeper feelings versus when you're working with your mood. Are you trying to talk yourself out of feeling hurt by someone's actions? Or are you simply trying to lift your spirits after a tough morning?

Try this: Next time you're experiencing difficult feelings, instead of trying to change them, just acknowledge them. "Yes, I feel this way, and that's okay." You might find that accepting your feelings while managing your mood is a more authentic way to navigate your emotional life.

Remember, it's perfectly fine to use healthy strategies to improve your mood – exercise, music, time with friends – while still honouring your deeper feelings. The wisdom lies in knowing the difference and not expecting ourselves to change our fundamental feelings as easily as we might change our playlist.

August 6th

"We have to dare to be ourselves, however frightening or strange that self may prove to be."

— May Sarton

What a profound reflection from May Sarton about one of life's most challenging journeys – being authentically ourselves. The word "dare" really strikes me here because it acknowledges something we often don't talk about: being yourself takes genuine courage. It's not just a gentle act of self-discovery, but sometimes a bold, even defiant choice to show up as who we truly are.

I find it especially touching that Sarton acknowledges the fear and strangeness we might encounter along the way. She's not sugar-coating the journey – sometimes what we find within ourselves can feel alien or unsettling. But there's deep wisdom in her suggestion that we need to embrace these parts too, not just the comfortable, socially acceptable aspects of who we are.

Here's a small but meaningful practice you might try today: Choose one small aspect of yourself that you usually hide or downplay – maybe it's an unusual interest, a quirky habit, or even just a genuine opinion you typically keep to yourself. Find one safe moment to let that part of you be seen. It doesn't have to be dramatic; perhaps it's mentioning your passion for collecting vintage bottle caps in a casual conversation, or wearing that colourful scarf you love but usually think is "too much."

Remember, authenticity isn't about making grand declarations – it's about those small, brave moments where we choose truth over comfort, even when it makes us nervous. Each time we do this, we create more space for others to do the same.

August 7th

"I spent my childhood learning how to fear, and now I spend my adulthood learning how not to."

— Gemma Troy

This quote hits deep in its raw honesty about the journey many of us are on. What strikes me most is how Gemma Troy captures this universal yet rarely discussed truth – that many of our fears aren't innate, they're learned, often in childhood when we were too young to understand what was happening. And now, as adults, we find ourselves doing the patient, sometimes painful work of unlearning those old protective patterns.

The parallel between learning and unlearning is particularly powerful here. It acknowledges that feeling safe isn't just about "getting over" our fears – it's an active process of re-education, just as complex and demanding as the original learning was. It's like we're being both student and teacher to ourselves, gradually rewriting lessons that were etched into our hearts long ago.

Here's something meaningful you might try today: Take a quiet moment to identify one small fear that you know is a learned response from your past. It might be fear of speaking up in meetings, fear of trying new things, or even fear of letting people get too close. Then, instead of pushing against it, simply acknowledge it with compassion: "I understand why young-me learned this fear. It made sense then." Sometimes, just recognising that our fears were once survival tools can be the first step in gently laying them down.

Remember, unlearning fear isn't about being fearless – it's about building a new relationship with fear, one where we're in conversation with it rather than controlled by it.

August 8th

"Stop being tormented by everyone else's reaction to you."

— Joyce Meyer

This quote speaks to one of the heaviest burdens many of us carry – the exhausting weight of constantly monitoring and worrying about how others perceive us. I find it especially powerful that Meyer uses the word "tormented," because that's exactly what it feels like, isn't it? A constant internal torment of replaying conversations, second-guessing ourselves, and adapting our behaviour to please others.

The simplicity of "stop" is striking too. Of course, it's not really that simple – but sometimes we need that direct reminder that we actually have the power to choose whether to continue this pattern. We've often been doing this emotional labor for so long that we forget it's not mandatory.

Here's a practical step you might take today: When you notice yourself worrying about someone's reaction, try this brief practice. Take a breath and ask yourself: "Is this person thinking about me as much as I'm thinking about their thoughts about me?" The answer is almost always no. Most people are too caught up in their own lives and concerns to scrutinise us the way we imagine they do.

Then, redirect that energy you would have spent worrying about their reaction into something that actually serves you – maybe that's focusing on your work, enjoying your lunch, or simply being present in your own experience rather than living in someone else's imagined judgement of you.

Remember, everyone's reactions say more about their own story than yours. You're not responsible for managing other people's perceptions – you're only responsible for living authentically and kindly.

August 9th

"Sometimes skulls are thick. Sometimes hearts are vacant. Sometimes words don't work."

— James Frey

This quote from Frey captures something about human connection and its limitations. I appreciate how it acknowledges, with such stark imagery, that sometimes our best efforts to reach others or be understood simply don't succeed – not because we're not trying hard enough, but because there are real barriers we can't always overcome.

I find particular wisdom in how it points to different types of obstacles: the "thick skulls" suggesting resistance to new ideas, "vacant hearts" pointing to emotional unavailability, and the limitation of words themselves. It's a reminder that communication breakdowns can happen for various reasons, and not all of them are within our power to fix.

Here's a practical way to work with this insight today: When you encounter resistance or disconnection with someone, instead of trying harder and harder to make your point (which often leads to frustration), pause and ask yourself: "What kind of barrier might I be facing here?" Sometimes just identifying whether it's an intellectual disconnect, emotional unavailability, or simply a limitation of language can help you either find a different approach or – equally important – accept that this particular conversation might need to wait for another time.

Remember, recognising when "words don't work" isn't admitting defeat – it's showing wisdom about where to invest your emotional energy and when to step back.

August 10th

"We fall in love with the little things about someone, like the sound of their voice, the way they laugh, and the way they smile."

— Gary Hardy

This quote beautifully captures how love often works in the most unexpected ways. It's rarely the grand gestures or obvious features that capture our hearts - it's those tiny, precious details that make someone uniquely them. I find it fascinating how we might meet hundreds of people, but suddenly one person's particular way of wrinkling their nose when they laugh just melts our heart.

These little things become the threads that weave together our deepest connections. They're the details we find ourselves missing most when someone's not around - the way they hum while cooking, or how they always tap their fingers on the steering wheel to their favourite song.

Here's a simple practice for today: Take a moment to notice and appreciate the small, endearing things about the people you care about - whether it's a romantic partner, family member, or close friend. Maybe it's how your friend always sends you random funny memes when you're having a tough day, or how your parent has a specific way of saying "hello" on the phone. Share your observation with them - something as simple as "I love how you always...".

You'll be amazed at how noting these little things can deepen your appreciation for the relationships in your life and make both you and them feel more seen and valued.

Remember, it's these seemingly insignificant details that often hold the most significance in our hearts. They're what make each relationship uniquely special and irreplaceable.

August 11th

"A friend is someone who knows all about you and still loves you."

— Elbert Hubbard

This beautiful observation by Hubbard touches something profound about true friendship. What moves me most about this quote is how it captures both the vulnerability and the safety of deep friendship – that incredible feeling of being fully known, even the parts we're not proud of, and still being embraced completely.

The word "still" is particularly powerful here. It acknowledges that there are parts of all of us that might be hard to love – our flaws, our mistakes, our complicated histories – and yet real friendship persists despite, or perhaps even because of, knowing all these layers of who we are. It's not about being loved for our carefully curated public self, but for our whole, messy, authentic being.

Here's something meaningful you might try today: Think of one friend who knows your complicated parts and loves you anyway. Send them a message sharing one specific thing about them that you know and love – maybe even something others might see as a quirk or flaw, but that you appreciate as part of who they are. Sometimes acknowledging how deeply we see each other strengthens that beautiful circle of being known and loved.

Remember, when we find people who love us with this kind of full awareness, it's not just acceptance we're experiencing – it's an invitation to be more fully ourselves in a world that often asks us to be less.

August 12th

"It is better to be hated for what you are than to be loved for what you are not."

— Andre Gide

This quote cuts straight to the heart of authenticity and the real price we sometimes pay for being true to ourselves. What I find particularly powerful about Gide's insight is how it challenges our natural instinct to seek approval and acceptance at any cost.

There's something both terrifying and liberating in this wisdom. It acknowledges that yes, being authentic might actually lead to being disliked or even hated – that's the hard truth many similar quotes skip over. But it also suggests that the alternative – being loved for a false version of yourself – is actually a heavier burden to bear. It's like carrying around a costume that gets heavier every day.

Here's a practical way to bring this wisdom into your life today: Think of one small way you've been adjusting your true self to be more "likeable" – maybe it's laughing at jokes you don't find funny, agreeing with opinions you don't share, or hiding an interest you think others might judge. Choose one moment today to let your genuine response show instead. It might feel uncomfortable, but notice how it also feels to put down that mask, even briefly. Remember, the love and acceptance we get for our false selves never really satisfies us because deep down, we know it's not really meant for us – it's meant for the person we're pretending to be. The disapproval we might face for being genuine, while painful, at least has the merit of being a response to our true self.

August 13th

"A good scare is worth more to a man than good advice."

— E. W. Howe

I've noticed how true this is - often we don't really internalise lessons until we experience something that shakes us up a bit. Think about how many people don't take their health seriously until they have a health scare, or don't save money until they face a financial crisis.

Here's a practical way to use this wisdom without waiting for those scary wake-up calls: Take a moment today to identify one area of your life where you've been ignoring good advice. Maybe it's about your health, relationships, or work. Now, instead of waiting for a crisis, try to vividly imagine the consequences of continuing to ignore it. Use that controlled "scare" as motivation to take action now.

What makes this quote particularly powerful is that it taps into how we're wired - our brains tend to respond more strongly to potential threats than to logical advice. But rather than waiting for life to provide those scares (which can be quite costly), we can use this understanding to motivate positive changes before problems arise.

Remember, the best lessons don't always have to come from actual crises - sometimes just honestly facing potential consequences can be enough to spark meaningful change.

August 14th

"Mindfulness gives you time. Time gives you choices. Choices, skilfully made, lead to freedom."

— Bhante H. Gunaratana

This layered wisdom from Gunaratana elegantly breaks down how mindfulness creates a path to personal freedom, step by step. What I find especially insightful is how it reveals the hidden gift of mindfulness – it's not just about being present, but about how that presence creates a space between our triggers and our reactions.

That space, that pause, is where the magic happens. When we're mindful, we gain those precious moments to actually see our choices rather than just reacting on autopilot. It's like time slows down just enough for us to notice there's more than one path forward.

Here's something you might try today: The next time you feel a strong emotional reaction coming on – maybe frustration with a coworker or anxiety about a decision – try taking one conscious breath before responding. Just that tiny pause. Notice how even this brief moment of mindfulness gives you time to choose your response rather than just react.

Remember, freedom doesn't always mean making different choices – sometimes it's simply knowing that we chose our response consciously rather than letting our habits choose for us. Each mindful moment is a small step towards greater personal freedom, one conscious choice at a time.

August 15th

"Nothing kills love faster than secrets."

— Cornelia Funke -Tintentod

This is such a powerful observation about the nature of intimacy and trust. What makes this quote particularly insightful is how it captures the way secrets act like a slow poison in relationships - they create invisible barriers between people, even when everything looks fine on the surface.

Today, choose one thing you've been holding back from someone important in your life - not necessarily a dark secret, but perhaps a concern, a hope, or a feeling you've been hesitant to express. Set aside 10 minutes to share it with them. The goal isn't to unload everything at once, but to practice the habit of open communication before small withholdings grow into relationship-damaging secrets.

What makes this perspective so valuable is that it reminds us that love thrives on transparency. When we keep secrets, we're not just withholding information - we're actually actively creating distance between ourselves and those we care about. Each secret becomes a tiny wall, and over time, those walls can become insurmountable.

Remember, being open doesn't mean sharing every thought that crosses your mind. It means being honest about the things that matter, even when it's uncomfortable. The temporary discomfort of vulnerability is usually far less damaging than the long-term erosion of trust that secrets can cause.

August 16th

"One thing I've learned.. life is a paradox. In order to heal you must hurt, in order to love you must break open and in order to have peace you must face chaos. Never regret any experience in your life, because it is always meant to bring you balance. The light always follows."

— Unknown

This quote resonates deeply with me. It speaks to one of life's fundamental truths - that growth often comes through challenges, not despite them. The author beautifully captures how life's most meaningful transformations often require us to go through difficult experiences first.

Think about how a broken bone heals stronger at the point of fracture, or how going through heartbreak can teach us to love more deeply and wisely. Even our most painful experiences can be doorways to greater wisdom and resilience. The key is not to resist these challenging moments, but to understand that they're part of our journey towards wholeness.

Here's a practical suggestion for today: The next time you face a difficult situation - whether it's a disagreement with someone, a setback at work, or an emotional struggle - instead of immediately trying to escape the discomfort, pause for a moment. Take a deep breath and ask yourself: "What might this challenge be trying to teach me? How could this experience help me grow?"

Sometimes just shifting our perspective from "Why is this happening to me?" to "What is this teaching me?" can transform how we experience life's inevitable difficulties. Remember, just as the darkest part of night comes right before dawn, our most challenging moments often precede our greatest breakthroughs.

August 17th

"She understood that the hardest times in life to go through were when you were transitioning from one version of yourself to another."

— Sarah Addison Allen

This quote captures something we all experience but often struggle to name. Those periods of transition - whether we're changing careers, ending relationships, moving to new places, or simply growing into a different version of ourselves - can feel incredibly disorienting. It's like being caught between two worlds, no longer fully who we were but not yet fully who we're becoming.

Here's something to consider today: If you're in one of these transition periods right now, try to be gentler with yourself. These transformative times often feel messy and uncomfortable because we're literally rewiring our sense of self. Think of it like a caterpillar in its chrysalis - the transformation process itself isn't pretty, but it's necessary for growth.

One practical way to handle this today is to take a moment to acknowledge and honour both versions of yourself - the one you're leaving behind and the one you're becoming. Maybe write down what you're grateful to your past self for teaching you, and what you're excited about in your emerging self. Remember that feeling unsettled during these transitions isn't a sign that something's wrong - it's often a sign that you're growing in exactly the way you need to.

These transitional periods, though challenging, are often where our most significant growth happens. They're the spaces between chapters where we rewrite our story.

August 18th

"Adaptability is a great asset to have because life is so unpredictable, and things can change overnight for any of us."

— Chanda Kochhar

This quote captures such an essential truth about life. I've seen countless times how the ability to adapt can make the difference between thriving and struggling when life throws its inevitable curveballs. No matter how carefully we plan, change is the one constant we can count on.

Think about how the most resilient people you know handle unexpected changes - they bend rather than break. They might not always like the changes, but they find ways to work with new situations rather than fighting against them.

Here's a practical way to build your adaptability muscle today: Try taking a different route to work or school, or intentionally change one small part of your daily routine. Maybe have breakfast for dinner, or if you usually exercise in the morning, try the evening instead. These small, controlled changes help us practice being flexible in low-stakes situations, making it easier to adapt when bigger changes come along.

The beauty of developing adaptability is that it's not just about surviving change - it's about discovering new opportunities and possibilities we might have missed if we'd stayed rigidly attached to our original plans. Each time we successfully adapt to something new, we build confidence in our ability to handle whatever comes next.

August 19th

"Mental health and physical health are one and the same for me - they go hand in hand. If you aren't physically healthy, you won't be mentally healthy either - and vice versa. The mind and body is connected and when one is off, the other suffers as well."

— Kelly Gale

This quote is something I've observed repeatedly in both research and real life - the profound interconnection between our physical and mental well-being. Kelly Gale expresses perfectly how these two aspects of our health are really just different sides of the same coin.

Think about those days when you're physically exhausted - how much harder it is to stay positive or think clearly. Or conversely, when you're anxious or stressed, how your body responds with tension, digestive issues, or fatigue. It's like an ongoing conversation between mind and body.

Here's a practical suggestion for today: Try what I call the "mood-movement check-in." Once today, when you're feeling mentally down or stressed, pause and do just 5 minutes of gentle movement - it could be stretching, walking, or even dancing to one song. Notice how your mental state shifts, even slightly. Alternatively, when you're feeling physically sluggish, take a moment to practice a brief mindfulness exercise or deep breathing. This simple practice helps us tune into and strengthen that mind-body connection.

The beautiful thing about understanding this relationship is that it gives us multiple entry points for improving our overall well-being. Sometimes when we're struggling mentally, the best intervention might be physical - like going for a walk. And when we're physically under the weather, practices like meditation or positive visualisation can help support our body's healing process.

August 20th

"Life is short, and we must make the most of every moment."

— Rosamunde Pilcher

This quote touches something deep and universal - that precious awareness of how fleeting our time really is. It's not meant to create anxiety, but rather to wake us up to the richness of each moment we're given. I've found that when we truly grasp how finite our time is, it can transform how we choose to live each day. Think about how we often postpone joy or meaningful experiences, telling ourselves "someday" or "when the time is right." But life doesn't pause while we wait for the perfect moment. Every day we wait is a day we can't get back.

Here's a simple practice for today: Take what I call a "moment pause." Three times today, stop whatever you're doing for just 30 seconds. Really notice where you are, who you're with, what you're feeling. Maybe it's during your morning coffee, while walking to your car, or during dinner with family. These brief pauses help train us to be more present and appreciate the small moments that make up our lives.

The beauty of this awareness isn't just about making grand changes - it's about bringing more intentionality to our everyday choices. Maybe it means finally sending that message to an old friend you've been thinking about, or spending an extra few minutes reading with your child instead of rushing through bedtime. These small choices, made with awareness of life's brevity, add up to a life lived more fully and with fewer regrets.

August 21st

"Success is not measured by wealth, but by the impact you have on others."

— Kurt Vonnegut

This quote strikes at something really profound about how we often misunderstand what truly matters in life. While society tends to push us towards chasing material success, Vonnegut reminds us that our real legacy lies in how we touch others' lives. I've seen time and again how the people we remember most fondly aren't usually the wealthiest, but those who showed kindness, offered support, or helped us grow.

Think about the people who've had the biggest positive impact on your own life - maybe a teacher who believed in you, a friend who was there during tough times, or even a stranger whose small act of kindness changed your day. Their value to you probably had nothing to do with their bank account.

Here's a practical way to implement this wisdom today: Choose one person in your life - it could be someone you see regularly like a coworker or neighbour - and look for one small way to make their day better. Maybe it's offering a genuine compliment, taking time to really listen to them, or helping with a task they're struggling with. Notice how this kind of intentional positive impact creates a different kind of richness in your life - one that no amount of money can buy.

The beautiful thing about measuring success through impact is that it's available to everyone, regardless of their circumstances. Every single day offers countless opportunities to make a difference in someone's life, and these moments of connection and support often create ripples that extend far beyond what we can see.

August 22nd

"Dealing with other people reminds me of why I like to be alone."

— Raine Cooper

While this quote might make us chuckle in recognition, I want to explore it with some nuance. It speaks to something many of us feel - that pull between connection and solitude, especially when social interactions become challenging. But I think there's a deeper wisdom we can find here. It's perfectly natural to want to retreat when dealing with others becomes overwhelming. Solitude can be healing and necessary. However, I've noticed that the key isn't to completely withdraw, but to find the right balance that works for you and to develop healthy boundaries.

Here's a practical suggestion for today: Instead of seeing it as an all-or-nothing choice between people and solitude, try what I call "mindful boundaries." When you feel socially drained, rather than completely withdrawing, take intentional breaks. Maybe it's a 15-minute quiet walk between meetings, or setting aside one evening this week just for yourself. Think of it like charging your social battery - you need both connection and solitude to function at your best.

The goal isn't to avoid people altogether, but to approach interactions with more awareness of your own needs and limits. This way, when you do engage with others, you're doing so from a place of genuine energy rather than depletion.

August 23rd

"There is as much attachment in wanting to be rid of something as there is in holding on to it. It is our attachment that seeds our suffering. Peace lies between embracing what we would push away and letting go of what we would cling to."

— Anna Zieo

This quote delves into one of life's most subtle but profound paradoxes. I've seen how often our desperate attempts to push away what we don't want can actually keep us more tightly bound to it - whether it's an uncomfortable emotion, a difficult memory, or an unwanted situation. Think about how struggling against quicksand only makes you sink faster, while relaxing helps you float. The same principle applies to our inner experiences. When we fight against anxiety, it often intensifies. When we desperately try to forget something, it seems to stick more firmly in our minds.

Here's a practical suggestion for today: Try what I call the "middle way pause." When you notice yourself either strongly resisting something or clinging tightly to something, take a moment to simply observe that tension. Don't try to change it, but don't feed it either. Maybe it's resistance to a coworker's irritating habit, or attachment to how you think your day should go. Just notice the push or pull, and experiment with letting your grip loosen just a little. The beauty of this approach is that it offers a different kind of freedom - not from the thing itself, but from our exhausting battle with it. True peace often comes not from achieving perfect circumstances, but from finding that delicate balance between acceptance and letting go.

August 24th

"Sometimes compromise is important. Sometimes it's better to give in to someone else's wishes in order to have fun as a group or as a couple, or for the benefit of the team. Sometimes compromise is dangerous. We need to guard against compromising our standards to gain the approval or love of someone else. Decide when you can, and when you cannot, compromise. If it's not harmful and you are ambivalent about a decision, then compromise. If it could lead to breaking your values, compromise isn't a good idea."

— Melody Beattie

This quote captures the delicate balance we need to strike in relationships and life decisions. I appreciate how Beattie distinguishes between healthy and unhealthy compromise - it's not a simple "compromise is good" or "compromise is bad" situation, but rather about understanding when it serves growth and when it might harm our core values.

Think of it like a tree in the wind - it needs to be flexible enough to bend with strong gusts (healthy compromise), but if it bends too far, it will break (compromising core values). The wisdom lies in knowing the difference between the two.

Here's a practical suggestion for today: When faced with a situation requiring potential compromise, try what I call the "values check."

Take a moment to ask yourself two questions:

- "Will this compromise bring genuine connection or mutual benefit?"
- "Does this compromise ask me to cross any of my fundamental ethical lines?"

If the first answer is "yes" and the second is "no," it's likely a healthy compromise - like agreeing to watch your partner's choice of movie even though it's not your favourite genre. But if you're being asked to compromise your honesty, integrity, or self-respect, that's when you need to stand firm.

The real art lies in communicating these boundaries with grace - being able to say "no" to harmful compromises while staying open to the kind of give-and-take that builds stronger relationships and communities.

August 25th

"There are good days and there are bad days, and this is one of them."

— Lawrence Welk

I love the playful wisdom in this quote! It perfectly captures how life often feels both good and bad at the same time, with a dash of humour that helps us not take ourselves too seriously. It reminds me that even the way we label our experiences as "good" or "bad" can sometimes miss the complexity of what we're going through.

Think about those days that seem to be going terribly, but then something wonderful happens, or those "perfect" days that have their own little challenges. Life rarely fits into neat categories of purely good or bad.

Here's a simple practice for today: When you catch yourself labelling a day as entirely "good" or "bad," try what I call the "both/and pause." Take a moment to notice one thing that's going well on a "bad" day, or acknowledge one small challenge on a "good" day. Maybe the morning meeting was rough, but your coffee was perfect. Or perhaps it's a fantastic day overall, but you stubbed your toe.

This kind of perspective helps us develop resilience and a sense of humour about life's ups and downs. It reminds us that no day is completely one thing or another - and sometimes, like Welk humorously suggests, it's perfectly okay to let it be both at once.

August 26th

"Apologies aren't meant to change the past, they are meant to change the future."

— Kevin Hancock

This quote captures something really profound about the true purpose of apologising. So often we get caught up thinking that an apology is about erasing what happened, when really it's about creating a path forward. I've seen how genuine apologies can transform relationships and create openings for healing that seemed impossible before. Think about how when someone truly apologises to us, what matters most isn't the words themselves, but feeling that they understand the impact of their actions and are committed to doing better. It's like building a bridge across a divide - the apology isn't about pretending the divide never existed, but about creating a way to cross it.

Here's a meaningful practice for today: If there's a situation weighing on you where you know you've hurt someone, try what I call the "future-focused apology." Rather than just saying "I'm sorry" and focusing on the past event, take a moment to express your understanding of how your actions affected them and share one specific way you'll act differently going forward. For example, instead of "Sorry I was late," try "I know my being late made you miss part of the event - I'm going to start leaving 15 minutes earlier for our meetings." The beauty of this approach is that it transforms an apology from just words about the past into a commitment that can strengthen relationships and trust going forward. It shows that we're not just acknowledging our mistakes, but learning and growing from them.

August 27th

"Until you've finished it, tell nobody."

— Gary Hardy

There's a fascinating psychological effect at play here - when we talk about our goals and plans prematurely, we often get a false sense of accomplishment that can actually reduce our drive to complete the real work.

I've seen this happen countless times in myself and others: someone announces their big plans to write a book, start a business, or begin a fitness journey, and that initial burst of social validation feels so good that it partially satisfies the psychological reward we're seeking. It's like our brain gets a small "hit" of achievement without having done the actual work.

Today, I'd encourage you to think about one goal or project that's important to you. Instead of sharing it widely, try keeping it close to your chest. Channel that energy you might have spent talking about it into actually doing it. Notice how different it feels to work in this quiet, focused way.

The beauty of this approach is that it lets you maintain full ownership of your journey until you have something concrete to show. When you do finally share your achievement, it won't be about what you're going to do - it'll be about what you've actually done. And that's a much more powerful story to tell.

August 28th

"How do you know when it's over? Maybe when you feel more in love with your memories than with the person standing in front of you."

— Gunnar Ardelius

That's a deeply insightful quote that touches on something many of us experience but struggle to acknowledge. When we find ourselves constantly retreating into memories of "better times" instead of being present with someone, it's often a sign that we're holding onto what was rather than engaging with what is. It's like keeping a beautiful pressed flower - while it preserves a moment perfectly, it can never grow or change.

I think the real wisdom here isn't just about romantic relationships - it's about recognising when we're living in the past instead of embracing the present.

Here's a simple practice you might find helpful: Each day, when you're with someone important in your life (partner, friend, family member), try to notice one new thing about them - a different laugh, a new interest, or even just how the light catches their eyes differently. This helps train us to stay present and remember that people, like life itself, are always evolving.

When we truly see the person in front of us, rather than the memory we're holding onto, we give ourselves and others the chance to grow together rather than apart.

August 29th

"What's the point of having a voice if you're gonna be silent in those moments you shouldn't be?"

— Angie Thomas

That quote really strikes at the heart of personal responsibility and moral courage. It reminds me of those moments we've all experienced - when we see something wrong happening and feel that knot in our stomach, that voice inside telling us to speak up, but fear or convenience makes us hesitate.

What Angie Thomas captures so powerfully here is that having a voice isn't just a gift - it's a responsibility. It's like being given a powerful tool but keeping it locked away when it's needed most. The true test of our character often comes in those uncomfortable moments when speaking up might cost us something - maybe popularity, comfort, or even opportunities.

Here's a practical way to build this muscle daily: Start with small moments of truth-telling. When you hear a casual comment that perpetuates harm or see someone being treated unfairly in a meeting, take a deep breath and speak up respectfully. It could be as simple as saying "I see this differently" or "That makes me uncomfortable." Each small act of speaking up builds our courage for the bigger moments that matter.

Remember, your voice gains strength through use, just like any other muscle. The more you use it when it matters, the stronger and more natural it becomes to speak up when you need to.

August 30th

"Any idiot can face a crisis; it's this day-to-day living that wears you out."

— Anton Chekhov

This quote hits home with its raw honesty about the human experience. Chekhov captures something deeply true - that while we often romanticise big moments of crisis where adrenaline kicks in and we rise to the occasion, it's the quiet weight of everyday life that can really test our resilience.

It's like how people can often find extraordinary strength during emergencies, but might struggle with the simple discipline of making their bed each morning or maintaining healthy relationships through the mundane moments. The daily grind - bills, responsibilities, small disappointments, routine maintenance of life - that's what truly challenges our spirit.

This evening, try to identify and celebrate one small victory from your day. Maybe you finally answered that email you've been avoiding, had a meaningful conversation with your kid over breakfast, or simply managed to stay patient during a frustrating commute. By acknowledging these tiny triumphs, we build resilience for the daily marathon that is life.

The beauty in Chekhov's insight is that it validates our daily struggles while reminding us that mastering the ordinary days is perhaps our greatest achievement. When we can find peace and purpose in the routine, that's when we're truly living well.

August 31st

"Instead of seeing how much pain I can dish out towards those I disagree with, or who I believe have done me wrong, I seek to follow the golden rule and use my words and behaviour to create more of what the world needs – love, compassion, and connection."

— Aspen Baker

This quote really speaks to a fundamental choice we all face in our interactions with others, especially during conflicts. It's about breaking that instinctive cycle of responding to hurt with more hurt. I've seen how choosing compassion over retaliation, though often harder in the moment, creates lasting positive change both in our relationships and within ourselves.

You know how tempting it is when someone wrongs us to want to "give them a taste of their own medicine"? But Baker points to a more powerful path - one that doesn't just avoid adding more negativity to the world, but actively creates something better. It's like having two seeds to plant: one that grows thorns, and another that grows flowers. The choice is always ours.

Here's a practical suggestion for today: When you encounter someone who frustrates or upsets you, try what I call the "pause and reframe." Before reacting, take a breath and ask yourself: "What would make this interaction better, not worse?" Maybe it's responding to criticism with curiosity instead of defensiveness, or meeting anger with calm understanding. Even if the other person doesn't immediately reciprocate, you're creating space for potential connection rather than guaranteed conflict.

Remember, choosing compassion doesn't mean being a doormat - it means being strong enough to break the cycle of negativity and create opportunities for understanding. It's about recognising that every interaction is a chance to either build walls or bridges.

September 1st

"Ah, September! You are the doorway to the season that awakens my soul."

— Peggy Toney Horton

This quote beautifully captures that special feeling so many of us experience when September arrives, marking the transition into fall. What's particularly striking is how it frames September not as the end of summer, but as a beginning - a doorway opening to something enriching and meaningful.

I find it especially powerful how it speaks to the way seasons can deeply affect our inner world. For many people, fall brings a sense of renewal and awakening, perhaps even more so than the traditional spring renewal. There's something about the crisp air, the changing colours, and the subtle shift in light that can stir us emotionally and creatively.

Today, take a moment to notice one small sign of the changing season - maybe it's a leaf starting to turn, the angle of the afternoon light, or the first time you need to grab a light jacket. Let that observation be a mini-doorway to presence and appreciation. This kind of mindful attention can help us feel more connected to nature's rhythms and our own internal seasons of change.

Remember, just as September opens the door to Autumn, each day offers us a doorway to experience life with fresh eyes and an awakened spirit. It's about being present enough to walk through it.

September 2nd

"That's what careless words do. They make people love you a little less."

— Arundhati Roy

This is a powerful observation about the lasting impact of our words. It reminds me of how a single thoughtless comment can create tiny fractures in even our strongest relationships - not dramatic breaks, but small chips that accumulate over time.

What makes Roy's insight so profound is how it captures the subtle way words can erode love. It's rarely the big arguments that end relationships - it's often those small, careless remarks that slowly dim the warmth between people, like water gradually wearing away at stone.

Here's a practical daily practice that can help: Before speaking, especially in moments of frustration, try taking one deep breath and asking yourself, "Will these words make them feel closer to me or further away?" This tiny pause can be the difference between strengthening a bond and weakening it.

The beauty of this awareness is that it works both ways - just as careless words can make people love us less, mindful, kind words can make love grow stronger. Each interaction is an opportunity to either build or erode the connections we value most.

September 3rd

"What we have once enjoyed we can never lose. All that we love deeply becomes a part of us."

— Helen Keller

This is such a comforting perspective on love and loss. What strikes me about Keller's wisdom is how she transforms what we often see as loss into something permanent and precious. Rather than focusing on what's gone, she reminds us that meaningful experiences and connections literally shape who we become.

Think about it - every person who has touched our lives, every moment of joy we've experienced, has left an imprint that contributes to who we are today. Like rivers carving valleys over time, love shapes the landscape of our hearts permanently.

Today, spend a moment recalling one beautiful memory or connection that has shaped you. It could be a lesson from a grandparent who's no longer here, the courage you learned from a past challenge, or the joy from a childhood friendship. Notice how that experience still lives in you - maybe in your values, your smile, or the way you treat others.

What's powerful about this perspective is that it helps us move through loss with grace while honouring how love continues to live and work within us. Instead of viewing memories as just reminders of what we've lost, we can see them as active parts of who we've become - treasures that can never be taken away.

September 4th

"The most profound changes happen in quiet moments. Let your transformation speak for itself."

— Unknown

This quote speaks to a deep truth about authentic personal growth that often gets overlooked in our social media age, where every small change seems to need an announcement. It reminds me of how a seed transforms into a tree - the most important work happens silently, underground, before anything is visible. We often feel pressure to broadcast our progress, our healing, our improvements - but real, lasting change tends to happen in those quiet, private moments when we're just doing the work, without an audience. It's in those small daily choices, private revelations, and moments of quiet persistence that we truly transform.

Today, take 5 minutes for what I call "quiet growth time" - where you work on something meaningful to you without documenting or sharing it. Maybe it's reading, journaling, practicing a skill, or simply sitting in reflection. The key is to let this be purely for your own growth, with no external validation needed.

The beauty of letting your transformation speak for itself is that when changes are genuine, people notice naturally - not because you told them to look, but because real growth has a way of shining through in how you move through the world, how you handle challenges, and how you treat others. It's like the difference between announcing you're becoming more patient versus people naturally noticing you respond to frustration with more grace.

September 5th

"You cannot protect yourself from sadness without protecting yourself from happiness."

— Jonathan Safran Foer

This quote touches on one of life's paradoxes - that our attempts to avoid pain often end up limiting our capacity for joy. It's like trying to build a wall around your heart - sure, it might keep out some hurt, but it also blocks the sunlight of genuine happiness and connection.

I've noticed how often people try to "protect" themselves after being hurt - maybe by not getting too close to others, not dreaming too big, or not letting themselves get too excited about possibilities. But what Foer captures so beautifully here is that emotional armour doesn't discriminate - it blocks everything, both the pain and the pleasure.

Today, think about if you have ever noticed yourself pulling back from something because you're afraid of getting hurt, pause and ask, "What joy might I also be blocking?" Then try to stay open for just one more moment than feels comfortable. Maybe it's letting yourself fully enjoy a friendship even though people have left before, or fully celebrating a success even though you know nothing lasts forever.

The real wisdom here is that living fully means being vulnerable to both light and shadow. True resilience isn't about building walls - it's about learning to stay open even though we know there are no guarantees. Because in the end, a life half-felt in an attempt to avoid pain is perhaps the saddest outcome of all.

September 6th

"You may get to a stage of your life, when you have finished doing what was needed to get through the storm, but it has taken everything from you, and ask yourself...Is this all I am now ? The answer yes, but you can be more, so much more, if you wish to be, and better than before"

— Gary Hardy

This quote really speaks to me about the transformative nature of hardship. Sometimes we go through incredibly difficult periods that drain everything from us - our energy, our sense of self, even our direction in life. We survive, but we feel hollowed out, like a different person entirely. I've seen this happen to many people, and perhaps you've experienced it yourself.

But here's what I find beautiful about Hardy's message: it acknowledges this emptiness while simultaneously opening a door to possibility. It's saying "Yes, this is where you are now, and that's okay" - but it doesn't leave you there. Instead, it gently suggests that this emptied space within you can actually become fertile ground for new growth.

Let me offer a practical suggestion: Take a moment today to write down five small things you'd like to try or learn - things that have nothing to do with your past or your struggles. Maybe it's learning to bake bread, taking up photography, or simply starting a daily walking routine. The key is to choose something fresh, something that has no emotional connection to what you've been through. This can be your first step towards becoming "more" - not by trying to rebuild what was lost, but by creating something entirely new.

Remember, you're not starting over - you're starting fresh, with all the wisdom your struggles have given you. That's an incredibly powerful foundation to build upon.

September 7th

"I don't care if you're black, white, straight, bisexual, gay, lesbian, short, tall, fat, skinny, rich or poor. If you're nice to me, I'll be nice to you. Simple as that."

— Robert Michaels MD

This is such a refreshingly straightforward take on human interaction. At its core, this quote captures what I believe is the essence of genuine human connection - the simple principle of mutual respect and kindness, stripped of all the labels we tend to put on each other.

Dr. Michaels highlights something profound here: while we often make things complicated with prejudgements and biases, the basic formula for positive human interaction is actually quite simple. It's about how we treat each other, nothing more, nothing less.

Here's a practical way to embody this wisdom today: Try approaching each interaction with a clean slate. Whether it's the barista at your coffee shop, a colleague you don't normally talk to, or someone who seems very different from you, focus solely on the interaction itself. Respond to their energy and kindness rather than any preconceptions. You might be surprised at the connections you make and how this simple shift can enrich your daily experiences.

This isn't just about being nice - it's about creating a ripple effect of positive interactions that can transform our corner of the world, one simple exchange at a time.

September 8th

"Grief has a way of changing us, shaping us into someone we no longer recognise."

— Javier Marías

This is such a profound observation about how loss reshapes us. When we think about grief, it comes in so many forms - the deep ache of losing a loved one, the heartbreak of a relationship ending, the surprising intensity of losing a beloved pet, or even the loss of a dream or life path we held dear. Each type of grief has its own unique fingerprint on our souls, yet they all share this power to fundamentally change who we are.

Sometimes we look in the mirror during or after these profound losses and barely recognise ourselves. Our laugh might sound different, our priorities shift dramatically, or we might find ourselves drawn to entirely new things while losing interest in what once excited us. What surprises many people is how similar the impact can be - the loss of a pet can hit us just as hard as losing a human relationship, or the end of a long-term relationship can shake our foundation as deeply as a death. This transformation can be unsettling, even frightening - but it's also deeply natural.

Let me share something practical that might help if you're going through any kind of grief today: Try to be gentle with this new version of yourself. Instead of fighting against these changes or trying to force yourself back to who you were "before," consider keeping a small journal where you document one new thing you notice about yourself each day. It could be as simple as "Today I preferred to be alone" or "I found myself drawn to different music." This practice helps us honour and understand our evolution rather than resist it.

Remember, the person you're becoming through grief isn't less than who you were before - you're being reshaped by one of the most profound human experiences possible. Whether it's the loss of a person, a pet, a relationship, or a dream, there's a deep wisdom that often emerges from this transformation, even though the path to it can be incredibly painful.

September 9th

"Sometimes the hardest part of life is simply showing up."

— Ann-Marie MacDonald

There's such raw honesty in this simple statement. Some days just getting out of bed, facing the world, and doing what needs to be done takes more courage than any grand gesture. Whether it's showing up to work when you're struggling emotionally, attending a social event when anxiety is high, or simply facing another day when you're feeling overwhelmed - these seemingly small acts can require immense strength.

Here's a practical perspective that might help when you're having one of those days today: Break "showing up" into smaller victories. Maybe today, showing up means just taking a shower and making your bed. Maybe it means attending that meeting, even if you don't speak up as much as usual. Or maybe it means simply answering one text from a friend when you're feeling low.

You're not letting yourself down by finding some days harder than others. Sometimes, just being present - even if you're not at your best - is an act of incredible resilience. And here's something I've learned: those who seem to have it all together? They have these days too. We all do.

If you're in this space right now, try celebrating the small act of showing up today, whatever that looks like for you. Sometimes that's enough, and that's perfectly okay.

September 10th

"Blame is the coward's way out, the easy way to explain away our own failures."

— Jeff Abbott

This hits at something really fundamental about human nature and personal growth. I've noticed that when we point fingers at others for our setbacks, we might feel better in the moment, but we rob ourselves of something incredibly valuable: the power to change and grow.

Think about it - when we blame others or circumstances for our situations, it might protect our ego temporarily, but it leaves us feeling helpless, stuck in a narrative where we have no control over our lives. It's like handing over the keys to our own development to everyone else.

Here's a practical way to shift this mindset today: The next time something goes wrong, before your mind automatically searches for someone or something to blame, pause and ask yourself, "What part of this situation was within my control? What could I have done differently?" This isn't about beating yourself up - it's about finding the aspects of any situation where you have the power to make changes.

For example, instead of blaming traffic for being late, we might recognise we could have checked the route beforehand or left earlier. Rather than blaming a colleague for a project's failure, we might consider how we could have communicated more clearly or followed up more consistently.

This shift from blame to responsibility isn't always comfortable, but it's incredibly empowering. Because when we own our part in our failures, we also own our ability to create different outcomes in the future.

September 11th

"Accept what you are able to do and what you are not able to do."

— Mitch Albom

This is one of those pieces of wisdom that seems so simple on the surface, yet it's one of the hardest lessons for many of us to truly embrace. I find this quote especially powerful because it speaks to both sides of self-awareness - recognising our strengths and accepting our limitations. We often put immense pressure on ourselves to be capable of everything. We see others succeeding in various areas and think we should be able to do it all too. But there's such freedom in honest self-assessment and acceptance. It's not about giving up or settling - it's about understanding your unique combination of abilities and limitations so you can focus your energy where it truly matters.

Here's something practical you might try today: Make two lists. On one side, write down things you know you're genuinely good at - skills you've developed, natural talents you have. On the other, acknowledge areas where you struggle or things that simply aren't your strength. Then, instead of feeling bad about that second list, ask yourself: "How can I work with this reality rather than fight against it?" Maybe it means delegating certain tasks, asking for help, or simply choosing to focus your energy elsewhere. Remember, accepting your limitations isn't weakness - it's wisdom. It frees up mental and emotional energy you might have spent feeling inadequate and redirects it to areas where you can truly shine. After all, no one person is meant to be capable of everything.

September 12th

"Endings are not bad things. They just mean that something else is about to begin."

— C. Joybell C

    This is such a powerful reframing of how we view endings. We often approach endings with dread or sadness - whether it's the end of a relationship, a job, a phase of life, or even a cherished routine. But there's profound wisdom in seeing endings as doorways rather than dead ends. Think about how nature demonstrates this truth: A sunset isn't just the end of a day - it's the beginning of night with its own unique beauty. When leaves fall from trees, they're not just ending their life cycle - they're making way for new growth and nourishing the soil for what's to come.

Here's a practical way to embrace this perspective: Next time you face an ending in your life, try this simple reflection exercise. Take a piece of paper and draw a line down the middle. On one side, acknowledge what's ending and honour the feelings that come with that. On the other side, write down the possibilities this ending opens up - the new beginnings it makes possible. Maybe the end of a job creates space to pursue a passion you've put aside, or the end of a relationship allows you to rediscover parts of yourself you'd forgotten. The key isn't to deny the sadness or difficulty of endings, but to recognise that they're not the whole story. They're transitions, making space for new chapters we can't yet imagine. Sometimes the most beautiful beginnings are only possible because something else ended first.

September 13th

"Life is too short to waste your time on people who don't respect, appreciate, and value you."

— Roy T. Bennett

This is such a powerful reminder about the importance of protecting our energy and time. Sometimes we get caught up in trying to win over people who consistently show us they don't value us - whether it's in relationships, friendships, or even professional connections. We keep pouring our energy into these situations, hoping things will change, while precious time slips away. Here's what I find particularly meaningful about this quote: it's not just about the obvious cases of disrespect, but also about those subtle situations where people don't actively appreciate or value who we are and what we bring to the table. Life really is too brief to spend it trying to prove our worth to those who don't see it.

Take a moment today to assess your relationships and interactions. Ask yourself, "Do I consistently feel respected, appreciated, and valued in this connection?" If the answer is no, consider taking one small step to either set a boundary or redirect that energy towards people and situations where you are valued. This might mean declining an invitation from someone who consistently dismisses your feelings, or spending more time with those who celebrate your presence. Remember, choosing to distance yourself from those who don't value you isn't selfish - it's self-respect. It creates space in your life for connections that will nurture and uplift you, rather than drain you.

September 14th

"Today I read that butterflies rest when it rains because it damages their wings. It's okay to rest during the storms of life. You'll fly again when it's over."

— Unknown

This is such a beautiful metaphor that captures a profound truth about self-care and resilience. Nature often provides us with these perfect analogies for our own lives, and the butterfly in the rain is particularly touching because it speaks to something many of us struggle with - the feeling that we should keep pushing through difficult times, no matter what.

Just like butterflies, we sometimes need to pause and take shelter during our personal storms - whether that's grief, burnout, illness, or any overwhelming life challenge. There's deep wisdom in recognising that pausing isn't weakness; it's a necessary part of survival and eventual thriving.

Today or when you're going through a difficult period, try asking yourself, "What would a butterfly do right now?" Sometimes the bravest thing we can do is acknowledge that we need to rest, to shelter, to protect ourselves until the storm passes. This might mean taking a mental health day, saying no to extra commitments, or simply allowing yourself to be less productive than usual.

The beautiful promise in this quote is that the storm will pass. Just as butterflies emerge to fly again when the rain stops, you too will find your wings again. Your pause isn't permanent - it's protective. And when you do take flight again, you'll be stronger for having had the wisdom to rest when you needed it.

September 15th

"You don't have to have it all figured out at 21, or 30, or even 40. You'll bloom when you're ready. The only thing that matters is never giving up."

— Aaron Mahnke

This is such a comforting and liberating truth. I appreciate how it challenges our culture's obsession with early achievement and arbitrary age milestones. It's fascinating how we often pressure ourselves to meet these imaginary deadlines for life accomplishments, when nature itself shows us that different things bloom in their own perfect time.

The comparison to blooming is particularly beautiful because it acknowledges that growth is a natural process that can't be rushed. Just as some flowers bloom in spring and others in late summer, each person's journey unfolds according to their own unique timeline. What matters isn't when you bloom, but maintaining that persistent spirit that keeps you growing towards the light.

For today, I'd suggest this: Write down one thing you've been feeling "behind" on or anxious about not having figured out yet. Then, instead of seeing it as a failure to meet some arbitrary timeline, reframe it as part of your unique growing season. What if you're not behind at all, but rather gathering exactly the experiences and wisdom you need for your particular journey?

The real power in this quote lies in its final line about never giving up. It suggests that the only true failure isn't in blooming late, but in stopping your growth altogether. Whether you're 21, 45, or 70, as long as you keep nurturing your growth and staying open to possibilities, you're exactly where you need to be.

September 16th

"Good listeners, like precious gems, are to be treasured."

— Walter Anderson

I really connect with this quote from Walter Anderson. It reminds me of how rare and valuable truly good listeners have become in our fast-paced world, where everyone seems eager to speak but few take the time to genuinely listen.

Think about those moments when someone really listened to you – not just waiting for their turn to talk, but truly hearing you. It makes you feel seen, understood, valued. That's why Anderson compares good listeners to precious gems – they bring light and value to our lives in ways that are hard to measure but deeply felt.

Here's a simple way to put this wisdom into practice today: In your next conversation, try this technique I call "the pause." When someone finishes speaking, take a brief moment – maybe 2-3 seconds – before responding. Use that pause to really absorb what they've said rather than jumping in with your thoughts. You'll be amazed at how this tiny change can deepen your connections and help others feel truly heard. Plus, you might be surprised by how much more you learn and understand when you're not busy planning your next response.

Remember, becoming a better listener isn't just a gift to others – it's also a gift to yourself. The insights and connections you gain through deep listening can bring unexpected richness to your own life.

September 17th

"The desire to be loved is the last illusion. Give it up and you will be free."

— Margaret Atwood

This is such a profound observation by Atwood that cuts right to the core of human desire and suffering. There's something deeply paradoxical about our pursuit of love – the more desperately we chase it, the more it seems to elude us.

When Atwood calls it "the last illusion," she's touching on how this desire can become a prison of sorts. We often build our entire lives around being loved – seeking approval, moulding ourselves to others' expectations, fearing rejection. It's usually the last attachment we're willing to let go of, even after we've seen through other illusions in life.

Here's a practical thought for today: Try spending just one hour making choices without considering what others will think or how it will affect whether they love you. Maybe it's ordering what you truly want for lunch rather than what seems sophisticated, wearing something that makes you feel good regardless of others' opinions, or expressing an honest view even if it might not be popular. Notice how different it feels to act from this place of freedom rather than from a place of seeking love and approval.

The irony, of course, is that when we stop desperately needing to be loved, we often become more authentic and centred – and paradoxically, more lovable. But that's not the goal anymore, and that's exactly what makes it powerful.

September 18th

"When all else fails, go hiking."

— T.J. Burr

I love the simplicity and wisdom in this quote. It's fascinating how Burr captures something so profound in such a straightforward statement. When life gets complicated, nature has this remarkable way of helping us reset and find clarity.

I've noticed that there's something almost magical about how putting one foot in front of the other on a trail can untangle the knots in our minds. Maybe it's the rhythm of walking, the fresh air, or just the way nature has of making our "big problems" feel smaller against the backdrop of ancient trees or vast horizons.

Here's a practical suggestion for today: Even if you can't go on a full-blown hike, try taking a 15-minute walk somewhere with a bit of nature – maybe a local park or just a tree-lined street. Leave your phone in your pocket (or better yet, at home), and let your mind wander as your feet move. Notice how the simple act of moving through open space can shift your perspective on whatever's troubling you.

Remember, the quote isn't just about hiking – it's about returning to basics when things get overwhelming. Sometimes the simplest solutions are the most powerful, and few things are simpler than putting one foot in front of the other in the open air.

September 19th

"If you stay humble and keep your humility embedded in your behaviour then no circumstances can erode your core. You will keep on shining evermore."

— Bhuwan Thapaliya

This quote really speaks to a timeless truth about personal strength and character. What I find particularly meaningful here is how Thapaliya connects humility not just to being modest, but to having an unshakeable core – it's like building your house on solid rock rather than shifting sand. Think about how humble people you know handle both success and failure. They usually maintain their balance because their sense of self isn't tied to external achievements or others' opinions. There's incredible freedom and strength in that stability.

Here's a practical way to cultivate this kind of grounded humility today: When something good happens – maybe a compliment or an achievement – try responding with genuine gratitude while acknowledging the factors and people that helped make it possible. Instead of saying "Thanks, I worked hard on this," try "Thanks, I learned so much from working with the team on this." Notice how this slight shift in perspective helps you stay connected to the bigger picture.

And perhaps most beautifully, as Thapaliya suggests, when we approach life this way, our light actually shines brighter – not because we're trying to outshine others, but because we're steady and authentic in who we are. That kind of inner stability has a way of naturally radiating outward.

September 20th

"To forgive is to refuse to contaminate the future with the errors of the past."

— Craig D. Lounsbrough

This is such a powerful reframing of forgiveness that really gets to the heart of why it matters. Most of us tend to think of forgiveness as something we do for others, but Lounsbrough reveals it as an act of self-preservation and wisdom. I love how he uses the word "contaminate" – it perfectly captures how holding onto past hurts can poison our present and future moments. It's like carrying around a toxic substance that affects everything we touch, every new relationship, every fresh opportunity.

Here's something practical you could try today: Think of a small grudge or resentment you're holding – maybe something minor like a colleague who took credit for your work or a friend who forgot an important date. Now imagine this grudge as a dark cloud that's casting a shadow not just on that person, but on all your future interactions with others in similar situations. Ask yourself: "Am I willing to let this past event colour all my future experiences?"

The real power of forgiveness isn't in excusing what happened – it's in choosing to keep your future clear and open, free from the shadows of old wounds. It's about giving yourself permission to experience new people and situations with fresh eyes, unburdened by past disappointments. Remember, forgiveness doesn't mean what happened was okay – it just means you're choosing not to let it define what happens next.

September 21st

"The only journey is the one within."

— Rainer Maria Rilke

What a beautifully profound observation by Rilke. When I reflect on this quote, I see how he's captured something essential about the human experience – that beneath all our external travels and achievements, the most significant journey is the one we take in understanding ourselves.

It's fascinating how we often look outward for fulfilment – seeking new places, experiences, relationships – when the most transformative territory lies within our own hearts and minds. All those external journeys, while valuable, are really just different paths leading us back to ourselves.

Here's something you might try today: Take 10 minutes of genuine solitude (not just being alone with your phone). Find a quiet spot and check in with yourself – not just about what you're doing or planning, but about how you're evolving as a person. What internal landscapes have you been avoiding exploring? What parts of yourself have you yet to understand or accept? Sometimes just acknowledging these inner territories can be the first step in a profound internal journey.

The beauty of this inner journey is that it's always available to us, regardless of our circumstances. We don't need special equipment or tickets – just the courage to look inward with honesty and compassion. And unlike external journeys, this one never really ends; it just keeps revealing new depths and dimensions of who we are.

September 22nd

"Life has taught me that you can't control someone's loyalty. No matter how good you are to them, doesn't mean they'll treat you the same. No matter how much they mean to you, doesn't mean they'll value you the same. Sometimes the people you love the most, turn out to be the people you can trust the least."

— Unknown

This quote touches on one of life's hardest but most important lessons about relationships and expectations. There's a deep wisdom here about accepting what we can and cannot control in our connections with others.

It's interesting how we often approach relationships like an equation: if we give loyalty, kindness, and value, we expect the same in return. But human hearts don't work like mathematical formulas. Each person carries their own wounds, fears, and capabilities for connection that have nothing to do with how well we treat them.

Here's something practical to consider today: Look at one relationship that's causing you pain because of unmet expectations. Instead of focusing on what you deserve from them, try shifting your energy to what you can control – your own boundaries and choices. Ask yourself: "Am I maintaining this relationship in a way that honours both their freedom to be who they are AND my need for genuine, reciprocal connection?"

The real strength comes not from trying to ensure others' loyalty, but from being wise about where we invest our trust and energy. Sometimes the most loving thing we can do – both for ourselves and others – is to accept that not everyone can or will meet us at the level of commitment we offer, and that's okay. It doesn't diminish the value of what we gave; it just means we need to be more discerning about where we place our trust going forward.

Remember, recognising this truth isn't cynical – it's actually freeing. It allows us to love and give authentically while maintaining healthy boundaries that protect our well-being.

September 23rd

"Some wounds never vanish. Yet little by little I learned to love my life."

— Mary Oliver

This quote by Mary Oliver touches something so deep and real about healing. There's profound wisdom in how she acknowledges both the permanence of certain wounds and our capacity to find joy despite them – even because of them. I find it especially moving how she uses the phrase "little by little." It's such an honest way to describe how we make peace with our scars. There's no dramatic moment of transformation, no sudden leap to acceptance. Instead, it's a gradual process, like learning to walk with a limp or finding beauty in broken pottery mended with gold.

Here's a gentle suggestion for today: Take a moment to acknowledge one of your wounds – not to try to fix it or make it disappear, but simply to recognise how you've learned to carry it. Maybe even notice one small way you've learned to love your life despite (or even through) this wound. It could be as simple as appreciating your morning coffee more deeply because you know what it means to struggle, or feeling greater compassion for others because of what you've endured.

Oliver's words remind us that healing isn't always about becoming "whole" again in the way we once were. Sometimes it's about learning to embrace life as it is, scars and all, and discovering that our capacity for joy hasn't been diminished by our wounds – it's been deepened by them.

September 24th

"The problem with people is they forget that most of the time it's the small things that count."

— Jennifer Niven

This observation by Niven really hits home, especially in our world of big gestures and grand moments. It reminds me of how we often overlook the quiet power of small kindnesses and everyday moments while chasing after bigger, more dramatic experiences. Think about the times that really touched your heart – often it's not the expensive gifts or elaborate events, but the small, thoughtful gestures. Maybe it was someone remembering how you like your coffee, a friend sending a text just to check in, or a partner quietly doing a chore they know you hate.

Here's a simple way to put this wisdom into practice today: Choose three tiny acts of mindfulness or kindness. Maybe leave a sticky note of encouragement on a coworker's desk, send a specific thank-you text mentioning something you appreciate about someone, or simply take a moment to really listen when someone speaks instead of planning your response. These might seem insignificant, but they're the threads that weave the fabric of our relationships and daily happiness.

The beauty of focusing on small things is that they're always available to us. We don't need special occasions or resources – just attention and intention. And often, it's these small moments of connection and awareness that build into something far more meaningful than any grand gesture could achieve.

September 25th

"We increasingly find ourselves at the mercy of our devices."

— Tony Reinke

This quote from Reinke really captures something crucial about our modern predicament. I'ts fascinating how we've shifted from being the users of our technology to sometimes feeling like we're being used by it.

I appreciate how Reinke uses the word "mercy" here – it perfectly captures that feeling of powerlessness many of us experience when we realise we've just spent an hour scrolling without meaning to, or when we feel that reflexive urge to check our phones even in the middle of important moments with loved ones.

Here's a practical suggestion for today: Try creating one intentional "device-free zone" in your life. It could be as simple as putting your phone in another room during dinner, or not checking it for the first hour after you wake up. Notice how this small act of reclaiming control might shift your relationship with your devices. Pay attention to any initial discomfort – that's often a sign of how dependent we've become.

The key isn't to demonise technology – after all, these tools bring incredible benefits to our lives. Instead, it's about consciously shifting from being at their mercy to being their mindful master. Sometimes just recognising our dependence is the first step towards regaining our agency.

September 26th

"You will find out who you are not a thousand times, before you ever discover who you are."

— William Chapman

This quote beautifully captures something I've observed so many times in life's journey. It's a gentle reminder that self-discovery is often more about elimination than immediate revelation. Think about it - when you try something new and realise "this isn't quite me," that's not a failure. It's actually a valuable piece of your personal puzzle.

Here's a practical suggestion for today: Take a moment to reflect on something you once thought defined you, but later realised wasn't truly aligned with who you are. Maybe it was a career path, a relationship style, or even just a hobby you thought you should love but didn't. Instead of viewing these past "misses" as mistakes, try seeing them as important stepping stones that helped clarify who you really are.

You could even start a simple "Not Me" journal entry today. Write down one thing you've learned about yourself through the process of elimination - something you've discovered isn't authentic to who you are. This kind of self-awareness is incredibly powerful because each "no" brings you closer to your genuine "yes." Remember, feeling lost or unsure isn't a sign you're doing life wrong - it's often evidence you're doing the important work of finding your true self. Every "this isn't me" moment is actually a gift of clarity, leading you closer to who you really are.

September 27th

"Maybe today is that day. The day you finally do that thing you have been wanting to do for years, that thing you know you can do but you never do it, today can be that day."

— Gary Hardy

Here I am gently challenging that gap between our potential and our action – that space where so many of our dreams live. There's something both encouraging and quietly urgent in his words, isn't there? He's not demanding action, but rather opening a door of possibility. It's interesting how we often carry these dreams around for years, like seeds we never quite get around to planting. Sometimes we wait for the 'perfect' moment, forgetting that today – this ordinary, imperfect day – could be exactly the right time to begin.

Here's a practical thought for right now: Take a moment to bring to mind that one thing you've been carrying around – maybe it's writing that first page of your book, making that phone call you've been avoiding, or finally signing up for that class. Now, instead of thinking about the whole journey ahead, just focus on the smallest possible first step you could take in the next hour. Not tomorrow, not next week – today.

Remember, you don't need to complete the entire journey today. You just need to take that first step that transforms "someday" into "day one." Sometimes the simple act of beginning can break the spell of perpetual postponement. So what's that thing for you? What small step could you take today that your future self would thank you for?

September 28th

"May you find somebody who always knows how to make your soul smile."

— Mark Anthony

This quote really touches on something beautiful about human connection. It's not just about finding someone who makes you laugh or keeps you entertained - it's about finding that person who can reach your soul, who understands you at a deeper level and brings out your inner light.

But here's a thought for today: Instead of just waiting to find that special someone, why not start by being that person for others? Try this - reach out to someone you care about today and do something specific that speaks to their soul. Maybe it's sending a thoughtful message remembering something important to them, or asking about that project they're passionate about.

When we learn to make others' souls smile, we often discover that our own souls begin to smile too, and we become the kind of person who naturally attracts deeper, more meaningful connections.

It's amazing how shifting our focus from receiving to giving can transform both our relationships and our daily experience of life. Plus, it helps us recognise and appreciate those soul-brightening qualities in others when we encounter them.

September 29th

"Sometimes the best goal you can set is just to get out of bed every day. If you can succeed at this, then other things become possible."

— Cynthia Patterson

This quote really hits home, especially for those going through tough times. We often put so much pressure on ourselves to achieve big things, but sometimes life requires us to step back and recognise that the smallest victories can be the most meaningful.

Getting out of bed might seem simple to some, but for anyone dealing with depression, grief, burnout, or overwhelming challenges, it can feel like climbing a mountain. And that's perfectly okay. What Patterson captures here is a profound truth about healing and progress: it starts with these basic acts of showing up for ourselves.

For today, if you're struggling, try this: instead of overwhelming yourself with a long to-do list, make getting out of bed your win. Celebrate it. And if you're in a good place right now, keep this perspective in your back pocket – it's a gentle reminder to be kind to yourself during future difficult times. Remember that sometimes the bravest thing we can do is simply begin again, one morning at a time. Each time you get up, you're creating possibility, and that's incredibly powerful.

Think of it like building a house – you need a foundation before you can put up the walls and roof. Getting out of bed is that foundation. Everything else can follow, but it all starts with that first step.

September 30th

"No matter what has happened in your lives, or how different you both are, sisters can always be there for each other and make sure neither of them ever feel alone. They are in a unique position of having a shared history which can help them understand each other more than most."

— Gary Hardy

This really speaks to the unique bond between sisters, doesn't it? There's something incredibly powerful about having someone who's witnessed your life from the beginning - who knows all the family stories, remembers how the holiday dinners really went, and understands exactly why certain things make you laugh or cry. Sisters can be there for each other despite their differences or past conflicts. It's not about being perfect all the time - it's about that deep, underlying connection that remains even when life gets messy.

Here's a practical thought for today: If you have a sister, consider sending her a message or giving her a call, not about anything specific, but just to share a memory that only she would understand. Maybe it's about that ridiculous Halloween costume you both tried to make, or that time you covered for each other when things went wrong. These shared moments, even the small ones, are like secret threads that keep you connected.

Even if you've drifted apart or have had your differences, that shared history is always there as a foundation to rebuild upon. Sometimes just reaching out with "Remember when..." can open doors that seemed long closed.

October 1st

"In October any wonderful unexpected thing might be possible."

— Elizabeth George Speare

This quote captures something magical about October - that sense of possibility that hangs in the autumn air. I love how it speaks to both the literal and metaphorical changes that come with this time of year. The shifting colours, the cooling air, the way the world seems to transform itself - it all creates this atmosphere where anything feels possible.

For today, I'd encourage embracing this "October mindset" in a specific way: Choose one area of your life where you've been stuck in routine thinking and consciously open yourself to unexpected possibilities. Reach out to someone you've lost touch with, or start that project you've been hesitating about. October's energy of transformation gives us permission to believe in wonderful unexpected things.

What makes this quote particularly powerful is how it reminds us that magic and possibility often come with changes in season - both in nature and in our lives. Sometimes all we need is that gentle reminder that wonderful unexpected things aren't just possible, they're practically invited during times of transition.

Have you ever noticed how certain seasons seem to carry their own special kind of possibility?

October 2nd

"Never tell your problems to anyone...20% don't care and the other 80% are glad you have them."

— Lou Holtz

While I understand the cynical wisdom Lou Holtz is trying to share here, I'd like to offer a more nuanced perspective. Yes, it's true that not everyone we meet will have our best interests at heart, and we should be thoughtful about who we trust with our vulnerabilities. But this quote might push people towards harmful isolation if taken too literally.

Here's a more balanced approach for today: Instead of never sharing your problems, focus on being selective about who you confide in. Try to identify one or two people in your life who have consistently shown up for you, who listen without judgement, and who genuinely care about your wellbeing. These might be family members, close friends, or mental health professionals.

Think of it like having a valuable piece of jewellery - you wouldn't show it to everyone you meet, but you also wouldn't lock it away forever where no one can see it. You choose carefully who to share it with.

The reality is that while some people might be indifferent or even take satisfaction in others' struggles, there are also many compassionate individuals who genuinely want to help. Sometimes sharing our problems isn't just about finding solutions - it's about feeling less alone in our challenges. The key is discernment, not total isolation.

October 3rd

"The truth of love lives in the choices made."

— Unknown

This is such a profound insight about the real nature of love. What strikes me about this quote is how it cuts through all the flowery sentiments and romantic declarations to focus on what truly matters - our actions and choices.

It's easy to say "I love you" or feel intense emotions, but love reveals itself most truthfully in those daily decisions we make. It's choosing to listen when we're tired, showing up when it's inconvenient, or staying present during difficult times. It's also in the small choices - making someone's coffee just the way they like it, remembering to ask about something that matters to them, or choosing patience when it would be easier to react.

For today, I'd suggest something practical: Pay attention to the choices you make in your relationships, especially the small ones. Maybe choose to put your phone down and really listen when someone's talking, or take a moment to do something thoughtful for someone you care about without being asked. These seemingly minor decisions are actually the building blocks of genuine love.

Remember, love isn't just a feeling that happens to us - it's an active choice we make over and over again. Each choice is like adding another brick to the foundation of a relationship, making it stronger and more reliable over time.

October 4th

"But don't forget who you really are. And I'm not talking about your so-called real name. All names are made up by someone else, even the one your parents gave you. You know who you really are. When you're alone at night, looking up at the stars, or maybe lying in your bed in total darkness, you know that nameless person inside you."

— Louis Sachar

This quote really touches on something profound about our inner identity - that core self that exists beneath all the labels, roles, and names we accumulate throughout life. It's fascinating how we all have this private inner world that's so real to us, yet often hard to express to others.

For today, I'd encourage you to spend a few minutes in quiet solitude - maybe right before bed or early in the morning - and just be with that nameless person Sachar describes. No phones, no distractions, no need to be anyone's parent, employee, partner, or friend. Just you, being with yourself. You might be surprised what you discover.

Think about times when you've felt most authentically yourself. Often it's not in the big moments where we're performing for others, but in those quiet, private moments - when we're lost in creating something we love, or feeling deeply moved by music, or experiencing a moment of perfect peace in nature. That's often when we touch that true self that exists beyond all the names and roles we carry.

This practice of connecting with our core self isn't just philosophical - it can help us make better decisions, set boundaries that align with our values, and feel more grounded in our daily lives. When we know who we are at our centre, it becomes easier to navigate all the external pressures and expectations that life throws at us.

October 5th

"The difference between school and life? In school, you're taught a lesson and then given a test. In life, you're given a test that teaches you a lesson."

— Tom Bodett

This quote really captures something profound about how life's learning process works. In school, everything feels neat and orderly - you study, prepare, and know exactly when the test is coming. But life? Life throws pop quizzes at us when we least expect them, and often in subjects we didn't even know we needed to learn about.

Here's a thought for today: Instead of dreading or resisting the unexpected challenges that come your way, try to approach them with curiosity. Ask yourself, "What might this situation be trying to teach me?" Maybe that difficult conversation with a colleague isn't just an obstacle to get through, but a lesson in communication or boundary-setting. Perhaps that project that's not going as planned is teaching you something valuable about adaptability or resilience.

Think of it like being in a massive open-world classroom where every experience - good or challenging - is part of the curriculum. The beauty of this perspective is that it turns setbacks into stepping stones. When we view life's tests as lessons in disguise, we stop seeing ourselves as failing and start seeing ourselves as learning and growing.

Remember, unlike school tests, life's lessons often don't reveal their full meaning until much later. That's okay - sometimes the most valuable insights take time to sink in. The key is staying open to the learning, even when (especially when) we didn't sign up for the class.

October 6th

"The soul that gives thanks can find comfort in everything; the soul that complains can find comfort in nothing."

— Hannah Whitall Smith

This quote really cuts to the heart of how our perspective shapes our entire experience of life. It's not suggesting we should ignore difficulties or force positivity, but rather pointing to a deeper truth about gratitude's power to transform our inner landscape.

Here's something practical to try today: When you encounter your next challenge or discomfort (even a small one like traffic or a minor inconvenience), pause for a moment. Instead of immediately reacting with complaint, try to find just one thing to be thankful for in that situation. Maybe the traffic gives you time to listen to your favourite podcast, or maybe that annoying task at work is helping you develop new skills.

Think of it like wearing different pairs of glasses. The lens of complaint makes everything look darker and more difficult, while the lens of gratitude helps us spot the hidden gifts in our circumstances. It's not about denying reality - it's about choosing which aspects of reality we focus on.

This shift isn't always easy, and it takes practice. But starting with small moments of gratitude can gradually reshape how we experience everything - from life's big challenges to its everyday moments. The beautiful thing is that the more we practice finding things to be thankful for, the more naturally our minds begin to spot them, creating a kind of positive feedback loop that can lift our entire mood and outlook.

October 7th

"Perhaps too much of everything is as bad as too little."

— Edna Ferber

This seemingly simple quote carries such deep wisdom about balance in life. We often think "more is better" - more money, more success, more possessions, more activities - but Ferber touches on something really crucial here about the nature of excess.

For today, try this: Look at one area of your life where you might be operating in extremes. Maybe you're working too many hours, spending too much time on social media, being too rigid with your exercise routine, or even being too giving to others at the expense of yourself. Pick just one area and ask yourself: "What would 'enough' look like here?"

Think of it like seasoning a meal - too little salt and the food is bland, too much and it's inedible. The magic lies in finding that sweet spot. Sometimes cutting back on something, even something good, can actually enrich our lives. It's counterintuitive, but often true.

The real art is in finding your personal balance point. What's "too much" for one person might be "too little" for another. The key is being honest with yourself about when abundance starts becoming excess in your own life, and having the wisdom to adjust accordingly.

October 8th

"Because a song can take you back instantly to a moment, or a place, or even a person. No matter what else has changed in you or the world, that one song stays the same, just like that moment. Which is pretty amazing, when you actually think about it."

— Sarah Dessen

This quote beautifully captures the almost magical power of music in our lives. It's fascinating how a few notes can act like a time machine, instantly transporting us back to specific moments with all their emotions and sensations intact.

Here's something meaningful you could try today: Take a moment to intentionally listen to a song that holds special meaning for you. Not as background music while you work or drive, but sitting quietly and really experiencing it. Notice how it makes you feel, what memories it brings up, who it makes you think of. Maybe it's the song that played during your first dance, or one that got you through a tough time, or simply reminds you of driving around with friends in summer.

Think of these songs like emotional photographs - they capture not just the moment, but the feeling of that moment. Unlike actual photos, though, they can trigger all our senses: the smells, the feelings, the atmosphere of that time. It's remarkable how a three-minute song can hold such a complete snapshot of who we were and what we felt at a particular point in our lives.

This preservation of moments through music gives us something precious - a way to reconnect with parts of ourselves and our history that might otherwise fade with time. It's like having an emotional anchor that keeps certain experiences vivid and accessible, no matter how much time passes or how much we change.

October 9th

"About all you can do in life is be who you are. Some people will love you for you. Most will love you for what you can do for them, and some won't like you at all."

— Rita Mae Brown

I really appreciate how this quote cuts through the endless self-help advice about changing ourselves to be more likeable or successful. It offers something much more valuable: permission to be authentic and a clear-eyed view of how others will respond to that authenticity.

Here's a thought for today: Instead of spending energy trying to make everyone like you (which is exhausting and impossible), try focusing on being more genuinely yourself in one small situation. Maybe it's sharing your real opinion in a meeting, saying "no" to something you don't want to do, or expressing an interest you usually keep hidden. Notice how it feels to drop that mask, even briefly.

Think of it like having a garden. You can't control which bees will be attracted to which flowers - you can only focus on growing healthy plants. Similarly, you can't control how others respond to you - you can only focus on being authentic and letting the right people naturally gravitate towards that authenticity.

The beauty of this approach is that while it might seem scary at first, it's actually deeply liberating. When we accept that some people won't like us no matter what we do, it frees us from the exhausting task of trying to please everyone.

And when we find those people who love us for who we really are - not for what we can do for them - those relationships tend to be far more fulfilling than any we could build on a foundation of pretence.

October 10th

"We're so engaged in doing things to achieve purposes of outer value that we forget that the inner value, the rapture that is associated with being alive, is what it's all about."

— Joseph Campbell

This Campbell quote really speaks to something I've noticed in how many of us live today. We get so caught up in chasing external markers of success - the next promotion, a bigger house, more followers on social media - that we can lose touch with the simple joy of being present in our own lives.

Think about children playing - they're completely absorbed in the moment, finding delight in simple things like jumping in puddles or watching ants march across the sidewalk. Somewhere along the way, many of us traded that natural state of wonder for an endless checklist of goals and achievements.

Here's something practical you could try today: Set aside just 10 minutes to do something solely because it brings you joy. Maybe it's listening to your favourite song with your eyes closed, taking a slow walk and really noticing the world around you, or simply sitting quietly with a cup of tea. Don't document it for social media, don't try to make it "productive" - just experience it fully for your own satisfaction.

The beauty of being alive isn't in what we accomplish, but in how deeply we can experience and appreciate each moment we're given. When we reconnect with that inner sense of wonder and aliveness, the external achievements often flow more naturally anyway.

October 11th

"Resting in the breath, the inward breath and the outward breath, I am held in present moment awareness."

— Elisabeth Blaikie

This quote beautifully captures one of the most powerful yet simple tools we have for finding peace and presence - our own breath. When you think about it, it's remarkable that our most basic life-sustaining function can also be our anchor to the present moment.

What strikes me most about Blaikie's words is how they describe breath as something that "holds" us. It's not just about breathing - it's about allowing ourselves to be cradled by this natural rhythm that's always with us, always flowing, always connecting us to now.

Here's a gentle suggestion for today: Next time you're feeling scattered, overwhelmed, or just disconnected, try this for just 30 seconds. Stop whatever you're doing and simply notice your breath. Don't try to change it or control it - just feel the sensation of breathing in, and breathing out. Notice how your body moves with each breath. It's amazing how just this brief moment of attention can bring you back to yourself and clear your mind.

This isn't about perfect meditation or achieving some special state - it's about remembering that you always have this tool available to you, this way of coming home to the present moment, no matter where you are or what's happening around you.

October 12th

"If you're reading this...Congratulations, you're alive. If that's not something to smile about, then I don't know what is."

— Chad Sugg

I love the beautiful simplicity of this quote - it's like a gentle wake-up call to one of the most incredible gifts we often take for granted. Just being here, breathing, experiencing this moment... it's actually quite extraordinary when you really stop to think about it.

You know what's amazing? Right now, your heart is beating, your lungs are working, billions of cells in your body are orchestrating an incredible symphony of life - and most of the time we're too busy worrying about deadlines or scrolling through our phones to even notice.

Here's a tiny practice for today: When you brush your teeth tonight, take just a moment to look in the mirror and give yourself a genuine smile. Not because everything's perfect, but simply because you're here, alive, experiencing this wild and wonderful adventure called life. It might feel a bit silly at first, but there's something powerful about acknowledging the sheer miracle of your existence.

Sometimes we get so caught up waiting for big reasons to be happy that we miss the most fundamental one - we're alive, and that alone is pretty remarkable. Every single breath is a fresh opportunity, every heartbeat a reminder that we get to be here, now, experiencing this world in all its complexity and beauty.

October 13th

"Show respect to people who don't even deserve it; not as a reflection of their character, but as a reflection of yours."

— Dave Willis

This quote touches on something profound about personal growth and dignity. It reminds me of how true strength often shows itself in the most challenging moments - not when it's easy to be kind, but when it's difficult.

Think about it - when someone is difficult or disrespectful, our natural instinct might be to mirror their behaviour. But choosing to remain respectful isn't about validating their actions; it's about staying true to our own values. It's like keeping your torch lit even when walking through darkness.

Here's a practical way to put this into action today: When you encounter someone who tests your patience - maybe a rude cashier, an aggressive driver, or a difficult coworker - challenge yourself to respond with calm respect. Not because they've earned it, but because that's who you choose to be. Notice how this choice affects not just the interaction, but how you feel about yourself afterward.

Remember, being respectful doesn't mean being a doormat or accepting mistreatment. It's about handling challenging situations with dignity and grace, which often says more about your character than any accomplishment could. Sometimes, maintaining your own standards of behaviour, especially when others don't, can be one of the most powerful forms of self-respect.

October 14th

"Living a meaningful life is not being financially wealthy, being in the limelight and having thousands of followers. It's about being authentic, showing humility, vulnerability and making a real difference to the lives of others."

— Gary Hardy

This resonates deeply with how our culture often confuses external success with genuine fulfilment. It captures something vital about what truly nourishes the human spirit - it's not about the metrics we can measure or display, but about the authentic connections and impact we create.

In my experience working with people, those who find the deepest satisfaction in life are rarely the ones with the most impressive social media profiles or the biggest bank accounts. They're often the ones who've learned to drop their masks, to be real with themselves and others, to admit when they're struggling, and to reach out and help others along the way.

Here's a small challenge for today: Try sharing something genuine about yourself with someone - maybe a fear you're dealing with, a dream you haven't told anyone about, or even just admitting that you don't have everything figured out. This kind of authentic connection, even in a small moment, often creates ripples of positive impact we might never even see.

The beautiful thing about making a difference in others' lives is that it doesn't require grand gestures or public recognition. It might be as simple as truly listening to someone who's struggling, offering genuine encouragement, or helping in a way that nobody else will ever know about. These moments, though they'll never show up on a resume or social media feed, are what weave the real fabric of a meaningful life.

October 15th

"It's okay to be broken - just make sure that you won't lose a piece of yourself while healing."

— Laura Chouette

This is such a tender and wise perspective on healing. I find it particularly meaningful how Chouette acknowledges both the reality of being broken and the importance of mindful healing. It's like she's giving us permission to be wounded while also gently warning us about a pitfall many people fall into during recovery.

Sometimes in our rush to heal, to "get better," to move past pain, we can try to cut away or deny parts of ourselves that we think caused our suffering. But often those very parts - our sensitivity, our ability to love deeply, our willingness to be vulnerable - are also sources of our strength and humanity.

Here's something you might try today if you're going through a difficult time: Take a moment to write down one quality or aspect of yourself that feels painful right now, but that you know deep down is also a source of beauty or strength. Maybe it's your big heart that got broken, your trust that was betrayed, or your dreams that didn't work out. Instead of trying to harden that part of yourself, can you hold it gently, acknowledging both its hurt and its value?

Remember, healing isn't about becoming someone new - it's about learning to carry your experiences with more wisdom and self-compassion. The goal isn't to erase the cracks, but to understand how they've made you more complete, more understanding, more authentically you.

October 16th

"Say no to everything until you arrive at a definitive yes!"

— Swati Sharma

I find this quote particularly powerful because it flips our usual approach to decision-making on its head. Many of us default to "yes" out of obligation, fear of missing out, or a desire to please others - but Sharma suggests something much more intentional.

Think of it like being a curator of your own life. The best curators don't fill a gallery with every piece of art they see - they carefully select works that align with their vision. When you start with "no" as your default, each "yes" becomes a conscious choice rather than a habitual response.

Here's a practical way to apply this today: The next time someone asks you to commit to something - whether it's a social engagement, a project, or even a small favour - pause before automatically saying yes. Ask yourself: Does this align with my values and priorities? Does it energise me or drain me? Will saying yes to this mean saying no to something more important?

This isn't about becoming rigid or closed off - it's about being intentional with your time and energy. A well-chosen "yes" carries more power and commitment than a dozen half-hearted ones. And when you do say yes, you can give that commitment your full presence and enthusiasm, knowing it's something you truly want to do.

Remember, every "yes" you give is automatically a "no" to something else - your time and energy are finite resources. Making them count is one of the most powerful forms of self-respect.

October 17th

"Burnout will have you taking a pause for weeks, months, and even years. Take care of yourself and prioritise your overall needs. You will actually have better results after some much-needed time of relaxation. If you don't take this more seriously, you can run the risk of losing passion for something you once loved. And it takes an immensity of work to get the urge back."

— Robin S. Baker

This quote really hits home because it addresses something we often overlook until it's too late - the true cost of pushing ourselves too hard. Baker captures something crucial here: burnout isn't just feeling tired; it can fundamentally change our relationship with work we once loved.

I've seen this pattern play out so many times - people ignore the early warning signs, thinking they can push through just a little longer, only to find themselves completely depleted and needing much more recovery time than if they'd paused earlier. It's like continuing to drive a car with the check engine light on - eventually, you're looking at major repairs instead of simple maintenance.

Here's something practical you could do today: Take 10 minutes to do an honest check-in with yourself. Look for those subtle signs of approaching burnout - are you feeling less excited about things you usually enjoy? Having trouble sleeping? Finding yourself more irritable? Instead of pushing these signals aside, treat them as valuable information from your body and mind.

Then, schedule one small act of recovery for this week. Maybe it's blocking off a full evening with no work emails, taking a long walk, or saying no to an optional commitment that's been draining you. Think of it as preventive maintenance for your well-being - much easier than having to rebuild from complete exhaustion.

Remember, passion isn't an infinite resource that we can keep drawing from without replenishment. Just like a garden needs periods of rest between harvests, our creative and emotional energy needs time to regenerate. Taking care of yourself isn't a luxury - it's essential maintenance for sustainable success.

October 18th

"No matter how honestly you open up to someone, there are still things you cannot reveal."

— Haruki Murakami

This Murakami quote touches on something deeply true about human connection and self-knowledge. It's fascinating how even in our most intimate relationships, there remain parts of ourselves that are either too complex to express or perhaps not fully understood even by us. I think sometimes we put pressure on ourselves to be completely transparent in our close relationships, as if total disclosure equals authentic connection. But there's a kind of wisdom in recognising that some parts of our inner landscape are meant to remain private - not out of deception, but as part of the natural mystery of being human.

Here's a gentle suggestion for today: Practice being comfortable with this reality. When you're sharing something important with someone, notice if you feel that subtle pressure to explain everything perfectly or reveal every aspect. Try allowing yourself to share what feels natural while respecting those spaces within yourself that aren't ready or meant to be shared. It's not about holding back - it's about honouring the complexity of your inner world.

The beauty of deep relationships isn't in knowing everything about each other, but in creating a space where we can be authentic while respecting the natural boundaries of our individual experiences. Sometimes, acknowledging what cannot be fully shared is just as intimate as sharing itself.

October 19th

"To hide feelings when you are near crying is the secret of dignity."

— Dejan Stojanovic

I have a slightly different take on this quote that I'd like to share. While Stojanovic's words capture something powerful about human resilience and composure, I believe there's also profound dignity in allowing ourselves to be vulnerable when we need to be.

Think about someone you deeply respect who has allowed themselves to cry in front of you. Did they lose their dignity? Often, it's quite the opposite - there's something incredibly powerful and brave about being authentic with our emotions, about trusting others enough to let them see our raw humanity.

Here's a gentle suggestion for today: If you find yourself holding back tears in a situation where it's actually safe to express them, ask yourself what you're protecting. Sometimes maintaining composure is absolutely necessary - in a professional setting or when we need to be strong for others. But in private moments or with trusted loved ones, allowing yourself to fully feel and express emotion can be an act of self-respect rather than a loss of dignity.

The real secret of dignity might not be in hiding our feelings, but in knowing when it's appropriate to show them and having the courage to do so. After all, our tears often come from the same place as our deepest compassion, our strongest loves, and our most profound connections to what matters in life.

October 20th

"See the world as it is, not as you wish it would be."

— E. Lockhart

This quote really cuts through to something essential about living wisely and effectively. It reminds me of how often we can get caught between reality and our expectations, causing ourselves unnecessary suffering.

You know what's interesting? Our tendency to see the world as we wish it to be isn't always obvious to us. It shows up in small ways - like expecting people to react the way we would, or assuming things "should" work out a certain way because that seems most logical to us.

Here's a practical way to work with this wisdom today: Pick one situation in your life that's causing you frustration. It might be a relationship, a work situation, or even something as simple as your daily commute. Take a moment to identify the gap between how you wish it was and how it actually is. What would change if you fully accepted the reality of this situation, even if just for today? Sometimes, seeing things clearly is the first step to either making effective changes or finding peace with what is.

This isn't about giving up on improving things or settling for less. Rather, it's about starting from an honest place. When we see things as they truly are, we can respond with wisdom rather than react from wishful thinking. It's like trying to read a map - you can only find your way forward if you're clear about where you actually are, not where you wish you were.

October 21st

"If you would be a real seeker after truth, it is necessary that at least once in your life you doubt, as far as possible, all things."

— Rene Descartes

This Descartes quote touches on something profound about genuine wisdom and personal growth. There's a special kind of courage required to pause and question our most deeply held beliefs and assumptions - the things we've perhaps never even thought to examine.

Think about how many of our views about life, success, relationships, or even ourselves we've inherited from others or absorbed from our environment without really examining them. It's like we're living in a house someone else built, never checking if the foundation is solid.

Here's something transformative you might try today: Pick one belief you hold strongly - maybe about yourself, about how relationships should work, or about what makes a life successful. Then, just for a moment, hold it up to the light and ask yourself: "How do I know this is true? What if the opposite were true?" Don't try to reach any immediate conclusions - just sit with the questions.

The point isn't to demolish everything we believe, but to develop a more nuanced understanding of why we believe what we believe. When we dare to question deeply, we often emerge with either stronger convictions because we've tested them, or with new insights that better serve us.

Remember, doubting isn't about becoming cynical - it's about developing the intellectual honesty and courage to seek truth beyond our comfort zone. Some of the most profound certainties come after periods of genuine questioning.

October 22nd

"Acting like you don't care is not letting it go."

— Penelope Douglas

This quote really strikes at something I see people struggle with all the time. When we're hurt or disappointed, it's tempting to put on that "whatever, I don't care" mask. We might even convince ourselves that's what moving on looks like. But there's a world of difference between genuinely letting go and just pretending something doesn't affect us.

True letting go is about acknowledging our feelings, processing them, and then consciously choosing to move forward. Acting like we don't care? That's often just suppressing those emotions, where they'll likely resurface later in unexpected ways.

Here's something practical you could try today: When something bothers you, instead of immediately brushing it off with "I don't care," take a quiet moment to ask yourself, "What am I actually feeling right now?" Just name it - whether it's disappointment, anger, or hurt. You don't have to solve it immediately, but acknowledging it is the first step towards genuinely letting go. It's like opening a window in a stuffy room - sometimes just letting the air in is exactly what you need.

October 23rd

"You have not seen strength and courage before until you have witnessed a child battling a terminal illness."

— Gary Hardy

This quote strikes an even deeper chord knowing it comes from my personal experience as a father. The strength I witnessed in my two-year-old daughter battling leukaemia - that's the kind of courage that changes how we see the world forever. When you watch your own child face such an enormous challenge at such a tender age, it redefines everything you thought you knew about strength.

What's particularly moving is how these tiny warriors face their battles with a resilience that's both heartbreaking and inspiring. At two years old, my daughter shouldn't have had to know what it means to be that strong, yet she showed kind of courage that many adults would struggle to muster. She fought a battle that no one, let alone a toddler, should have to face - and she won.

Here's something meaningful we could all do today: Let's take a moment to appreciate our health or our children's health if we're fortunate enough to have it. And for those currently in the midst of similar battles - whether personally or supporting a loved one - remember that the strength shown by children like my daughter proves that incredible courage can come in the smallest packages. My daughter's victory over leukaemia is a powerful reminder that even in our darkest moments, hope and strength can prevail.

October 24th

"Let your attitude attract someone because beauty is not a lifetime asset."

— Papa Jack

You know what I love about this quote? It cuts through all the surface-level stuff and gets to what really matters in the long run. Sure, physical beauty can catch someone's eye, but it's your attitude - how you approach life, treat others, and carry yourself - that creates lasting connections and relationships.

Think about the people who've had the most positive impact in your life. Chances are, it wasn't their looks that made them special - it was their warmth, their kindness, their humour, or their inspiring outlook on life. These qualities don't fade with time; they often grow richer and more compelling.

Here's a simple way to put this wisdom into practice today: Pay attention to your reactions and responses in your interactions. When something frustrating happens, try to respond with patience instead of irritation. When you meet someone new, focus on being genuinely interested rather than trying to impress. These small shifts in attitude can totally change how people experience you - and more importantly, how you experience life.

Remember, your attitude is something you can actively cultivate and improve. Unlike physical beauty, it's an asset that's completely under your control and only gets better with intention and practice.

October 25th

"Most women outlive their spouses. Divorce remains at record rates. It's important for a woman to be able to control her finances."

— Maria Bartiromo

This is such an important and practical piece of wisdom that often gets overlooked. Financial independence isn't just about having your own money - it's about having the knowledge and confidence to manage it effectively, regardless of your relationship status.

The reality is that life can change in unexpected ways. Whether through divorce or becoming a widow, many women find themselves suddenly responsible for managing finances they may have previously delegated to their spouse. And even in healthy relationships, having financial literacy and autonomy strengthens both partners and the relationship itself.

Here's something tangible you could do today: Take a clear look at your financial picture. If you don't already have one, open your own bank account. Review your retirement accounts and make sure you understand how they work. If you share accounts with a spouse, ensure you have access to all passwords and know where important documents are kept. Even something as simple as reviewing last month's expenses can be a powerful first step towards financial empowerment. Think of financial literacy like learning a new language - it might feel overwhelming at first, but taking it one step at a time builds confidence and capability. And just like any other skill, the best time to start learning is now, before you actually need it.

October 26th

"Taking care of yourself isn't a luxury - it's an essential part of being strong enough to be there for others."

— Gary Hardy

This quote really gets to the heart of why self-care isn't selfish - it's actually fundamental to our ability to help others. It reframes self-care from something that might feel indulgent to something that's actually a responsibility, especially if we want to be there for those we care about. It reminds me of the classic airplane oxygen mask instruction - you have to secure your own mask first before helping others. It's not selfish; it's necessary. If you're depleted, how can you possibly have the strength to lift others up?

For today, I'd suggest this practical step: Identify one area where you've been running on empty while trying to care for others. Maybe it's lack of sleep, skipped meals, or postponed medical check-ups. Choose just one small act of self-care you can do today - whether that's taking a proper lunch break, going to bed 30 minutes earlier, or finally making that doctor's appointment you've been putting off. Think of it not as taking time away from others, but as investing in your capacity to be there for them.

The beauty of this perspective is how it removes the guilt that often accompanies self-care. When we understand that taking care of ourselves is actually part of taking care of others, it becomes easier to prioritise our own wellbeing. After all, you can't pour from an empty cup.

October 27th

"Your mind is programmable, if you're not programming it, then someone else will program it for you."

— Jeremy Hammond

This quote really hits home for me when I think about how our minds are constantly being influenced - whether we're aware of it or not. In today's world, we're bombarded with messages from social media, advertising, news, and other people's opinions. If we're not intentional about what we allow into our minds and what we choose to focus on, we essentially hand over the controls to others.

Here's a practical way to take back that control today: Set aside 10 minutes to do a "mental audit." Pay attention to what content you're consuming and how it makes you feel. Does scrolling through certain social media feeds leave you feeling drained or negative? Do particular news sources increase your anxiety? Once you identify these patterns, you can make a conscious decision about what deserves space in your mind.

Think of your mind like a garden - you can either actively plant and tend to the thoughts and beliefs you want to grow, or weeds will naturally take over. The choice is yours, but it requires awareness and action. Consider starting a simple morning routine where you consciously choose what goes into your mind first thing - maybe it's reading something inspiring, practicing gratitude, or quiet reflection. This puts you in the driver's seat of your mental programming, rather than letting the world's noise take the wheel.

October 28th

"This idea of shared humanity and the connections that we make with one another - that's what, in fact, makes life worth living."

— Clint Smith

This quote touches on something so fundamental to the human experience - how our connections with others give our lives depth and meaning. It's fascinating that in an age where we can feel more isolated than ever, despite all our digital connections, this basic truth remains: genuine human connection is what makes us feel truly alive. We often get caught up in chasing achievements, success, or material goals. But at the end of the day, it's those moments of real connection - when we truly see and are seen by others, when we share our struggles and joys, when we recognise our common humanity in someone else's story - that give our lives its richest meaning.

Here's something you could do today that builds on this wisdom: Have one conversation where you go a little deeper than usual. Maybe instead of the usual "How are you?" and "Fine," share something genuine about your day or ask someone about something they care about. Listen not just to respond, but to understand. These small moments of authentic connection, where we drop our guards and connect as human beings, create ripples that enrich both lives. Think about it - years from now, you probably won't remember that extra hour you spent at work, but you'll remember the meaningful conversations and connections you made along the way. These shared moments of humanity aren't just nice to have - they're essential to living a life that feels truly worthwhile.

October 29th

"It's okay to love something a little too much, as long as it's real to you."

— Gerard Way

This quote really touches on something beautiful about human nature - the depth of our capacity to feel passionate about the things and experiences that matter to us. There's a wonderful authenticity in allowing ourselves to love deeply, even if others might not understand or share our enthusiasm.

We often feel pressure to tone down our excitement or hide how much we care about certain things - whether it's your partner, a hobby, a creative pursuit, a fictional world, or even a way of seeing life. We worry about being "too much" or caring "too intensely." But there's something powerful about embracing that part of ourselves that loves deeply and cares intensely, as long as it comes from a genuine place.

Here's something you could try today: Instead of downplaying something you're passionate about, share it with someone - your enthusiasm included. Maybe it's telling a friend about that book that changed your perspective, that song that moves you deeply, or that hobby that brings you joy. Don't apologise for your enthusiasm or try to make it seem "cooler" or more distant than it is. When we're genuine about what matters to us, we often give others permission to be genuine too.

Remember, your authentic emotions and passions are part of what makes you uniquely you. There's no such thing as loving something "too much" if that love enriches your life and helps you connect with what's meaningful to you.

October 30th

"Successful people are not gifted. They just work hard, then succeed on purpose."

— G.K. Nielson

I really connect with this quote because it challenges that common myth that successful people are just "naturally talented." From what I've seen, success is much more about showing up every day and putting in consistent effort - it's not about waiting for some magical talent to appear.

What I find especially powerful is that last part - "succeed on purpose." It suggests that success isn't accidental. It's about making conscious choices and taking deliberate actions towards your goals, even when it's not easy or convenient.

Here's something practical you could try today: Pick one important goal you have and break it down into a small, specific action you can take. Instead of saying "I want to be more fit," decide "I'll do 10 minutes of exercise right after breakfast." The key is making it concrete and doable. This way, you're not relying on inspiration or talent - you're creating success through intentional action, just like the quote suggests.

Remember, every significant achievement in your life will likely be the result of consistent, purposeful effort rather than innate ability. That's actually pretty encouraging, isn't it? It means success is within your control.

October 31st

"You're rare, so people are gonna fall in love with the idea of having you, but most of them aren't used to rare, they're foreign to it, so they'll lack the capacity to treat you as such. And that's where they lose you."

— Unknown

This quote touches on something really profound about self-worth and relationships. It's about understanding that being unique - having depth, complexity, or qualities that make you stand out - can attract people, but not everyone is equipped to appreciate or nurture those qualities in a meaningful way.

Think of it like having a rare book or instrument. Many people might be drawn to the idea of possessing something special, but fewer understand how to properly care for it, appreciate its nuances, or invest the time to really understand its value. The same goes for relationships - some people might be attracted to what makes you unique, but aren't prepared for what it means to truly connect with and understand someone who doesn't fit into their usual patterns or expectations.

Here's something valuable you could reflect on today: Pay attention to whether the people in your life (romantic or otherwise) appreciate you for who you actually are, or just the idea of who they think you should be. Do they make space for your complexity? Do they put in the effort to understand your depth? Sometimes, realising the difference between being admired and being truly understood can help us make better choices about who we let into our inner circle.

Remember, it's better to be appreciated authentically by a few who understand your worth than to be superficially desired by many who don't know how to value what makes you unique.

November 1st

"November at its best, with a sort of delightful menace in the air."

— Anne Bosworth Greene

This quote captures something so visceral about November that many of us feel but struggle to put into words. There's this unique tension in November's atmosphere - you can feel winter's approach in the crisp air and see it in the bare branches, yet there's something oddly thrilling about that impending change.

It's like that feeling when storm clouds are gathering - there's both excitement and apprehension in the air. November has that same quality - shorter days, the last stubborn leaves clinging to trees, morning frost that hints at the winter ahead. It's not just about the weather though - it's about that feeling of anticipation, of nature holding its breath before winter makes its full entrance.

Here's a way to embrace this "delightful menace" today: Take a moment to step outside and really notice these November qualities around you. Maybe it's the sharp edge to the wind, the particular quality of the late autumn light, or the way the clouds move across the sky. Sometimes just acknowledging these transitional moments makes us feel more connected to the natural rhythm of things.

Remember, there's something special about these threshold times - they remind us that change, even when it brings challenges, can have its own kind of beauty and excitement.

November 2nd

"I can't change where I come from or what I've been through, so why should I be ashamed of what makes me, me?"

— Angie Thomas

There's such strength and wisdom in this quote. It speaks to a universal truth about self-acceptance that many of us struggle with - that our past experiences and origins, whether challenging or privileged, have shaped who we are today.

We often spend so much energy trying to hide or apologise for parts of our journey, especially the difficult or uncomfortable parts. But every experience, every struggle, every triumph - they're all threads in the tapestry of who we've become. Our backgrounds and experiences give us unique perspectives and strengths that no one else has.

Here's something powerful you could do today: Take a moment to reflect on an aspect of your background or experience that you've felt self-conscious about. Instead of seeing it as a limitation, try to identify how it has made you stronger, more compassionate, or more resilient. Maybe growing up with limited resources made you creative and resourceful. Perhaps facing challenges early in life gave you empathy for others' struggles.

Remember, authenticity is one of your greatest strengths. When we stop apologising for our journey and start embracing it as part of our story, we free up so much energy that can be used for growth and connection instead. Your experiences aren't just things that happened to you - they're part of what makes you uniquely equipped to understand and impact the world in your own special way.

November 3rd

"You deserve something you don't have to question. You deserve someone who is sure of you."

— Reuben Holmes

This quote really touches on something fundamental about human relationships and self-worth. When Holmes talks about deserving something (or someone) you don't have to question, he's pointing to that deep sense of security we all crave – and rightfully so.

Think about how exhausting it is to constantly wonder where you stand, whether in a relationship, friendship, or even at work. That mental energy spent questioning and doubting could be used for growth, joy, and actually living your life.

Here's a practical suggestion for today: Take a moment to notice which relationships or situations in your life feel secure, where you don't have to question your place. Maybe it's a friend who always has your back, or a family member who loves you unconditionally. Spend a few extra minutes appreciating those relationships today. And if you find yourself in situations where you're constantly questioning your worth or someone's commitment to you, ask yourself: Is this doubt serving me, or is it time to either have an honest conversation or reevaluate that relationship?

Remember, certainty in relationships isn't about having constant reassurance – it's about having that quiet confidence that comes from consistent actions and clear communication. You deserve that peace of mind.

November 4th

"I want to protect your smile, your peace, everything I know about you."

— Kyuugou

This is such a tender and profound expression of love and care. What strikes me about this quote is how beautifully it captures the essence of genuine love - not just romantic love, but any deep caring relationship where we want to be a guardian of another person's happiness and wellbeing.

Think about those small moments when someone you care about is truly happy - their authentic smile, their relaxed demeanour when they're at peace. There's something incredibly precious about witnessing that, isn't there? This quote reminds us that true care goes beyond just being present for the big moments - it's about wanting to preserve all those little pieces that make someone who they are.

Here's something practical you could do today: Think of one person whose happiness matters deeply to you. What's one small thing you could do to protect their peace or bring out their smile? Maybe it's sending them a message remembering something specific they once told you, taking a task off their plate when they're stressed, or simply creating a quiet moment for them to decompress. Sometimes the smallest gestures can be the most powerful shields for someone's wellbeing. Remember, protecting someone's peace doesn't mean shielding them from all of life's challenges - it means being that safe harbour where they can be completely themselves, knowing their joy and authenticity are valued and protected.

November 5th

"Having an emotionally mature partner is incredibly valuable. With them, you can express yourself without fear. They don't insult, judge, blame or give you the silent treatment. They aren't aggressive or manipulative. Instead, they listen, respond, and work towards resolving issues together."

— Gary Hardy

This quote really gets to the heart of what makes relationships healthy and sustainable. It is describing something that many people don't realise they need until they experience it - the incredible relief and freedom of being with someone who handles emotions and conflicts with maturity.

It's interesting how we often focus on surface-level compatibility - shared interests, attraction, chemistry - but emotional maturity is this foundational element that affects every single interaction in a relationship. It's like having a solid foundation for a house - you might not see it every day, but it's what keeps everything stable and secure.

Here's something practical you could do today: Take a moment to reflect on your own emotional responses in your relationships (romantic or otherwise). When someone brings up an issue, what's your first reaction? Do you get defensive, shut down, or do you stay present and listen? Maybe pick one challenging emotional response you tend to have and consciously practice a more mature approach today - like taking a deep breath and asking questions to understand better instead of immediately defending yourself.

The beautiful thing about emotional maturity is that it's a skill we can all develop. Even if you recognise some immature patterns in yourself, being aware of them is the first step to growing. And by working on our own emotional maturity, we not only become better partners but we also start naturally attracting and recognising similarly mature people in our lives.

Remember, you're not just looking for someone who makes you happy in the good times - you're looking for someone who knows how to handle the tough times with grace and respect.

November 6th

"You can learn from anyone even your enemy."

— Ovid

What a timeless piece of wisdom from Ovid. There's something really profound about being able to set aside our ego and personal feelings to recognise that valuable lessons can come from unexpected sources - even from people we might strongly dislike or disagree with.

Think about it - sometimes our strongest opponents can be our greatest teachers, not because they're right, but because they challenge us in ways that force us to grow. They might reveal our blind spots, test our patience, or push us to strengthen our own convictions and understanding.

Here's something practical you could try today: Think of someone who really challenges you or someone whose views oppose yours. Instead of dismissing them entirely, ask yourself: "What can I learn from this person?" Maybe it's how NOT to do something, maybe it's understanding a different perspective better, or maybe it's developing stronger emotional resilience. Even if you learn patience from dealing with an impatient person, that's valuable growth.

Remember, learning from someone doesn't mean you have to like them or agree with them - it just means you're wise enough to recognise that growth opportunities can come from any interaction, positive or negative. This kind of open mindset can turn your challenges into stepping stones for personal development.

November 7th

"The availability of choice is the downfall of mankind."

— Haresh Sippy

This is quite a thought-provoking statement that touches on something we all struggle with in modern life. Sippy captures a paradox that psychologists and philosophers have long studied - how having too many choices can actually make us less happy and more paralysed.

Think about it: We live in an age of unprecedented options - from the 50 kinds of toothpaste at the store to the endless career paths we could take, or the countless potential partners we could meet through apps. While having choices is generally good, too many options can lead to decision paralysis, constant second-guessing, and a nagging feeling that we might have made the wrong choice. Sometimes having fewer options can actually bring more peace and clarity.

Here's something practical you could try today: Pick one area of your life where you feel overwhelmed by choices (maybe your morning routine, your workout plan, or your entertainment options). Try simplifying it by deliberately limiting your options to just two or three choices. For example, instead of scrolling through endless streaming options tonight, pick between just two shows or movies. Notice how it feels to make decisions with fewer options - you might find it brings a sense of relief and helps you actually enjoy what you choose more fully.

Remember, sometimes the key to happiness isn't having more choices, but being content and fully present with the choices we've made. Freedom isn't always about having endless options - sometimes it's about the peace that comes from simplicity.

November 8th

"Our goodness, our badness all develop from social experience, the company we keep, the things we're taught when we're young. We start with a clean slate. It's everyone else who fucks us up."

— S. Walden

This is quite a raw and honest perspective on human nature that touches on something really fundamental about how we develop as people. Walden's observation speaks to the profound impact that our environment, relationships, and early experiences have on shaping who we become.

There's something both liberating and sobering about this idea. On one hand, it suggests that none of us are inherently "bad" - we all start with potential that could go in any direction. But it also highlights the immense responsibility we have in shaping others' lives, especially children's, and how the ripples of our actions can affect people in ways we might never fully understand.

Here's something meaningful you could do today: Take a moment to reflect on the positive influences in your life - those people who helped write good things on your "slate." Then think about how you might be influencing others' "slates" right now. Could you make one small change in how you interact with someone today - maybe showing a bit more patience with a colleague, or offering encouragement to someone who's struggling? Sometimes being conscious of our impact on others can help us break negative cycles and create more positive ones.

Remember, while we can't change our past experiences or how others have affected us, understanding this gives us the power to be more intentional about the company we keep now and the influence we have on others. We can choose to be the kind of person who writes something positive on others' slates.

November 9th

"I love the big fresh starts, the clean slates like birthdays and new years, but I also really like the idea that we can get up every morning and start over."

— Kristin Armstrong

This is such an empowering perspective that balances both the big picture and day-to-day opportunities for renewal. What I love about Armstrong's insight is how it reminds us that we don't have to wait for major milestones to begin again. We often put so much pressure on those big moments - New Year's resolutions, birthday promises, Monday morning commitments. While those are wonderful opportunities for reflection and change, there's something incredibly liberating about recognising that each morning carries the same potential for a fresh start. Every sunrise is like a mini New Year, offering us a chance to reset, adjust our course, or simply try again.

Here's something you could do today: Before you go to bed tonight, take a moment to think about tomorrow morning not just as another day, but as a fresh page. Pick one small thing you'd like to do differently - maybe it's starting your day with a moment of gratitude, having a proper breakfast, or being more patient with yourself. The beauty of seeing each day as a fresh start is that if it doesn't work out perfectly tomorrow, you get another chance the very next morning. Remember, you don't need to wait for a big occasion to make a change or start over. The power to begin again is available to you every single morning - and sometimes even in the middle of the day. There's something quite wonderful about that kind of everyday magic, isn't it?

November 10th

"You are capable of more than you know. Choose a goal that seems right for you and strive to be the best, however hard the path. Aim high. Behave honourably. Prepare to be alone at times, and to endure failure. Persist! The world needs all you can give."

— E. O. Wilson

This quote from E.O. Wilson carries such profound wisdom about human potential and perseverance. What strikes me most is how it balances ambitious encouragement with honest acknowledgment of the challenges ahead.

It's interesting how Wilson doesn't just say "you can do anything" - instead, he gives us this nuanced message about choosing goals that feel right for us personally, while still pushing our boundaries. He's acknowledging that each person's path is unique, but the principles of persistence and honour are universal.

Here's something meaningful you could do today: Take a quiet moment to think about a goal that's been tugging at your heart - something that excites you but maybe also scares you a little. Write it down. Then, instead of focusing on the entire mountain you need to climb, identify just one small step you could take today towards that goal. It doesn't have to be dramatic - even tiny steps forward count.

The part about being prepared for solitude and failure is particularly wise. It's like Wilson is saying, "Yes, chase your dreams, but know that the path won't always be comfortable or crowded." Sometimes the most meaningful pursuits require us to stand alone for a while or face setbacks that others might not understand.

Remember, when he says "the world needs all you can give," he's reminding us that our personal growth and achievements aren't just for ourselves - they're contributions to the larger human story. Your unique talents and perspectives, when developed and shared, become your gift to the world.

November 11th

"I cannot compromise my respect for your love. You can keep your love, I will keep my respect."

— Amit Kalantri

This is such a powerful statement about personal boundaries and self-worth. Kalantri captures something essential about the relationship between love and respect - that love without respect isn't really love at all, and that our self-respect shouldn't be negotiable. It's easy to get caught up in the desire to be loved, to be accepted, to belong. Sometimes we find ourselves slowly compromising our values, our boundaries, or our self-respect in small ways, thinking it's a fair trade for someone's love or attention. But as this quote suggests, that's a dangerous bargain that often leaves us feeling diminished rather than cherished.

Here's something valuable you could do today: Think about a situation in your life where you might be feeling the tension between maintaining your respect and keeping someone's love or approval. It could be in a relationship, at work, or with family. Ask yourself: "What would my choice look like if I prioritised my self-respect in this situation?" Sometimes just clearly seeing where we're compromising our respect can be the first step to making healthier choices.

Remember, true love - whether it's romantic, familial, or friendship - should enhance your self-respect, not erode it. When someone asks you to choose between their love and your self-respect, they're not really offering love at all. The right people in your life will value both your love and your respect, understanding that they're inseparable.

November 12th

"To tell someone not to be emotional is to tell them to be dead."

— Jeanette Winterson

This is such a profound observation by Winterson that cuts right to the heart of what it means to be human. There's something almost absurd about how often we're told to "stop being so emotional" - as if our emotions aren't the very essence of being alive and human.

Think about it: our emotions are what make us feel deeply connected to others, what drive us to create art, what push us to fight for what's right, what make us fall in love, what help us grieve and heal. They're not just reactions - they're the colours with which we paint our lives.

Here's something meaningful you could try today: When you feel a strong emotion - whether it's joy, frustration, sadness, or excitement - instead of trying to suppress it or judge it, try to sit with it for a moment. Notice it, like you'd notice the weather. What's it telling you? What's it teaching you about what matters to you? Sometimes just acknowledging our emotions instead of fighting them can transform how we experience them.

Remember, being emotional doesn't mean being out of control - it means being fully alive. The goal isn't to eliminate emotions but to understand them and express them in healthy ways. After all, as Winterson suggests, the opposite of being emotional isn't being rational - it's being lifeless.

November 13th

"No one forgets the truth; they just get better at lying."

— Richard Yates

This is such a piercing observation about human nature from Yates. It speaks to something deep about how we handle uncomfortable truths in our lives and the stories we tell ourselves.

It's fascinating how we humans develop these layers of self-deception - not because we've actually forgotten what's true, but because we've gotten more sophisticated at avoiding it. It's like we build elaborate detours around the truths that make us uncomfortable, all while carrying those very truths deep inside.

Here's something valuable you could try today: Take a quiet moment to reflect on an area of your life where you might be "getting better at lying" to yourself. Maybe it's about a relationship that needs attention, a habit you know isn't serving you, or a dream you've been pushing aside. Just acknowledge it without judgement. Sometimes simply recognising where we're creating these detours around truth can be the first step to finding our way back to honesty with ourselves.

Remember, the capacity for self-honesty is like a muscle - it can weaken with disuse, but it can also be strengthened with practice. The truth doesn't disappear just because we've gotten good at looking away from it. It waits patiently for us to find the courage to face it again.

November 14th

"As you sit there judging, criticising, gossiping about your fellow humans failings and missteps, destroying someones reputation, have you ever thought about your own? Have you ever thought that you are in no position to judge anyone? No you haven't have you, and that says everything we need to know about you."

— Gary Hardy

This is something we all struggle with - that tendency to point fingers at others while forgetting to look in the mirror. This remind me of an important truth: we're all walking our own complicated paths, making mistakes, and trying to figure things out, trying to change and be better.

Here's a suggestion for today: The next time you catch yourself about to criticise someone or share some gossip, pause for just 10 seconds. In those moments, ask yourself: "What's going on in their life that I might not know about? When was the last time I made a similar mistake?" This brief pause can be transformative - not just in how we treat others, but in developing more self-awareness and compassion for ourselves too.

I've seen this work wonders in my own life and with others I've guided. When we spend less energy judging others, we free up so much mental space for personal growth and meaningful connections. Plus, there's something incredibly liberating about letting go of that need to criticise others - it's like putting down a heavy weight you didn't even realise you were carrying.

November 15th

"Sometimes a shock to the system is a good thing, you know? Like a reminder that you're alive."

— Jessi Kirby

This quote wonderfully captures something profound about how those unexpected jolts in life - even the uncomfortable ones - can actually wake us up to the present moment in a powerful way. Kirby is pointing to that strange paradox where sometimes it takes getting shaken up to truly feel the vibrancy of being alive.

Here's a thought for today: Instead of avoiding small discomforts, try deliberately stepping out of your comfort zone in one tiny way. Maybe take a cold shower for 30 seconds, try a food you've always avoided, or strike up a conversation with someone new. These little "shocks" can break us out of autopilot and make us feel more present and energised.

I've noticed that when people embrace these small challenges willingly, rather than just reacting to unexpected ones, they often discover a newfound appreciation for life's intensity. It's like deliberately turning up the contrast on a photo - suddenly everything becomes more vivid and real. Plus, choosing our own "shocks" helps build resilience for when life throws unexpected ones our way.

November 16th

"Detachment is not that you should own nothing, but that nothing should own you."

— Ali ibn abi Talib

This is such a profound piece of ancient wisdom that feels more relevant than ever in our modern world of constant consumption and attachment. Ali ibn abi Talib wasn't suggesting we need to live like ascetics - rather, he was pointing to something deeper about our relationship with... everything, really.

For today, try this: Pick one thing you feel particularly attached to - maybe your phone, a favourite possession, or even a rigid routine - and practice loosening your grip on it just a bit. If it's your phone, maybe put it in another room for an hour. If it's a possession you're protective of, practice letting someone else use it. The goal isn't to stop caring about things entirely, but to notice how our attachments might be controlling us more than we're controlling them.

What's beautiful about this approach is that it often leads to more freedom and joy, not less. When we hold things lightly instead of clutching them tightly, we can still enjoy them fully while maintaining our inner peace if they're not available or if things don't go as planned. It's about having things without letting them have us.

November 17th

"I thought about how you're shaped so much by the people who surround you, and how careful you have to be in choosing them for this exact reason, and then I thought, despite all that, in the end maybe you have to lose them all in order to truly find yourself."

— Jojo Moyes

This quote really touches on the delicate balance between connection and self-discovery. Moyes captures something profound about how our relationships shape us, but also how sometimes finding our true self requires a kind of solitude - even if that's uncomfortable or not what we planned.

Here's something meaningful you could try today: Take 15 minutes to sit quietly and write down the ways different people in your life have influenced who you've become. Not to judge whether that influence was good or bad, but just to become aware of it. Then ask yourself: "What parts of me are truly mine, and what parts am I borrowing from others?"

Sometimes we get so caught up in being who others need or expect us to be that we forget to check in with ourselves. This isn't about pushing people away - it's about finding that sweet spot where we can maintain meaningful connections while still nurturing our own unique identity. Sometimes the most powerful growth happens when we're brave enough to stand on our own two feet, even if just for a while, and listen to our own inner voice.

The key is finding the balance between being shaped by those we love and maintaining our own core identity. Think of it like a tree - strong roots in community, but growing in its own unique direction.

November 18th

"Good things take time, better things take a little longer."

— Sanhita Baruah

This is such a gentle reminder about something we often forget in our fast-paced world. Baruah is touching on a truth that runs counter to our instant-gratification culture - that truly meaningful growth and achievement often unfolds slowly, like a flower gradually opening.

Here's a practical way to embrace this wisdom today: Choose one thing you've been rushing or feeling impatient about. Maybe it's a personal goal, a relationship, or a project. Now, instead of focusing on when it will be "done," try to find one small aspect of the journey itself to appreciate. If you're learning a new skill, for example, celebrate those tiny moments of improvement rather than fixating on mastery.

I've seen how transformative it can be when people shift from fighting against time to working with it. Think of it like cooking a good stew - you can't rush the process of flavours melding together. The waiting and slow development are actually essential parts of creating something truly special. When we accept this, the journey itself becomes richer, and ironically, we often end up creating something even better than we initially imagined.

November 19th

"You will love again the stranger who was your self."

— Derek Walcott

This quote touches something deep in my understanding of the human journey. We often become strangers to ourselves - through hardship, through the daily grind, or just by losing touch with who we once were. Walcott is reminding us that reconciliation with ourselves isn't just possible - it's a natural part of healing and growth.

Think about how we sometimes look at old photos and barely recognise that version of ourselves - maybe someone who laughed more easily, dreamed more boldly, or simply lived more freely. The beauty in Walcott's words is the promise that we cannot only reconnect with that self but learn to love them again.

For today, I'd suggest taking just 10 minutes to write a letter to your younger self - maybe from five years ago. Not to give advice, but to remember who you were, what you loved, what made you smile. Often, in remembering who we were, we rediscover parts of ourselves we'd like to bring back into our present lives. Maybe it's an old hobby you used to love, or a quality you possessed that you'd like to nurture again. This simple act of remembering can be the first step in rekindling that love for all versions of yourself - past, present, and future.

November 20th

"Those who love you are not fooled by mistakes you have made, or by dark images you hold about yourself. They remember your beauty when you feel ugly; your wholeness when you are broken; your innocence when you feel guilty; and your purpose when you are confused."

— Alan Cohen

This quote really touches on something profound about true love and friendship. It's fascinating how the people who truly love us seem to have this amazing ability to see through our moments of self-doubt and hold onto the best version of who we are - even when we can't see it ourselves.

I think what makes this quote particularly powerful is how it acknowledges that we all have these moments where we feel broken or lost. It's part of being human. But real love acts like this incredible mirror that reflects back our truest self, not the temporary shadows we're struggling with.

For today, I'd suggest something that might feel a bit vulnerable but could be deeply meaningful: Think of someone who loves you this way - maybe a parent, a friend, or a partner - and ask them what they see in you that you might sometimes forget about yourself. Their perspective might be exactly what you need to hear right now. And if you're not ready for that conversation, try writing down a moment when someone believed in you when you didn't believe in yourself. Often, just remembering these instances can help us reconnect with our own worth.

The beautiful thing is, we can also be this kind of person for others. Today, if you notice someone in your life being particularly hard on themselves, take a moment to remind them of their light that you see, even if they're currently having trouble seeing it themselves. Sometimes, being that mirror for someone else can be just as healing as having others be that mirror for us.

November 21st

"What you seek out and feed your mind affects your soul, so be mindful of what that is, because it's what you will eventually become."

— Gary Hardy

This quote is about how we shape ourselves through what we choose to consume mentally and spiritually. It's like that old saying "you are what you eat," but for our minds and souls — everything we take in, whether it's the content we read, the conversations we have, or the thoughts we dwell on, gradually transforms who we are.

It's fascinating how our minds work like gardens — whatever we feed and water will grow. If we constantly feed our minds with negativity, anxiety, or shallow distractions, those things take root and flourish. But if we nourish ourselves with wisdom, beauty, and meaningful connections, those qualities begin to define us instead.

Today, do a "mental diet check." Take a few moments to reflect on what you've been feeding your mind over the past 24 hours. What kind of social media content? What conversations? What thoughts have you been ruminating on? Then, consciously choose one nourishing "mental meal" to add to your day — maybe it's reading something uplifting, having a meaningful conversation, or spending time in quiet reflection.

Think of it like creating a nutrition plan for your soul. Just as we might plan our meals for physical health, we can be intentional about planning what we feed our minds and spirits. The beautiful thing is, once we start being mindful of this, we often naturally begin craving more of what truly nourishes us.

What kind of mental nourishment have you noticed makes you feel most aligned with who you want to become?

November 22nd

"They say a person needs just three things to be truly happy in this world: someone to love, something to do, and something to hope for."

— Tom Bodett

This quote touches on something so fundamentally true about human happiness. I find it beautiful in its simplicity - how it distills the complexity of human fulfilment into these three essential elements that beautifully complement each other. Love gives us connection and meaning, purpose gives us direction and growth, and hope gives us the energy to keep moving forward even when things get difficult. It's like a three-legged stool - each element supports the others and creates stability in our lives.

What I particularly appreciate about this wisdom is that it's adaptable to any life situation. The "someone to love" could be family, friends, a partner, or even a community you care about. The "something to do" might be your career, a hobby, volunteer work, or creating art. And "something to hope for" could be any goal or dream that lights up your future.

For today, I'd suggest taking a moment to check in with these three areas of your life. Pick one that maybe needs a little more attention right now. If it's love, perhaps reach out to someone you care about. If its purpose, take one small step towards a goal or project. If it's hope, spend a few minutes visualising something you're looking forward to or dreaming up a new possibility for your future.

Remember, these three elements don't have to be grand or dramatic - sometimes the simplest forms of love, purpose, and hope create the most sustainable happiness.

November 23rd

"This is how we reveal ourselves: these tiny flashes of discomfort, the reactions we can't hide."

— Christina Lauren

This quote really touches on something subtle but profound about human nature. It's those small, unguarded moments - a slight flinch, a quick change in expression, an unconscious gesture - that often reveal more about who we truly are than our carefully crafted words or deliberate actions.

What I find most compelling about this insight is how it speaks to our authenticity. In those tiny flashes of discomfort, we can't maintain our social masks or keep up our practiced responses. It's like catching a glimpse of someone's true reflection in a window when they don't realise they're being observed.

For today, I'd suggest something that might feel a bit challenging but potentially enlightening: Pay attention to your own "tiny flashes" throughout the day. When do you feel that slight internal wince? What makes you unconsciously pull back or lean in? These small reactions often point to our true values, boundaries, or unresolved feelings that we might not be fully aware of.

This kind of self-observation isn't about judging these reactions or trying to change them - it's about understanding yourself better through these honest, unfiltered moments. Sometimes our discomfort has important things to tell us about what we truly need, value, or should pay attention to in our lives.

November 24th

"I'm thankful for my struggle for without it I wouldn't have stumbled across my strength."

— Alex Elle

This quote really speaks to me because it captures something profound about how we grow through difficult times. It's so natural to wish away our struggles - I catch myself doing it too. But Elle points out something beautiful here: those very challenges we face often reveal inner resources we didn't even know we had.

Think about it - maybe you've gone through something tough recently, like a failed project or a difficult relationship. In the moment, it probably felt awful. But looking back, you might realise you developed resilience, learned to set boundaries, or discovered creative problem-solving skills you now use every day.

Here's a simple suggestion for today: Take 5 minutes to reflect on a current challenge you're facing. Instead of seeing it purely as an obstacle, ask yourself: "What strength might this situation be helping me discover about myself?" Maybe it's patience, adaptability, or courage. Just shifting your perspective like this can transform how you approach difficulties and help you recognise your own growth in real-time.

November 25th

"Your truest friends are the ones who stand by you in your darkest moments, because they are willing to brave the shadows with you, and in your greatest moments, because they are not afraid to let you shine."

— Nicole Yatsonsky

This quote beautifully captures the essence of authentic friendship. In my experience helping others, I've noticed how many people struggle to differentiate between genuine friends and fair-weather companions. What Yatsonsky describes here is that rare, precious kind of friendship that's both a shelter in the storm and a cheerleader in the sunshine.

What really strikes me about this insight is how it highlights two equally challenging aspects of true friendship. Standing by someone in their darkness takes courage and selflessness - it's about being willing to sit in discomfort with someone you care about. But sometimes, it can be just as challenging to genuinely celebrate another's success without letting jealousy or insecurity creep in.

Here's a practical suggestion for today: Think about one person in your life who has shown up for you in both ways. Send them a specific message expressing your gratitude, mentioning a time they supported you during a struggle and a time they celebrated your success. This kind of intentional acknowledgment not only strengthens your bond but also helps you become more aware of showing up for others in the same way.

Remember, being this kind of friend ourselves is just as important as finding such friends. Consider how you can embody these qualities today - whether it's checking in on a friend going through a tough time or wholeheartedly celebrating someone else's achievement without letting your own ego get in the way.

November 26th

"You can't just switch off your feelings because the other person did."

— Sophie Kinsella

This quote really cuts to the heart of what makes heartbreak and rejection so challenging. Having worked with many people through their emotional journeys, I've seen how much people struggle with this exact situation - feeling like they're somehow wrong for still caring when someone else seems to have moved on effortlessly.

Here's what I find deeply true about this insight: our emotions don't come with an off switch, and that's actually a beautiful thing about being human. It's part of our capacity to love deeply and form meaningful connections. The pain you feel when someone else seems to have moved on isn't a weakness - it's evidence of your authentic ability to feel and connect.

For today, here's a gentle suggestion: Instead of trying to force yourself to "switch off" feelings that are still present (which usually just pushes them underground), try acknowledging them with self-compassion. Take a few minutes to write down what you're feeling without judgement, starting with "It's natural that I feel..." This simple act of accepting your emotions, rather than fighting them, can be the first step towards genuine healing.

Remember, your feelings moving at a different pace than someone else's doesn't diminish their validity. Sometimes the people who feel the longest are also the ones who love the deepest.

November 27th

"The best way to not be compared to others is to be beyond compare. And if they are comparing you, walk away, and they will quickly find out exactly how beyond compare you really are."

— Gary Hardy

This is a powerful perspective on dealing with comparison - It flips the usual anxieties about being compared to others completely on its head. Instead of worrying about measuring up, it suggests something far more empowering: being so uniquely yourself that comparisons become meaningless.

The second part is particularly clever - it's not about proving your worth or defending yourself against comparisons. It's about having the quiet confidence to walk away, knowing that your absence will speak louder than any argument could. It's like saying "My value isn't up for debate" through actions rather than words.

For today, here's a practical way to embody this wisdom: When you catch yourself in a moment of comparison (maybe scrolling social media, or in a work meeting, or even at home), pause and identify one thing you do in your own unique way. It could be how you solve problems, how you express care for others, or even something as simple as how you make your coffee in the morning. Then, instead of trying to adjust that uniqueness to match others' expectations, lean into it even more intentionally.

Remember, being "beyond compare" doesn't mean being better than everyone else - it means being so authentically yourself that comparisons simply become irrelevant. It's about recognising that your unique combination of qualities, experiences, and perspectives makes you invaluable in your own way.

November 28th

"She knew the power of her mind so she programmed it for success."

— Carrie Green

I love the elegant simplicity and profound truth in this quote. It captures something really powerful about personal development - the recognition that our mind is essentially programmable, like a sophisticated computer that we can intentionally direct towards success.

What's particularly striking is the awareness and intentionality implied here. She "knew" the power of her mind - suggesting a conscious recognition of her own potential - and then took active steps to shape it. It's not about waiting for success to happen or hoping for the right circumstances; it's about deliberately programming your thoughts and beliefs to align with your goals.

For today, I'd suggest a practical exercise in this kind of mental programming: Take 5 minutes this morning to write down three specific success-oriented thoughts that you want to "install" in your mind. These should be personal and specific to your goals - not just generic affirmations. For example, instead of "I am successful," you might write "I approach each challenge in my work project with creativity and confidence." Then, set reminders on your phone to read these thoughts at three different times during your day.

Think of it like running an update on your mental software - each time you consciously reinforce these success-oriented thoughts, you're strengthening those neural pathways. The key is consistency and specificity - just like any good programming requires clear, well-defined instructions executed regularly.

November 29th

"I know what it's like to be afraid of your own mind."

— Dr Reid

This is such a powerful and vulnerable truth that speaks to a universal human experience many of us face but rarely discuss openly. There's something deeply comforting about acknowledging this fear - it helps break through the isolation that often comes when we're struggling with our own thoughts.

Whether it's anxiety spinning worst-case scenarios, depression colouring our view of everything, or just those 3 AM thoughts that won't let us rest - feeling afraid of our own mind can be one of the most isolating experiences. Yet here's Dr. Reid, putting into words what so many people feel but can't express.

Here's a gentle suggestion for today: When you catch yourself feeling afraid of your thoughts, try this simple grounding practice - name 5 things you can see right now, 4 things you can touch, 3 things you can hear, 2 things you can smell, and 1 thing you can taste. This isn't about fixing everything, but rather giving yourself a gentle anchor back to the present moment when your mind feels overwhelming.

Remember, being afraid of your thoughts doesn't mean there's something wrong with you - it means you're human. And just like any other fear, acknowledging it often helps release some of its power over us.

November 30th

"Sometimes people think they know you. They know a few facts about you, and they piece you together in a way that makes sense to them. And if you don't know yourself very well, you might even believe that they are right. But the truth is, that isn't you. That isn't you at all."

— Leila Sales

I find this quote insightful. It's talking about how we sometimes let others' perceptions shape our understanding of ourselves.

Often, people take a few snapshots of our lives - maybe how we acted in a certain situation or decisions we made at a specific point in our lives - and based on that, they create their own story about who we are. It's like they're trying to complete a 5000 piece puzzle with only a handful of pieces.

What makes this quote especially powerful is the warning about believing their version of us, particularly when we're uncertain about ourselves. When we're searching for our identity or going through periods of self-doubt, it can be tempting to accept others' definitions of who we are simply because they seem so confident about their assessment of us. Usually, their assessment, based on their extremely limited knowledge of us, is not a positive one.

Today, take a moment to write down something about yourself that you know to be true, but that others often misunderstand or don't see. It could be an aspect of your personality, a deeply held value, or even just a preference that doesn't fit others' image of you. This isn't about proving anything to anyone else - it's about strengthening your own self-knowledge and being confident in who you really are.

Remember, you're the only one living your internal experience. Others may have their theories about who you are, but you're the author of your own story, not just a character in someone else's interpretation of that story. It is like reading the first chapter of a book and professing to know how exactly how it ends.

December 1st

"December, being the last month of the year, cannot help but make us think of what is to come."

— Fennel Hudson

This is such a timely reflection, especially as we find ourselves in December right now. Hudson captures something universal about how this month naturally pulls our thoughts towards both reflection and possibility.

Here's a gentle suggestion for today: Take 10 minutes to sit with a warm drink and write down not just goals for the future, but the feelings you want to carry forward. Rather than making a traditional resolution list, think about what you'd like to preserve from this year and what you'd like to leave behind. Maybe there's a quality you developed during a tough time that you want to keep nurturing, or perhaps there's a worry you're ready to set down.

December has this unique quality - it's both an ending and a beginning, like standing in a doorway between two rooms. Instead of feeling pressured to make grand plans, use this natural transition point to tune into what your heart is telling you about the direction you want to move in. Sometimes the quietest whispers of intuition in December become the loudest calls for change in the year ahead.

December 2nd

"Life goes on whether you choose to move on and take a chance in the unknown or stay behind, locked in the past, thinking of what could've been. I don't want to live in the past anymore. I'm so lonely here, there's nothing for me here anymore."

— Stephanie Smith

This quote touches on one of life's most challenging moments - that crossroads where we have to decide between clinging to what's familiar, even if it's painful, or taking that brave step into the unknown. Smith captures that ache of staying stuck, especially that powerful line "I'm so lonely here" - it really speaks to how emotionally draining it can be when we let our past anchor us down.

For today, here's something practical you might try: Take a sheet of paper and write down one small thing you've been avoiding or putting off because of past fears or old habits. Maybe it's calling an old friend, trying a new hobby, or even just taking a different route to work. Commit to doing just that one thing today. It doesn't have to be huge - what matters is taking that first step forward.

Remember, moving forward doesn't mean you have to have everything figured out. Sometimes just shifting your gaze from the rearview mirror to the road ahead is enough to start breaking free from that feeling of being trapped in the past. Each small step creates momentum for bigger changes when you're ready.

December 3rd

"Every man has his secret sorrows which the world knows not; and often times we call a man cold when he is only sad."

— Henry Wadsworth Longfellow

This quote from Longfellow touches something so deep about human nature and our tendency to misread each other. It's a powerful reminder that behind every stern face or distant demeanour, there's often a hidden story of pain or struggle that we know nothing about.

Here's something transformative you could try today: When you encounter someone who seems cold, unfriendly, or distant - maybe a cashier, a coworker, or even a family member - pause and remind yourself that they might be carrying a burden you can't see. Instead of matching their energy or labelling them, try offering a moment of unexpected warmth. It could be as simple as a genuine smile or asking "How are you?" and really meaning it.

I've seen how this shift in perspective can create ripples of compassion that transform both the giver and receiver. Sometimes that person who seems "cold" is just waiting for someone to see past their protective shell and acknowledge their humanity. And here's the beautiful thing - when we extend this understanding to others, we often find people extending the same grace back to us when we're the ones carrying hidden sorrows.

Remember, everyone you meet is fighting a battle you know nothing about. This awareness alone can change everything about how we move through the world and interact with each other.

December 4th

"No one can, or will, care more about your life than you do. So, it's time to start acting like it."

— Antonio Neves

This quote hits right at the heart of personal responsibility and self-advocacy. Neves is reminding us of something both empowering and challenging - that we're ultimately the primary stakeholder in our own lives, and our actions should reflect that.

Here's something powerful you could do today: Take 30 minutes to be your own best advocate. Think about something you've been putting up with that doesn't serve you well - maybe it's a situation at work you've been tolerating, a health concern you've been ignoring, or a boundary you've been hesitating to set. Then take one concrete step to address it, treating it with the same urgency you'd give if you were helping someone you deeply care about.

I've noticed that many people pour endless energy into caring for others while putting their own well-being on the back burner. But here's the thing - treating yourself as a priority isn't selfish; it's necessary. Just like on airplanes where they tell you to put on your own oxygen mask first, taking care of yourself actually puts you in a better position to care for others.

The real power in this quote lies in that last part - "start acting like it." It's not enough to just know we should care for ourselves; we need to demonstrate that care through our choices and actions, starting today.

December 5th

"December reminds us that endings are not empty spaces, but rather fertile ground where new beginnings take root."

— Mark Nepo

I find this quote particularly profound in how it reframes our perspective on endings. It reminds me of how nature itself uses winter - not as a final closing, but as essential preparation for spring's renewal. December, with its closing of the year, offers us this same wisdom.

What touches me deeply about this insight is how it transforms what could feel like loss or emptiness into something rich with potential. Just as a fallow field isn't truly empty but is quietly preparing for new growth, our endings - whether of a year, a relationship, or a chapter in our life - are creating space for something new to emerge.

For today, I'd suggest this reflective practice: Take a few moments to consider something that's ending or changing in your life right now. Instead of focusing on what's being lost, try to identify the new possibilities this ending might be making room for. What seeds of new beginnings might be taking root in this transition? Maybe write down three potential opportunities that this ending could create space for.

There's something especially meaningful about this message during December, when we're naturally drawn to both reflection and anticipation. It reminds us that endings and beginnings aren't separate events, but part of the same continuous cycle of growth and renewal.

December 6th

"There is an inner beauty about a woman who believes in herself, who knows she is capable of anything that she puts her mind to. There is a beauty in the strength and determination of a woman who follows her own path, who isn't thrown off by obstacles along the way. There is a beauty about a woman whose confidence comes from experiences; who knows she can fall, pick herself up, and move on."

— Unknown

This is such a powerful reflection on authentic feminine strength. What strikes me most about this quote is how it redefines beauty - not as something external or fleeting, but as something that radiates from within through resilience, self-belief, and lived experience.

I especially appreciate how it honours the journey of becoming. It's not about being perfect or never facing setbacks. Instead, it celebrates the woman who has weathered storms and emerged stronger, who has learned from her falls rather than being defined by them. There's something incredibly liberating about this perspective - it suggests that our challenges and "failures" aren't blemishes on our story, but rather the very things that can make us more beautiful.

For today, I'd encourage any woman reading this to take a moment and write down three challenges she's overcome in her life. Not just what happened, but how she grew from each experience, what strength it revealed in her that she might not have known she had.

Sometimes we're so focused on the next hurdle that we forget to acknowledge how far we've come and how much wisdom we've gained along the way. This simple exercise can be a powerful reminder of your own inner beauty and capability.

And for anyone, regardless of gender, who supports women in their lives - today might be a good day to acknowledge not just the outer beauty of someone you care about, but to specifically recognise and celebrate their strength, determination, or resilience. Sometimes seeing our own beauty more clearly starts with having it reflected back to us through the eyes of others.

December 7th

"Life's under no obligation to give us what we expect."

— Margaret Mitchell

This quote carries such a powerful truth, and what I find fascinating is how liberating it can be once we really absorb its meaning. At first glance, it might sound harsh or disappointing, but there's actually a profound freedom in releasing our grip on specific expectations. Think about it - how often do we cause ourselves unnecessary suffering simply because life didn't follow the script we wrote for it? Mitchell's words remind us that our expectations are just that - our own creations, not promises from the universe.

For today, I'd suggest a small but powerful practice: When you notice yourself getting frustrated because something isn't going as expected, pause and say to yourself, "Life is offering me something different right now. Let me be curious about what that might be." This slight shift from resistance to curiosity can completely transform your experience.

It's like going to a restaurant and being disappointed that your usual dish isn't available, only to try something new and discover it's even better than what you usually order. Sometimes life's greatest gifts come precisely when it doesn't give us what we expect.

This isn't about lowering our standards or giving up on our goals - it's about holding our expectations lightly enough that we can recognise unexpected opportunities and blessings when they appear in different packaging than we anticipated.

December 8th

"If you keep good food in your fridge, you will eat good food."

— Errick McAdams

This wonderfully practical quote gets right to the heart of how our environment shapes our choices. McAdams touches on something that's both simple and profound - success often comes down to setting ourselves up to make good decisions easy.

Think about it: When you're tired after a long day, or stressed, or just hungry and in a hurry, you're going to reach for whatever is most convenient. That's just human nature. If your fridge is stocked with nourishing foods, that's what you'll eat. If it's filled with less healthy options, well... that's what you'll reach for instead.

For today's reflection, let's expand this wisdom beyond just food. What "good things" can you stock in your life to make positive choices more natural? Maybe it's keeping a book by your bedside instead of your phone, or having your workout clothes ready the night before, or spending time talking to your partner who tends to bring out your best.

Consider taking 10 minutes today to arrange your environment - whether it's your fridge, your desk, or your living space - to make one healthy choice easier. Remember, we don't have to rely solely on willpower when we can use our environment to support our best intentions.

December 9th

"Letting go doesn't mean that you don't care about someone anymore. It's just realising that the only person you really have control over is yourself."

— Deborah Reber

This quote touches on one of life's most challenging truths. Having watched many people struggle with letting go, I find Reber's insight particularly powerful because it reframes letting go not as an act of giving up, but as an act of wisdom and self-awareness.

The key insight here is the distinction between caring and controlling. So often, we confuse the two, thinking that if we truly care about someone or something, we must be able to influence or change it. But real love and caring can exist – and often exist more purely – when we release our need to control outcomes.

Today, identify one situation where you're trying to control something that's ultimately not yours to control. It might be someone else's decisions, their feelings, or their journey. Take a moment to acknowledge that your desire for control likely comes from a place of caring deeply.

Then, practice what I call "loving release" – consciously choosing to step back while maintaining your care and compassion. You might try this simple exercise: When you feel the urge to step in and fix or control, take a deep breath and say to yourself, "I care about this, AND I recognise that this isn't mine to control."

Remember, letting go isn't a one-time event but a daily practice. Each time you choose to focus on what you can control – your own responses, boundaries, and actions – you're not just freeing others; you're freeing yourself to live more authentically and peacefully.

December 10th

"There's emotional reciprocity involved with giving compliments. Seeing someone else happy, especially when you were the one who made them happy, in turn makes you happy. It's one of the simplest ways to boost someone else's mood as well as your own."

— Hannah Owens

This quote beautifully captures the ripple effect of kindness - how genuine compliments create a circle of joy that benefits both the giver and receiver. It reveals a simple truth about human connection. It's fascinating how a sincere compliment can literally change the chemistry in both people's brains, releasing feel-good hormones that lift our spirits. Yet so often we hold back our positive thoughts about others, maybe feeling shy or worried they'll think we're strange. But really, we're just keeping little bits of happiness locked away.

Today, try this experiment: Give three genuine, specific compliments today. Not just "nice shirt" but something meaningful you've noticed - maybe someone's thoughtfulness, their creative approach to solving problems, or the way they light up when talking about their passions. Notice how it makes you feel to share these observations, and how the positive energy comes back to you. Remember, the key is authenticity. People can sense when a compliment comes from a real place of appreciation. And here's the beautiful thing - the more you practice noticing what you admire in others, the more you train your brain to see the good in the world. What genuine appreciation have you been holding back that you could share today?

December 11th

"Don't give them a taste of their own medicine. They already know what it tastes like. Give them a taste of your own medicine. If they lied, let your medicine be honesty. If they played with your emotions, let your medicine be maturity. Don't be afraid to be yourself, even if it means removing yourself from lives that you want to be in. You are, no doubt, worthy of being valued for who you are. So be who you are."

— Najwa Zebian

This quote by Zebian carries such profound wisdom about breaking cycles of hurt. What really moves me about it is how it redefines the concept of "medicine" - not as revenge, but as healing through our own integrity.

It's so natural to want to hurt back when we're wounded. I've seen countless people struggle with this impulse, this desire to show others how their actions felt. But Zebian points us towards something more transformative: responding to darkness with light, to pettiness with grace, to manipulation with authenticity.

The part about being willing to remove yourself from lives you want to be in - that's particularly powerful. It addresses one of the hardest truths about personal growth: sometimes maintaining our integrity means walking away from relationships we deeply wish could work. It's about recognising that staying true to your values isn't just about what you do, but also about what you refuse to compromise on.

Here's a practical suggestion for today: Think of a situation where you're feeling hurt or wronged. Instead of planning how to give that person "a taste of their own medicine," write down how you could respond in a way that reflects your highest self. Maybe it's choosing honesty where they chose deception, or responding with kindness where they showed cruelty. Then take one small action that aligns with that better choice.

Remember, choosing to respond with integrity isn't weakness - it's actually the harder path, and it's the one that helps you grow stronger while keeping your spirit intact.

December 12th

"Hiding your hurt only intensifies it. Problems grow in the dark and only become bigger and bigger. But when exposed to the light of truth, they shrink. You are only as sick as your secrets. So take off your mask, stop pretending you're perfect and walk into freedom."

— Rick Warren

This quote really resonates with my experience supporting people through difficult times. There's such deep truth in Warren's insight about how problems grow when we keep them hidden. It's like trying to hold a beach ball underwater - the harder you push it down, the more force it takes, and eventually, it's going to burst up to the surface anyway.

You know what's particularly powerful here? The connection between secrecy and shame. When we hide our struggles, we often do it because we're afraid of being seen as imperfect or weak. But that very act of hiding creates a prison of perfectionism that exhausts us and keeps us from healing.

Here's a practical suggestion for today: Choose one thing you've been carrying alone - maybe it's a fear, a regret, or a struggle - and share it with someone you trust. It doesn't have to be your biggest secret; start small. Maybe it's telling a friend about an insecurity you've never voiced, or admitting to someone close that you're having a harder time than you've let on.

The key isn't to dramatically unmask everything at once, but to take one step towards being more authentic. Often, you'll find that voicing what hurts takes away some of its power, and that most people respond with more understanding than you might expect. Remember, vulnerability isn't weakness - it's actually one of the bravest forms of strength.

December 13th

"Whatever you want emotionally, you have to start giving away."

— Mary Karr

This is such a deceptively simple yet profound truth about emotional fulfilment. I've seen how this principle plays out again and again in people's lives - those who desperately want love often hold back from giving it, those craving understanding sometimes struggle most to listen to others.

What I find fascinating about Karr's insight is how it challenges our natural instinct. When we're emotionally hungry, we tend to focus on what we're missing, what we need to receive. But she's pointing to a beautiful paradox: the path to receiving often begins with giving.

Here's something practical you could try today: Take a moment to identify what you're most emotionally hungry for right now. Is it appreciation? Understanding? Kindness? Then look for one opportunity to give exactly that to someone else. If you're feeling unappreciated, find someone whose efforts often go unnoticed and genuinely thank them. If you're craving understanding, practice deep listening with someone without waiting for your turn to speak.

Remember, this isn't about depleting yourself or giving to get something back. It's about recognising that giving creates a ripple effect - it not only opens us up to receiving but often helps us realise we had the capacity to generate what we needed all along.

December 14th

"You can't change how people treat you or what they say about you. All you can do is change how you react to it."

— Nicky Gumbel

This quote really gets at something fundamental about personal power and peace of mind. What strikes me most about Gumbel's insight is how it shifts our focus from what's outside our control to what's within it. It's not about letting people walk all over you - it's about recognising where your true power lies.

I've seen so many people exhaust themselves trying to control others' actions or opinions, essentially giving away their emotional well-being to people who might not even care. It's like trying to control the weather - frustrating and ultimately impossible.

Here's a practical suggestion for today: When someone does or says something that upsets you, try pausing for just 10 seconds before reacting. In that brief pause, ask yourself: "How do I want to feel about myself after responding to this?" This tiny moment of reflection can help you choose a reaction that aligns with who you want to be, rather than letting others' behaviour dictate your actions.

Remember, choosing how to react doesn't mean you have to accept mistreatment. Sometimes the most powerful reaction is setting a firm boundary or walking away. The key is that you're choosing your response thoughtfully rather than reacting automatically. This way, you keep your peace while others keep their chaos.

December 15th

"When you are feeling overwhelmed, stop, take a deep breath, and ask yourself what you need at this very moment, forget everything else, what does your soul need?"

— Gary Hardy

This quote offers practical wisdom for those moments when life feels like it's spinning too fast. It cuts through the noise of our busy minds to focus on something more essential - our core needs.

In our rush to handle everything at once, we often lose touch with what we truly need in the moment. Sometimes what our soul needs isn't another hour of work or another item checked off our to-do list - it might be as simple as five minutes of quiet, a walk outside, or a conversation with someone who gets us.

Here's a suggestion for today: The next time you feel that overwhelming sensation creeping in (and we all know that feeling - when everything seems urgent and too much), try this: Stop whatever you're doing. Take one slow, deep breath that lasts for a count of four in and four out. Then ask yourself this simple question: "What does my soul need right now?" Not what your schedule demands, not what others expect - just what YOU truly need in this moment. Maybe it's rest, maybe it's movement, maybe it's connection, or maybe it's just permission to let something go.

Remember, overwhelm is often our spirit's way of telling us we've drifted too far from what matters most to us. Taking that moment to check in isn't selfish - it's essential maintenance for your well-being.

December 16th

"You may not see it today or tomorrow, but you will look back in a few years and be absolutely perplexed and awed by how every little thing added up and brought you somewhere wonderful - or where you've always wanted to be. You will be grateful that things didn't work out the way you once wanted."

— Brianna Wiest

This quote carries such powerful wisdom about life's unexpected journey. What really strikes me about Wiest's insight is how it captures that mysterious way life has of weaving together moments that don't seem significant at the time, but later reveal themselves as crucial turning points.

I've seen this play out countless times, both in my conversations with others and in life patterns - how that job rejection led to an even better opportunity, how that relationship ending created space for personal growth, or how that apparent failure became the foundation for later success. It's like life is putting together a mosaic, and we're too close to see the full picture while it's happening.

Here's a thoughtful suggestion for today: Take a moment to write down something in your life right now that isn't going as planned or feels disappointing. Then, write "I'm curious to see how this fits into my larger story" next to it. This simple act can help shift your perspective from frustration to curiosity about how this moment might be setting up something you can't yet see.

Remember, you're in the middle of your story right now. Those things that feel like detours or dead ends? They might just be the universe's way of redirecting you to something better than you could have planned for yourself. Sometimes our greatest disappointments become our most profound redirections.

December 17th

"Before rushing to plan the next year, take time to honour the journey of this one."

— Cheryl Strayed

This quote talks about something essential for personal growth and self-awareness. What strikes me about Strayed's wisdom here is how it gently reminds us to pause and reflect before rushing forward - something we rarely give ourselves permission to do in our fast-paced world.

We often get caught up in the excitement of new goals and fresh starts, especially around transitions and year ends. But there's such richness in taking time to acknowledge where we've been, what we've overcome, and how we've grown. Every experience, whether triumph or challenge, has shaped who we are becoming.

Here's a meaningful suggestion for today: Take 15 minutes to sit quietly and write down three moments from your recent journey that changed you in some way. They don't have to be big dramatic events - sometimes it's the quiet revelations that transform us the most. What did these moments teach you? How did they help you grow? Honour these experiences by really acknowledging their impact on your path.

Remember, looking back isn't about dwelling in the past - it's about understanding your story so you can write the next chapter from a place of wisdom and self-awareness. The lessons from your journey are like hidden treasures that can illuminate your path forward.

December 18th

"When you love someone, you are sure. You don't need time to decide. You don't say stop and start over and over, like you're playing some kind of sport. You know the immensity of what you have and you protect it."

— Nina LaCour

What I find so compelling about LaCour's insight is how it cuts through all the games and uncertainty we sometimes create around love. She's speaking to something profound - that genuine love has a clarity to it, a certainty that doesn't waver like a weather vane in the wind.

In my experience helping others navigate relationships, I've seen how people often confuse drama and uncertainty for passion. But real love, as LaCour suggests, has this quiet certainty to it. It's not about the excitement of breaking up and making up - it's about recognising something precious and choosing to protect it, day after day.

Here's a suggestion for today: If you're in a relationship or close friendship, take a moment to reflect on what you're truly certain about with that person. Not what you wish was true, or what others say should be true, but what you know in your bones to be true. And if you're single, this is a beautiful standard to hold for future relationships - looking for that sense of certainty rather than settling for confusion dressed up as complexity.

Remember, love shouldn't feel like a sport with time-outs and do-overs. When it's real, it's more like finding a home you didn't even know you were looking for - you just know it's where you're meant to be.

December 19th

"Scars have the strange power to remind us that our past is real."

— Cormac McCarthy

This quote speaks to me about the transformative power of our wounds and challenges. McCarthy captures something - our scars, whether physical or emotional, aren't just markers of pain. They're proof that we've lived, struggled, and survived. They tell our story and shape who we become.

Here's a thought for today: Take a quiet moment to reflect on one of your own "scars" - maybe a difficult experience you've been through. Instead of seeing it only as a source of pain, try to identify one way it has made you stronger or more understanding of others.

Perhaps it taught you resilience, gave you deeper empathy, or helped you develop wisdom you now use to help others. Let that awareness guide how you approach today's challenges, knowing that even difficult experiences can ultimately contribute to your growth.

December 20th

"The only two important things in life are real love and being at peace with yourself."

— Jonathan Carroll

This is such a powerful distillation of what truly matters in life. Carroll cuts through all the noise - the endless chase for success, material wealth, status, and recognition - to focus on what genuinely brings fulfilment: authentic love and inner peace.

I find it fascinating that these two elements are deeply interconnected. It's challenging to find real love - whether giving or receiving it - if we're not at peace with ourselves. And often, being truly at peace with ourselves comes from experiencing and sharing genuine love.

Today, take 5 minutes to write down one thing you genuinely love about yourself and one thing you're still working on accepting. This small exercise can be a step towards both elements of Carroll's wisdom - it helps build self-love (real love for yourself) while also acknowledging and making peace with your ongoing journey of growth.

This kind of reflection often reveals that the parts of ourselves we struggle to accept are the very aspects that make us capable of deeper connections and more authentic love with others.

December 21st

"Be with someone who believes that everything is workoutable, and who doesn't walk out and go silent at the first sign of disagreement. But who rather stays and works just as hard as you do on your relationship."

— Gary Hardy

This is what makes relationships truly sustainable. It's not about finding someone perfect or never having conflicts - it's about finding someone who has that fundamental belief that challenges can be overcome through mutual effort and communication.

I particularly appreciate how this quote highlights the importance of emotional persistence. When someone goes silent or walks away during difficult moments, it can feel like a double wound - you're dealing with both the original issue and the pain of abandonment. But someone who stays, who sees disagreements as problems to solve together rather than reasons to retreat - that's a partner who understands the true meaning of commitment.

For today, I'd suggest this: If you're in a relationship, take a moment to recognise and appreciate moments when either you or your partner chose to stay and work things out, even when it was difficult. If you're single, reflect on this quality of "workoutability" - make it a core criterion in what you look for in future relationships. You might even practice this mindset in your friendships or family relationships today by approaching any disagreements with a "how can we solve this together?" attitude rather than withdrawing.

The beauty of relationships built on this foundation is that each successfully worked-through challenge makes the bond stronger and creates deeper trust. It's not just about avoiding conflict - it's about building confidence that together, you can handle whatever comes your way.

December 22nd

"Don't suffer in silence, reach out and ask for the help you need."

— Unknown

This quote touches on one of the most important lessons I've learned about emotional well-being - that there's incredible strength, not weakness, in asking for help. So many of us try to carry our burdens alone, thinking we should be able to handle everything by ourselves. But that's not how humans are wired - we're meant to connect and support each other.

Today, I'd suggest taking one small but meaningful step: Think of something you've been struggling with, even if it seems minor, and share it with someone you trust. It could be as simple as texting a friend "Hey, could we talk? I've been having a rough time with something." Or if that feels too big right now, you might start by just writing down what kind of help you need - sometimes naming it is the first step towards asking for it.

Remember, asking for help isn't just about getting support for yourself - it's also about giving others the chance to be there for you. When we reach out, we often find that not only do people want to help, but our vulnerability often creates deeper connections and gives others permission to be vulnerable too.

December 23rd

"Some people won't appreciate you no matter how much you do for them. Release yourself. Go where you're appreciated and understood."

— Robert Tew

This quote really hits home about a fundamental truth of relationships and self-worth. It's interesting - we often keep pouring energy into people who consistently fail to value it, almost like we're trying to earn appreciation that should come naturally in healthy relationships.

I especially connect with the word "release" here - it's gentler than "cut them off" or "walk away." It suggests freeing yourself from the weight of unmet expectations and unfulfilled hopes. It's about giving yourself permission to stop trying to prove your worth to people who can't or won't see it.

For today, here's a practical suggestion: Take a moment to identify one relationship in your life that consistently drains your energy without giving much back. Then make one small decision about how to redirect that energy towards someone or something that actually fills your cup. Maybe it's spending an extra 30 minutes with a friend who makes you feel valued, or joining a group where your contributions are recognised.

The beautiful thing about moving towards appreciation is that it often creates a positive cycle - when we're surrounded by people who value us, we tend to value ourselves more too. And when we value ourselves more, we naturally gravitate towards healthier relationships.

Remember, seeking appreciation isn't selfish - it's as essential as moving a plant to where it can get more sunlight.

December 24th

"I hope to live to be another man from what I was."

— Charles Dickens

This line from Scrooge's transformation in "A Christmas Carol" really captures something about the human potential for change. What strikes me is that Dickens didn't write "I hope to act differently" or "I hope to do better things" - but to "be another man." It speaks to that deep, fundamental kind of change that transforms who we are at our core, not just our surface behaviours.

Today, take a piece of paper and write down one quality of the person you want to become. Not just a behaviour you want to change, but a characteristic of your future self - maybe it's "someone who leads with compassion" or "a person who faces challenges with courage." Then choose one small action you can take today that aligns with that future self. It could be as simple as responding to a frustrating situation with patience instead of anger, or showing kindness to someone who wouldn't expect it.

What makes this quote so powerful is that it acknowledges both our capacity for change and our agency in making it happen. Like Scrooge, we're not locked into who we've been - every day offers us the chance to take a step towards becoming "another" version of ourselves.

Have you thought about what qualities of your future self you'd most like to develop?

December 25th

"Christmas is about sharing the day with the people you love, may I ask you to be mindful of what a privilege it is to have the person or people with you by your side, some people have nobody and will be spending it alone."

— Gary Hardy

I wanted to talk about the true spirit of Christmas - it's both a celebration and a gentle reminder of gratitude and compassion. I bridge the joy of connection with awareness of loneliness, reminding us that while we're celebrating, others may be experiencing Christmas very differently.

For today, I'd suggest something practical that captures both aspects of this: While planning or thinking about your celebrations, take a moment to reach out to someone who might be feeling alone - maybe an elderly neighbour, a friend who's far from family, or someone who's recently lost a loved one. It doesn't have to be grand - even a simple text saying "I'm thinking of you" can mean the world to someone who's feeling isolated.

I am also inviting you to practice present-moment appreciation. During Christmas gatherings, try to pause for just a moment to really look at the faces around you, to fully take in the privilege of having these specific people in your life, knowing that their presence is not guaranteed but rather a gift to be cherished.

There's something powerful about how this perspective can transform our experience of Christmas - from simply going through traditional motions to deeply appreciating each moment of connection while maintaining awareness of those who might need our attention and care.

December 26th

"May the spirit of giving extend beyond Boxing Day, filling your year with generosity and kindness."

— Unknown

This quote beautifully captures something vital about the holiday spirit and challenges us to expand it into a year-round practice. It's interesting how the magic of the holiday season often opens our hearts to giving more freely - we become more attuned to others' needs and find joy in generosity. But why limit that wonderful energy to just a few weeks?

For today, I'd suggest creating a simple "kindness calendar" for the upcoming month. Pick just one small act of giving per week that you can sustain beyond the holiday rush. It could be as simple as dropping some items of groceries off at a food bank once a month, setting aside an hour to call someone who might be lonely, or regularly contributing small amounts to a cause you care about. The key is choosing something sustainable that you can maintain throughout the year.

What makes this quote particularly meaningful is how it reframes giving from a seasonal activity to a way of life. When we extend that spirit of generosity beyond Boxing Day, we're not just helping others - we're nurturing a mindset that can transform our own daily experience of life.

Think about how different our communities might be if we all carried that holiday spirit of giving through every season. What kind of sustainable giving practice resonates most with you?

December 27th

"The best thing I did this year is learning to accept that whatever happens, happens. And whatever it was, it was okay."

— Gary Hardy

There's something incredibly freeing about this simple realisation. It reminds me of the difference between swimming against a strong current versus learning to float and navigate with it. This quote captures that moment when someone discovers they don't have to wrestle with every single thing that happens in their life.

What makes this particularly powerful is that it's not about giving up or becoming passive. It's about finding peace with the flow of life while still doing your best. It's the wisdom to know that despite our best plans and efforts, some things will unfold in their own way - and that's okay.

For today, I'd suggest a simple practice: When something doesn't go as planned (even something small), pause and say to yourself, "This too is part of my day, and that's okay." Then take a deep breath and ask yourself, "How can I flow with this rather than fight against it?" This small shift in perspective can transform frustrating moments into opportunities for practicing acceptance.

The beauty of this approach is that it actually gives you more energy for the things you can influence, because you're not wasting emotional energy resisting what you can't change. It's like learning to dance with life rather than trying to control every step.

December 28th

"If you find someone who makes you smile, who checks up on you often to see if you're okay. Who watches out or you and wants the best for you. Who loves and respects you. Don't let them go. People like that are hard to find."

— Franz Kafka

This quote resonates with the deep truth about meaningful relationships in our lives. Kafka captures something profound here - it's not just about finding someone who brings joy or love, but someone who demonstrates consistent care through small, everyday actions. Those check-ins, that watchful care, that genuine interest in your well-being - these are the quiet signs of authentic love and friendship.

For today, I'd encourage this practice: Think about who these people are in your life - the ones who consistently show up in these ways. Then, take a moment to actively appreciate them through a specific action. Send them a message describing a time their support meant a lot to you, or tell them about something good that happened in your day before they even ask. Turn the watching out for them into a two-way street.

What's particularly striking about this quote is how it emphasises the rarity of such connections. In our world of casual relationships and surface-level interactions, finding someone who invests deeply in your well-being is truly precious. These aren't just nice-to-have relationships - they're essential anchors in our lives.

I find it beautiful how Kafka, often known for darker themes, captured this tender observation about human connection. It reminds us that recognising and holding onto genuine care is one of life's most important skills.

December 29th

"Promise yourself to be so strong that nothing can disturb your peace of mind. Look at the sunny side of everything and make your optimism come true. Think only of the best, work only for the best, and expect only the best. Forget the mistakes of the past and press on to the greater achievements of the future."

— Christian D. Larson

This quote is about the power of intentional mindset and self-commitment. What strikes me most is that it starts with making a promise to yourself - not to others, but to you. That's often the most important and binding commitment we can make.

The beauty of this quote lies in how it presents mental strength not as something we're born with, but as something we actively choose and cultivate. It's like building an internal fortress of peace that external circumstances can't easily breach.

I particularly appreciate how it balances optimism with action - it's not just about thinking positively, but about actively working for the best while maintaining that positive outlook. And that final line about forgetting past mistakes? It's not suggesting we ignore our lessons, but rather that we don't let our past define our future potential.

For today, I'd suggest something practical: Create what I call a "peace of mind protocol" - a simple 3-minute routine you can use whenever you feel your peace being disturbed. It might look like this:

Take three deep breaths, then ask yourself: "What's one positive aspect of this situation I can focus on right now?" Then, identify one specific action you can take to move towards your best outcome. This combines the quote's wisdom about maintaining peace of mind with its emphasis on active optimism and forward movement.

Remember, strength of mind isn't about never feeling disturbed - it's about having a reliable way to return to your centre when disturbances come. That's what makes the peace sustainable.

December 30th

"When you look at your life and feel at peace because of changes you've made, that's recovery."

— Unknown

This quote captures the truth about healing and growth - that real recovery isn't just about stopping harmful behaviours or fixing what's broken, but about reaching a place where you can look at your life with genuine peace about the changes you've made.

Here's something gentle you could try today: Take a few quiet moments to acknowledge one positive change you've made in your life, no matter how small. Maybe you started going to bed a little earlier, learned to say "no" when needed, or began a small healthy habit. Instead of focusing on how far you still have to go, really let yourself feel good about that one shift you've already made.

I've seen how transformative it can be when people start recognising their progress this way. Often we're so focused on the next goal that we forget to acknowledge how far we've already come. Recovery - whether from trauma, addiction, unhealthy patterns, or just difficult times - isn't just about reaching some final destination. It's about creating a life that feels increasingly authentic and peaceful to live in.

The beauty of this quote is that it defines recovery not by external markers but by that internal sense of peace with our own journey of change. Sometimes the smallest shifts can bring the deepest sense of rightness and calm.

December 31st

"I've learned a lot this year. I learned that things don't always turn out the way you planned, or the way you think they should. And I've learned that there are things that go wrong that don't always get fixed or get put back together the way they were before. I've learned that some broken things stay broken, and I've learned that you can get through bad times and keep looking for better ones, as long as you have people who love you"

— Jennifer Weiner

What a beautifully honest reflection from Weiner. There's something deeply comforting about acknowledging that not everything can be fixed or restored to its original state. It's like accepting that some scars are permanent, but that doesn't mean we stop living fully.

Here's something you could try today: Reach out to one person who helped you through a difficult time this year. Not with a generic "thank you," but with a specific memory of how their presence made a difference. Something like "Remember when you brought me coffee and just sat with me that difficult morning? That meant more than you know."

I've noticed that when we acknowledge both the permanence of certain breaks and the healing power of loving connections, something shifts inside us. We stop exhausting ourselves trying to perfectly reconstruct what was lost, and instead learn to build something new with the support of those around us. It's like finding beauty in a mosaic made from broken pieces.

The real wisdom in Weiner's words lies in that balance - accepting what's irreparably changed while still holding onto hope for better days, anchored by the love of others. Sometimes our greatest strength isn't in fixing everything, but in learning to move forward with both our scars and our support system intact.

About the Author

Life's hardest lessons often come through our deepest struggles. My journey began in an abusive household with an alcoholic father and narcissistic mother, both members of a religious cult. At sixteen, I made the difficult choice to leave home, choosing an uncertain future over a destructive past.

Growing up with a debilitating stammer taught me early about persistence - eventually overcoming it at age 24. This victory showed me that change was possible, leading me to build a successful six-figure company from nothing. But life had other plans.

When my wife passed away from leukaemia, I was left to raise our two sons alone, without support. Trying to cope, I was prescribed antidepressants. Over eight years, these medications slowly altered who I was, eventually leading to a suicide attempt. This dark moment became a turning point when I realised the medications were the culprit.

During this time, while still under the influence of antidepressants and not thinking clearly, I entered into a new relationship too quickly after my wife's death. Though we welcomed a beautiful daughter together, the relationship couldn't survive - I simply wasn't ready, and the medication's effects on my judgment made everything more complicated. Then history seemed to repeat itself - my two-year-old daughter was diagnosed with leukaemia. Watching her endure the same treatment and fight the same disease that took my wife was heart-wrenching. But unlike before, this time brought hope - she survived and remains in remission.

Through these years, I lost everything that defined me - my wife, my company, my sense of self, my reputation and relationships. I felt I had failed my children and let down everyone who counted on me. My life became unrecognisable, stripped of everything I had loved and built.

But here's what I learned: rock bottom can become a foundation. Though I don't recommend it, I went cold turkey off the antidepressants, enduring years of withdrawal that still affects me today. Slowly, I began rebuilding my life, piece by piece. Every challenge, every loss, every moment of despair taught me something vital about resilience, healing, and the human spirit's capacity to rebuild.

Now, I share these hard-won insights with others. Not as someone who has all the answers, but as someone who understands struggle intimately and has found ways forward through life's darkest moments. My approach combines practical advice with deep empathy, born from real experience rather than theory.

Whether you're facing loss, searching for purpose, or simply trying to navigate life's complexities, this book offers perspectives and practices that have helped me and countless others find strength in difficult times.

If you're seeking personalised guidance, I offer one-on-one coaching sessions for anyone, anywhere in the world. No challenge is too big or small - whether it's relationships, career decisions, personal growth, or life transitions, I'm here to help you find your path forward.

Connect with me on Facebook, Instagram and YouTube for more insights, deeper discussions and personal guidance. Together, we can transform our challenges into stepping stones toward a more meaningful life.

With hope and solidarity,
    Gary Hardy

For more information about Gary's coaching services or to connect with his community, visit his website at www.gary-hardy.com or follow him on social media @officialgaryhardy

Gary Hardy is a Maxwell Life and Leadership Coach, specialising in transformational and empathetic coaching. Drawing from both professional expertise and profound personal experience, he helps individuals worldwide discover their inner strength and resilience through life's greatest challenges. He lives in London where he continues to inspire and guide others on their journey of personal growth and transformation.

youtube.com/@officialgaryhardy
instagram.com/officialgaryhardy
facebook.com/garyhardyofficial

Printed in Great Britain
by Amazon